THE PRODUCTIVE PERSONALITY

ALBION PUBLISHING COMPANY
san francisco

the productive personality

JOHN V. GILMORE
boston university

ALBION PUBLISHING COMPANY

1736 stockton street
san francisco, california 94133

designer, nancy clark

text set in melior with optima bold
by fairbanks-parker

Library of Congress Catalog Card Number 73-88382

ISBN O 87843 612 X

98765432

dedicated to Eunice, Peggy, Jack, and Marpie—
four wonderful and productive persons

contents

foreword by stanley coopersmith   viii
preface   x

CHAPTER ONE   THE QUALITY OF PRODUCTIVITY   1
historical perspective   2   productivity   6   measures of
productivity   9

CHAPTER TWO   THE ROLE OF SELF-ESTEEM   13
self-esteem   14   self-esteem in productive persons   17   dynamics
of productive functioning   41

CHAPTER THREE   THE FORMATION OF IDENTITY   43
identity   44   the identification process   51   sex
identity   67   identity and the productive personality   88

CHAPTER FOUR   SOCIAL RESPONSIBILITY   89
social responsibility in productive persons   90   formation of basic
values   99   the socialization process   114   social responsibility
and productivity   133

CHAPTER FIVE   COPING AND MASTERY   135
coping   136   coping skills   141   attributes for effective
coping   154   mastery: the final decision   174

CHAPTER SIX   THE ANTECEDENTS OF PRODUCTIVITY   177
the family structure   178   the family and personality
formation   188   family backgrounds of productive
persons   200   the family as a source   223

CHAPTER SEVEN   ENHANCEMENT OF PRODUCTIVITY   225
characteristics of the productive personality   226
development of the productive personality   230   social and
professional implications   235   nurturance of the
productive personality   250

bibliography   257
name index   277
subject index   283

foreword

In recent years advocates of a positive approach to personality functioning have raised serious questions about prevailing standards of normality, adjustment, and maturity. In general, however, they have been unable to provide specific guidelines for a description of positive mental health. Part of the problem stems from the use of social values as a basis for defining positive and negative traits and from the philosophical framework within which much of this theorizing has developed. At a time when social and moral values are undergoing vast change it has been difficult to formulate a standard of positive health that would meet with widespread agreement and be scientifically meaningful. Descriptions of healthy personalities have emerged which are couched in psychologically appealing terms, but they have been too vague to be of use in actually defining positive functioning or clarifying its antecedents. Nevertheless, they have served a very real function in illuminating the limitations of current approaches to adjustment and normality and have provided us with at least an idealized concept of positive personality functioning.

It is in this context of changing social standards and ambiguous definitions that this work by John Gilmore assumes its significance. Dr. Gilmore has presented an explicit definition of the productive personality, along with a comprehensive description of the antecedents and the consequences of this personality type. He has scoured and summarized the literature on positive personality traits and provides a synthesis that is founded on empirical results as well as on the intuition of a gifted clinician. For theorist and practitioner, teacher and student, this work stands as a summary statement of present knowledge on the personality traits, functioning, and family background of the productive person.

The definition of the productive personality formulated by Dr. Gilmore encompasses such characteristics as social responsibility and a sense of personal identity—a view which may not be shared by all investigators in this field. It is possible, of course, that these characteristics are not applicable to persons with other perspectives and value orientations. However, much of the theorizing about the goals and values of people in other cultures appears to be idealized speculation rather than actual knowledge. Zen philosophy may in fact have less impact on the actual value system of the Japanese peasant than it has on that of the American student. Far more detailed information is needed about the values by which others live before we can arrive at a cross-cultural definition of positive functioning. In the meantime, this work on the productive personality provides us with a formulation which applies in our own culture at this time. At some later point other variants may also emerge to offer a perspective on the person who takes hold of his life and achieves peace with himself.

Stanley Coopersmith

preface

Seldom is the material presented in a book entirely new; rather, it is a somewhat different version—a synthesis of the creative efforts and contributions of a great many other people. Usually it is also the culmination of many previous experiences and ideas which have germinated for some time.

A number of years ago my own experiences as consultant to the Veterans Administration hospitals brought me into contact with the difficulties and discouragements in implementing successful rehabilitation and treatment for the emotionally disabled. As a clinical psychologist in Boston University's Counseling Center I also found that efforts to help students improve low academic performance were only moderately successful. However, when their parents were counseled instead, and given specific advice on methods of enhancing their child's self-confidence, the child improved noticeably—and in some cases remarkably—in both academic achievement and general functioning. These results were sufficiently encouraging to arouse my interest in the actual origins of low achievement and its accompanying behavior problems, especially since the improvements were not explained by available theories of personality and abnormal psychology. During the early 1950s I attempted to construct a predictive test for achievement based on a quantification of the noncognitive factors involved in academic functioning. The results with tests of college and high school students were significant, but again they could not be explained by theories of defense mechanisms, since the high achievers were employing coping techniques, rather than defensive ones.

It often happens that some remark heard in passing serves to crystallize an idea. Dana Farnsworth, who has devoted his career to the physical and mental health of college students, exclaimed in conversation, "If we could only teach people to be better parents!" Another thought was set in motion by Abraham Maslow's sage comment that if we want to know more about mental health, we should study the functioning of self-actualizing persons, just as we study the techniques of the champion athlete to learn the secret of his success. Four years ago I began a concentrated study of the research literature on various aspects of productivity, most of which had been published only a few years before. As my thinking began to take form, it was given further direction by Stanley Coopersmith's reflection that there was a need in the field of psychology for some organized summary of this pioneer research as it relates to positive personality functioning.

What has emerged from the voluminous data on academic achievement, creativity, and leadership, as well as from some major studies in the more general areas of mental health, self-esteem, and self-actualization, is evidence of an underlying personality structure common to all individuals who, in one area

and no mention of Fromm?

or another, make some recognizable contribution to their own lives and the lives of others. There appears to be what we may call a *productive personality*, which can be defined and delineated in terms of certain basic personality traits.

This book is intended primarily to provide students interested in educational or developmental psychology and personality theory with an overview of the important research findings on the nature and antecedents of productivity. Both as future contributors to society and as future parents, they are in a position to make the most direct use of the insights afforded by these findings. I hope that this work will also be of value to teachers, counselors, psychologists, and others who are committed to the maximum development of the young.

Chapter One explains the choice of the term "productive" and the basis on which productivity has been defined. Chapter Two concerns the role of self-esteem—one of the most fundamental characteristics of the academic achiever, the creative person, and the leader. Chapter Three discusses the formation of identity, the productive person's awareness of himself as an individual. The productive individual is also characterized by a highly developed inner value system which governs his social behavior; the basis of this value system and the process through which it evolves are described in Chapter Four. Chapter Five details the specific attributes associated with the results of productive functioning, the coping skills and traits involved in competence. The family backgrounds from which productive persons have emerged, and some of the factors which may account for both their development and their differences, are outlined in Chapter Six. Chapter Seven concerns the implications of these research findings, both as a theoretical framework for the dynamics of productive functioning and as a basis for the enhancement of productivity in all individuals.

In summarizing the research reported in several hundred books, articles, and abstracts there has been no way to include, or even allude to, all the findings—and obviously not all of them can be generalized to a broad model of the productive personality. In this regard I should point out that the findings which have been reported are from research with groups rather than case studies of individuals. Also, in a work of such broad scope I have relied heavily on the expert knowledge of others. I owe special thanks to such authorities as Aronfreed, Bandura, Barron, Coopersmith, MacKinnon, Maslow, Rosenberg, and Schafer, from whose works I have quoted throughout. The definitions of *cope*, *empathy*, *productive*, *shame*, and *value* are quoted by permission from *Webster's Third New International Dictionary*, copyright 1971 by G. & C. Merriam Co., Publishers of the Merriam-Webster Dictionaries; the definitions of *expect*, *hope*, *independence*, and *self* are quoted by permission from *Webster's New World Dictionary of the American Language, College Edition*, copyright 1962 by the World Publishing Company; the passage on page 53 is quoted by permission from Roy Schafer, *Aspects of Internalization*, copyright 1968 by International Universities Press.

One is always indebted to many persons for their contributions to the completion of such an ambitious project. My greatest gratitude goes to my loyal and devoted wife, Eunice, not only for her constant support and encouragement, but for her many talents including excellent research and editorial skill. I am also deeply grateful to the members of my immediate and extended family, who, unavoidably neglected during the stressful final months of completing the manuscript, have nevertheless contributed much support and understanding.

Special appreciation is hereby expressed to Stanley Coopersmith for his initial interest in the project, for having read both preliminary and revised versions of the manuscript, and for having contributed both encouragement and a number of invaluable suggestions. I would also like to thank James Edmondson, the publisher of this volume, for his helpful advice, friendly cooperation, and patience and Nancy Clark for her painstaking and exceedingly skillful editing of the final manuscript. A number of unpublished research papers, particularly those of Margaret Gilmore, Stephen Shatkin, and Brian O'Callaghan, were helpful to me. The enthusiasm of my graduate students at Boston University has contributed much to the final formulation and clarification of the theoretical structure of the productive personality. Finally, I acknowledge gratefully the clerical assistance of Rebecca Rubin for many hours of skillful typing and much help in preparation of the manuscript.

John V. Gilmore   xiii

THE PRODUCTIVE PERSONALITY

During the last three decades psychologists have become increasingly interested in the competent, achieving person and the factors that enhance or impede his development. This interest is shared not only by psychologists, but also by those specialists in the allied fields of psychiatry and education who are concerned with the generative aspects of the mature and productive member of society. The origin of outstanding ability has long been a topic of study. In recent years, however, efforts to determine the causative factors in competence and achievement have shifted from an emphasis on heredity to an exploration of the personality factors that appear to be common to all outstanding individuals.

Early studies by Darwin (1859), Spencer (1864–1867), and Galton (1869) ascribed much of human personality functioning to hereditary factors. These studies were conducted primarily from a eugenic point of view, and genius was considered only in terms of genetic origin. Binet's first measure of intelligence (1905–1908),

the quality
of productivity

CHAPTER ONE

1

constructed as a predictor of scholastic achievement, also supported the concept that intelligence and outstanding ability were principally functions of heredity. The first serious effort to explore the development of special ability was Terman's long-range study of gifted children, begun in 1921. Terman was interested in discovering "what gifted children are like as children, what sort of adults they become, and what some of the factors are that influence their development."[1] Since that time a variety of important studies have provided us with new insight into the nature of the competent and productive personality.

historical perspective

Over the years concern with genius has gradually given way to interest in creativity and giftedness, as indicated by a survey of the studies published during the period from 1927 to 1965.[2] This interest was not marked, however, until the early 1950s, when research findings on various aspects of creativity opened the door to a new approach to the study of exceptional ability through exploration of the early childhood of outstanding persons. The work by Roe, Barron, Maslow, MacKinnon, Drevdahl, and others has given credence to the view that certain personality factors are intimately involved with creativity and success. At the same time, the writings of Erikson have enriched our understanding of productive functioning as an important aspect of the normal personality. As he contends:[3]

> I cannot accept the conclusion that just to be alive, or not to be sick, means to be healthy. . . .

More recently, the careful investigations of self-esteem by Rosenberg and by Coopersmith have given us valuable information about a personality characteristic which appears to be fundamental to all forms of productive behavior.

During this period the field of psychiatry was also reexamining its approach to the causes and treatment of mental illness. Horney (1939) had written convincingly concerning the influence

2   1 See Oden, 1968, p. 5   3 Erikson, 1950b, p. 93
       2 Albert, 1969, pp. 746, 748–750

of environmental factors in normal personality development, and Sullivan (1953) was outspoken on the need for a new approach to psychotherapy which included the role of environment. In 1955 Congress authorized a national survey under the Mental Health Study Act and appropriated funds for a Joint Commission on Mental Illness and Health. The first report of this commission, published in 1958, represented a two-year study of social, educational, economic, and other factors involved in mental illness and health.[4]

The Soviet Union's initiative in space exploration in 1957 spurred a feverish examination in this country of the factors associated with academic achievement. Studies of eminence and genius were replaced by research on giftedness, which was considered a more appropriate description of the attributes of the high achiever. These studies were concerned chiefly with the problem of identification, education, and training of the gifted child himself, rather than with the personality dynamics and characteristics of giftedness.[5] For the first time, however, concerned educators and psychologists began to give serious thought to factors other than heredity as possible elements in the acquisition of cognitive skills and general intellectual development. An inevitable part of such investigation was exhaustive research on the personality and noncognitive characteristics that might be associated with differences in academic achievement. Davis (1962) reported that in the twenty-year period from 1940 to 1960 there were approximately 1500 studies on the reliability of noncognitive measures in predicting actual performance. Fishman estimated that between 1935 and the date of his study (1962) approximately 1000 such research projects had been carried out at the college level alone.[6]

In the late 1950s, when it became apparent that the various factors associated with creativity would also require study, the emphasis turned to the cognitive abilities and personality characteristics associated with creativity. Because of the difficulty in agreeing on a definition of creativity which would effectively differentiate it from other traits or skills—verbal ability, for example—the research in this area has been less structured and less definitive than that on academic achievement. Until 1965 few

---

4 Jahoda, 1958

5 Albert, 1969, p. 750

6 See Cloninger, 1972, pp. 9–13

investigators attempted to define creativity or offer theories about it; more recent studies have dealt with the motivational dynamics and cognitive processes involved in creativity, but only 10 percent of this research has attributed even artistic creativity to personality factors.[7] There is a marked need for further exploration of the personality characteristics and family backgrounds of persons who are creative not only in artistic and scientific areas, but also in the various areas of scholarship.

A third form of competence that has received increasing attention is leadership. One of the first studies in this area was an investigation by Binet (1900) of suggestibility in children; a version of this experiment was also conducted in the United States by Terman (1904). However, there was little further work until the late 1930s, when sporadic studies began to appear on industrial psychology and on the effects of adult leadership on children's behavior. In recent years the research in academic achievement and creativity has stimulated investigations of the personality characteristics of business leaders, with specific reference to their early backgrounds. At the same time growing interest in a closely related subject—the organization and dynamics of groups—has led to extensive research on the manner in which groups identify and select leaders. Studies conducted at all age levels indicate that the person who is chosen as a leader, on either a formal or an informal basis, apparently possesses some quality or attribute to which others respond. One aspect of this quality, it seems, is competence in some specific academic or creative area. Evidently, demonstrated mastery in a specific area contributes to the confidence of others that a person is capable of leadership.

In fact, on closer examination of the research in all three of these areas of performance, it becomes apparent that the persons who are differentiated as outstanding in any one area also give evidence of competence in one or both of the other two. For example, the academic achiever often has a history of leadership activities, and the research scientist seems to have a particular affinity for music. There are occasional individuals, such as a Winston Churchill or an Albert Schweitzer, who have made no-

7 Albert, 1969, p. 749

table contributions in the areas of scholarship, creativity, and leadership alike. More often, however, the outstanding individual channels his productive efforts into one area as a matter of choice. The effective leader may be highly creative in his conceptual approach to the problems of the group, but his fulfillment lies in implementing his ideas through direct interaction with others. By the same token, the person who attains some exceptional level of knowledge or creative accomplishment is usually deeply concerned with the social and humanitarian implications of his work, but his actual reward lies in the work itself.

In view of the evident overlap in the competencies and skills of outstanding persons, regardless of their primary area of expression, it seems reasonable to believe that there is some underlying personality structure which is common to all of them. In describing the qualities of the self-actualizing person, Maslow made no distinction between the outstanding statesman (Thomas Jefferson), the noted musician (Fritz Kreisler), and the noted scientist (George Washington Carver). Recent research in the separate areas of scholarship, creativity, and leadership shows that outstanding persons in each of these areas share such personality qualities as independence, persistence, altruism, a high degree of self-control, and a highly developed sense of values.

Moreover, these qualities also appear to have common antecedents. In a study of honesty and altruism among sixth-grade boys and girls, Mussen et al. (1970) found an important factor to be warmly affectionate and supportive parents who stressed high standards of achievement and superior cognitive functioning as well as moral values and consideration for others.[8] In addition to the common personality characteristics which enable them to cope with daily problems, individuals who function effectively appear to have parental backgrounds noted for readily apparent nurturance, warmth, concern, and respect for each member of the family. Their parents may differ in educational level, socioeconomic status, cultural background, and aspirations for their children, but they all provide far beyond the minimum requirements for the physical and emotional needs of their offspring.

8   Mussen, Rutherford, Harris, and
    Keasey, 1970, p. 192

productivity

At this point we need some inclusive term to designate the individual who is making a tangible and significant contribution in his chosen field (achievement); who is imaginative, perceptive, and innovative in his approach to life problems and to the accomplishment of his own goals (creativity); and who is at the same time both responsible and responsive in his relationships with others (leadership). To refer to such a person as merely creative, self-actualizing, mentally healthy, mature, or competent seems neither appropriate nor adequate to express the sum total of these attributes.

One difficulty is that psychology has been handicapped for years by the lack of any suitable terms to denote positive aspects of personality functioning. The inadequacy of the labels "average" and "normal" is more or less self-evident. The widely abused designations "mental health" and "adjustment," in addition to their other limitations, have taken on unfortunate negative associations with mental hospitals and disordered behavior. White (1969) has suggested the term "emotional maturity" to denote a positive direction of growth and development which would apply to the adolescent and adult as well as to the child; he also proposes the terms "competence" and "effectance" to describe an individual's ability to deal effectively with his environment.[9] Maturity, however, is an elusive concept, and competence is similarly difficult to define in concrete terms; a person may be highly competent without accomplishing anything particularly productive.

Other borrowed or outdated designations such as "genius," "talent," "giftedness," and the like have never been satisfactorily defined; moreover, their connotation of some specific genetic structure implies an immutable distinction between the haves and the have nots which is, to say the least, a depressing prognosis for the latter. The term "eminence" is also limited by its implication that one must have reached a certain age and degree of fame in order to become effective.

6   9   R. White, 1966, p. 303; 1969, pp. 23, 28

A more useful term from a conceptual standpoint is "self-actualization," which refers to the expression of man's desire for self-realization. Jung defined self-actualization as a goal for personal growth which included the "fullest, most complete differentiation and harmonious blending of all aspects of man's total personality."[10] Probably the best-known work on this subject is Maslow's study (1954) of the characteristics of self-actualizing persons as he observed them in personal acquaintances and public and historical figures.[11] Although the concept of self-actualization as interpreted by Maslow and others does fill a need for some means of describing the positive qualities of human personality, it has lacked widespread acceptance and is, perhaps, too abstract to serve as a psychological description.

At a more concrete level, people have been designated as eminent, endowed with genius, gifted, or creative only on the basis of some tangible contribution to the world in which they were living. There is, after all, no basis for evaluating the qualities of a Mozart, a Goethe, or a Picasso except in terms of the recognized value of his works. Moreover, no value can be placed on an accomplishment unless it is produced. In short, it is the product that gives descriptive meaning to whatever designation is applied. On this basis it seems reasonable to describe the person directly in these terms, without reference to selective or arbitrarily ascribed factors such as genetic endowment, cultural or socioeconomic level, educational level, age, or sex. What is needed is a term which is both inclusive and definitive, and which designates an individual's effectiveness primarily in terms of the contribution he produces. We may describe such a person in the most inclusive terms as *productive*—from the Latin *producere*, meaning "to bring forth, beget, produce." To be productive means:[12]

> *having the quality or power of producing: bringing forth or able to bring forth [especially] in abundance: creative, generative, . . . yielding or furnishing results [or] benefits. . . .*

By definition, the productive individual generates either a tangible or an intangible product that is directly or indirectly

10 See Hall and Lindzey, 1957, p. 96

11 Maslow, 1954, chap. 12

12 Webster's third new international dictionary, 1971, sv productive

observable and of benefit to others. Thus any productive act is in some measure a creative one. MacKinnon (1962) has defined a creative act as having three essential characteristics: it must be original, novel, or at least statistically infrequent; it must in some way serve reality in providing the solution to a problem, the resolution of a situation, or the accomplishment of a goal; it must involve "a sustaining of the original insight, an evaluation and elaboration of it, [and] a developing of it to the full."[13] According to this definition of creativity, particularly its latter two aspects, the realization of full creativity is really synonymous with productivity, a process which, whether it is brief or extended, is characterized by adaptiveness, realization, and perhaps some element of originality. Most important, however, the process must produce a result.

The creative aspects of productivity are apparent in all dimensions of human endeavor. The contribution may be an innovative approach to some problem, a product unique in its quality or excellence, or simply the expression of a conviction or a personal example which serves to generate some change or crystallize the combined contributions of others. The result may be a new scientific theory, an immortal musical work, or some great social change such as that which revolved around Gandhi or Martin Luther King. Productivity does not refer to mere quantity of output. It denotes primarily the quality of the contribution with respect to its constructive impact on society. Thus it does not encompass antisocial acts, either directly or by inference; an antisocial act is a form of taking from society, whereas a productive act is one which gives to society. The highly productive individual, in some way and to some degree, is usually an instrument of constructive change, whether he is a scholar, a composer, a scientist, a writer, or a leader in the realm of politics, business, or his profession.

The ultimate judgment of who is and who is not a productive person obviously rests with others, whether the judgment is rendered by public recognition or by the consensus of experts. Thus productivity is subject to the same validation criteria as success, expertise, or intelligence: what is recognized as produc-

13 MacKinnon, 1962, p. 485

tive depends on the value a particular society places on the contribution. In Eastern societies, for example, an individual's tangible accomplishments may be considered of less value than a model of personal tranquility or withdrawal from the external environment. In Western societies the greatest value is placed on those contributions which are expected to lead in some way to less anxiety and pain or in greater comfort and pleasure for others.

If we hypothesize that the most important single criterion of productivity is some contribution of use to society, then it becomes apparent—since some people are more productive than others—that productivity must be relative. Moreover, a contribution that is intangible or not directly observable may go unrecognized. There are great numbers of individuals at all levels of society who are productive in every sense of our definition, but whose contributions are given little or no recognition. It is to be hoped that at some point, when our concepts have become more definitive and our measures more reliable, we shall be better able to evaluate both the quality and the quantity of productivity.

measures of productivity

In order to identify and describe the characteristics that comprise the productive personality, it is necessary to classify people in general as highly productive, average or low-productive, and nonproductive. The category of nonproductive persons consists of that relatively small proportion of the population who are emotionally and mentally handicapped and whose relationship to society is essentially a dependent one. The highly productive individuals—those whose unique or special contribution differentiates them from others—probably constitute, at the other end of the spectrum, a similarly small segment of the general population. Between these two extremes lies the bulk of the population, the millions of "average" persons who contribute to society with varying degrees of effectiveness. The nonproductive, or dysfunctioning, individual is a separate area of study and does not concern us here. However, in order to differentiate the highly productive person from those who are not highly productive, we need some means of referring to the large average group as a basis of comparison.

In general the designation highly productive refers to a group of subjects who have been labeled "high" by a given investigator according to his particular standard of differentiation. Thus in a given sample of high school students those with grade-point averages, SAT scores, or other ratings above a designated point might be termed high achievers and hence referred to as the high-productive group. The group whose level of performance or rating on some quantified measure is below this designated point is referred to as low-productive. The term "low" applies only in a relative sense; however, this term is used, rather than "average," because many research studies define only two groups—high and low.

In most studies the low-productive group is used as a source of validation for characteristics found in the smaller, high-productive group. However, some limiting factors should be noted with respect to the data reported for this group. Subjects in the low-productive group are in all probability less representative of their population group than those in the high-productive group, since their characteristics cover a much wider range. Moreover, unless both groups are identified as part of the same study, the comparison group is not likely to be matched in all variables. Some investigators have designed their research to include a control or comparison group for cross validation. Others have not, and in such cases an attempt has been made to compare findings on a similar population from some other study. When a study of the characteristics of the high academic achiever, for example, includes no data on the low achiever, it is often possible to find a study of low achievement which indicates the absence, or converse, of these characteristics. However, it is not always possible to find a comparison group that is matched in number and other variables, such as age, sex distribution, average IQ, and socioeconomic level. In some cases validation for a specific characteristic is available from a related study; if a study of high achievers reports independence as one of the characteristics, there may be a study of independence showing this trait to be associated with achievement.

As might be expected, the research data from widely disparate studies in three different fields do not always fit together neatly. Some of the studies are well designed, with careful statistical treatment of the information; some have lacked adequate control groups or have employed measures that were not subject to validation; in a few cases the method by which the data were collected is not fully described. One particular difficulty is in isolating the effects of education on the various aspects of academic achievement, creativity, and leadership. Most studies in any of these areas have involved persons with at least a minimum of education; several were conducted at the graduate level and with persons in business and professional areas that require advanced education. Nevertheless, it appears that productivity is not highly correlated with IQ or other measures of intelligence —at least above a certain level. In general the person with an IQ of 125 will be more productive than one with an IQ of 95; the person with an IQ of 150, however, may actually be less productive than the one with an IQ of 125. There is a correlation between IQ and academic achievement, but at the higher levels of education the correlation is lowest.

It should be borne in mind that a high percentage of the investigations with which we are concerned have been carried out in an educational or educationally oriented environment, and this may well color the findings on several aspects of productive functioning. Even so, academic achievement, creativity, and leadership have been explored at every educational level from nursery school to graduate school, and from the large number of reports, observations, and research studies some basic personality qualities have emerged with sufficient clarity to provide us with at least a preliminary picture of the productive personality.

The truly productive individual is unique in his own identity. It is possible to say of such a person, as Hamlet said of his father:[14]

I shall not look upon his like again.

14 Hamlet, Prince of Denmark, act I, scene ii

As a result, he makes a unique contribution to the lives of others. This contribution may be a professional skill, a work of art, some new insight into a situation or problem, or the influence to guide others in some worthwhile undertaking. The benefit may be immediate and dramatically apparent, as in the ringing performance of a Leontyne Price, or it may be less tangible and even unrecognized, as in the seeds of learning planted in generations of children by some unknown teacher. The insights gained from an understanding of productivity, the nature of the productive personality, and the factors involved in its development should have important implications for the development of our present generation of children and young people into competent and productive adults.

One personality factor which has appeared repeatedly in the findings on all types of productive functioning is self-esteem. Apparently any person, in order to function in a productive manner, must possess a favorable attitude toward himself and his capabilities. This attitude has been described in various ways. The concepts of ego strength and self-actualization, for example, have been discussed by widely respected authorities in the field of personality and child development. Each of these concepts does in fact encompass an important aspect of self-esteem; however, from the operational definitions provided by Rosenberg (1965) and Coopersmith (1967), it appears that self-esteem is a more basic and comprehensive psychological trait which is fundamental to the productive personality in general.

The role of self-esteem—or, perhaps more aptly, the manner in which self-esteem is expressed—varies somewhat in the three areas of productivity under study. There are, moreover, certain personality differences among these groups. Academic achievers, creative persons, and leaders differ from each other in cognitive characteristics, motivation, and areas of social competence. In

the role
of self-esteem

CHAPTER TWO

13

each of these groups, however, and at all age levels, self-esteem appears to be the one characteristic that differentiates the productive person from others. Thus a definition of this characteristic and an understanding of its relationship to academic achievement, creativity, and leadership provide us with a basic framework for describing the productive personality.

self-esteem

Self-esteem may be briefly defined as the individual's evaluative attitude toward himself. In a broader sense it is more or less synonymous with other frequently used designations, such as "self-acceptance," "self-respect," "self-confidence," "ego strength," "self-image," "self-concept," and "self-percept." All these descriptive terms have appeared in the recent proliferation of research literature, but they vary somewhat in clarity and usefulness. The connotations of such terms as "self-confidence" and "self-respect" are generally positive; such labels as "self-image" or "self-concept" are essentially neutral and require qualifying descriptions, whereas "self-acceptance" has the negative connotation of complacency, contentment with mediocrity, or lack of interest in self-improvement.

The term "ego strength" is much broader and more comprehensive in its implications. Ego strength is associated with various traits of both moral strength and moral development. It is associated with such traits as:[1]

> IQ; *reflective and analytic style of cognitive controls; future time perspective and capacity for delay of reward; capacity for sustained attention; desire for autonomous achievement . . . internal locus of control; and absence of low-self-esteem and anxiety.*

Considered in this broad sense, ego strength encompasses the trait of self-esteem. Moreover, it also includes a number of other personality strengths typical of productive individuals. Most of these traits are essentially "coping skills," the characteristics which enable an individual to deal effectively with problems. As we

1 National Institute of Child Health, 1968,
   p. 32; see also Kohlberg, 1964, pp.
   390–391

shall see in Chapter Five, the mastery of problems or situations requires a certain amount of intelligence, a capacity for reflection and analysis, the ability to control impulses and postpone immediate gratification in the interest of long-range goals, the power to focus attention on a stimulus or problem, and finally, independence and persistence in working toward goals. It is through all these skills, or personality strengths, that the productive person makes sound and effective decisions and meets the varied challenges and problems of his life. Basic to all these coping skills is his emotional security and freedom from anxiety.

The concept of ego strength does cover many aspects of the productive personality—as far as it goes. It is limited, however, to those traits which relate to performance and does not take into account the areas of personality which relate to social responsibility and concern. Definitions of ego strength do not mention, for example, such characteristics as empathy, altruism, and moral and ethical values, which also seem to be fundamental to the productive individual. This realm of personality function is encompassed by the term "self-actualization," which Maslow defines as the individual's full use and exploitation of his talents, capacities, and potentialities.[2] He describes the self-actualizing person as having "a genuine desire to help the human race" and refers specifically to his strong ethical and moral standards.

Although the concepts of ego strength and self-actualization are helpful in outlining the nature of the productive personality, both terms relate primarily to some result or net effect, rather than to the pivotal characteristic—or dependent variable—which might be responsible for this result. The differentiating characteristic in all productive individuals appears to be self-esteem. Self-esteem is not the sole determinant of productivity; the potential for productive achievement is also influenced by the environmental factors which determine an individual's personal values, his opportunities to develop competence, and his opportunities for productive expression. In light of current theory and research, however, the concept of self-esteem appears to be the most effective explanation of the differences between highly productive and less productive persons.

2 Maslow, 1954, pp. 200, 217, 222

Two leading authorities in the research on self-esteem are Rosenberg, who has studied family and sociological factors associated with self-esteem among high school juniors and seniors in New York State, and Coopersmith, who studied self-esteem in fifth- and sixth-grade students in Connecticut. Both researchers have contributed important definitions which help to clarify the parameters of this trait.

Coopersmith (1967) writes as follows:[3]

> By self-esteem we refer to the evaluation which the individual makes and customarily maintains with regard to himself: it expresses an attitude of approval or disapproval, and indicates the extent to which the individual believes himself to be capable, significant, successful, and worthy. In short, self-esteem is a personal judgment of worthiness that is expressed in the attitudes the individual holds toward himself. It is a subjective experience which the individual conveys to others by verbal reports and other overt expressive behavior.

Rosenberg (1965) characterizes a person with high self-esteem as one who "feels that he is a person of worth; he respects himself for what he is."[4] However, this attitude contains no element of conceit or self-satisfaction; rather, such a person has a positive attitude toward his further development and is concerned with growing, improving, and overcoming his present deficiencies. Rosenberg describes a person with low self-esteem as characterized, in contrast, by attitudes of self-rejection, self-dissatisfaction, and self-contempt. Coopersmith (1967) notes further that such persons typically feel inadequate and unworthy, helpless, and inferior and are frequently given to feelings of guilt, shame, or depression.[5]

It appears that the level of an individual's self-esteem —whether it is high, moderate, or low—remains fairly stable through the years. Engel (1959) found a correlation of .78 between the self-esteem levels of 172 middle-class junior and senior high school students remeasured two years later. Piers and Harris (1964) compared the stability of self-concept over a four-month interval among third-, sixth-, and tenth-graders and found that,

3 Coopersmith, 1967, pp. 4–5   5 Coopersmith, 1967, p. 3
4 Rosenberg, 1965, p. 31

irrespective of age, the correlations were all in the .70s.[6] Coopersmith retested fifty-six children after a three-year period and found a correlation of .70, suggesting "that at some time preceding middle childhood the individual arrives at a general appraisal of his worth, which remains relatively stable and enduring over a period of several years."[7]

In all these studies the subjects were at an age when they would ordinarily be living at home, presumably within a consistent family environment. However, longitudinal studies in other areas of behavior indicate that a child's early identifications and appraisals of himself are more or less permanent even in adulthood, since they also color his perceptions.

Another important aspect of self-esteem is the manner in which it is influenced by the attitudes of "significant others" in the individual's environment. As Douvan and Gold (1966) point out, although an individual's self-esteem reflects his own self-evaluation, this evaluation is in turn heavily dependent on the evaluations reflected to him by other people.[8] Self-esteem is also dependent on the degree to which a person's successes approach his expectations in those areas of behavior or accomplishment which are important to him.[9] Still, in the final analysis both his expectations and his successes are determined by his reaction to what those who matter to him think, or what he perceives them to think, whether his reference group is past, present, or future.

self-esteem in productive persons

THE ACADEMIC ACHIEVER

For many years academic achievement has been associated with cognitive ability as measured by standard IQ tests. Inasmuch as the initial IQ test developed by Binet was validated on the basis of classroom performance, one would expect some relationship between IQ scores and scholastic achievement. IQ tests have been useful in screening for abnormalities, neurological deficiencies, poverty of educational opportunities, and learning problems. On

6 See Douvan and Gold, 1966, p. 516

7 Coopersmith, 1967, p. 5

8 Douvan and Gold, 1966, p. 520

9 National Institute of Child Health, 1968, p. 28

17

the whole, however, they have proved relatively ineffective as a means of predicting subsequent academic achievement. In spite of this fact, the awe surrounding the terms "mental ability" and "IQ level" has made it difficult to view the limitations of such tests objectively.

The highest correlations between IQ and achievement are usually obtained at the high school level because of the wide distribution of ability in this age group; the next highest correlations are at the college level. Elementary school pupils come from such a wide variety of backgrounds that it is difficult to identify the relationships of background and IQ to achievement. At the graduate level, where ability in general is uniformly high, the correlations are lowest of all; discrepancies in academic performance at this level are presumably caused by factors other than intelligence.[10]

Even at the high school and college levels, where IQ scores are the most reliable measures of general ability, differences in IQ account for only 35 to 45 percent of the variance in academic performance. Since no other single factor or measure provides even this much correlation, the use of IQ tests continues in the absence of some better measuring instrument. The fact remains, however, that approximately half the variation in scholastic performance must be explained by factors other than those which are measured by an IQ test.[11]

One reason for the discrepancy between IQ scores and achievement ratings is that the IQ test fails to measure three important personality traits in the normal child. It does not measure the motivation or drive to do successful work in school; it does not measure impulsivity, which is often associated with lower achievement; and it does not measure memory, a skill or trait essential in all our educational programs.[12] For that matter, there are obviously factors other than intelligence involved in IQ scores themselves. For many years differences in measured IQ were ascribed to immutable differences in genetic makeup. Genetic factors undoubtedly play some role in general ability, and possibly in personality characteristics as well. However, owing to the fundamental interaction of any organism with its environment, there

10 Lavin, 1965, p. 58   12 Gilmore, 1968, p. 53
11 Lavin, 1965, p. 59

has so far been no way of determining the precise nature or influence of such factors.

Certain terms associated with academic achievement require clarification; among these are "underachievement" and "overachievement." Underachievement refers to the discrepancy between a student's ability (as measured by his score on a given intelligence test or other instrument) and his scholastic performance in terms of his grade-point average or rank in a given population of students. However, the concept of underachievement presupposes a comparison of achievement with some base line (usually established by an IQ test) which represents only one of the many factors involved in academic performance. Although the term "underachievement" appears frequently in the research literature, the simple designation "low achievement," without reference to any other variables, seems a more valid and meaningful one. For similar reasons, the designation "high achievement" is preferable to "overachievement" for students at the upper end of the continuum.

The research on academic achievement has dealt with a wide range of cognitive and noncognitive factors (personality traits). Some of these studies have related achievement to a single variable, such as study habits, interest in specific subject areas, and vocational interests (particularly as related to college major). Relationships have also been found between achievement and such variables as independence, impulsivity, anxiety, and self-image. Other studies have utilized a multivariate approach involving several personality traits. Lavin (1965) concludes from a survey of both single-variable and multivariate research that such factors as social maturity, emotional stability, achievement motivation, and certain aspects of cognitive style are generally associated with high academic achievement.[13]

The studies involving a single personality trait have proved somewhat more predictive than the multivariate investigations. These studies show that the high achiever is superior to the low achiever in self-image and cognitive flexibility, and is also less hostile and defensive. His interests are more clearly defined and are generally less dependent on the influence of others. He has

13 Lavin, 1965, pp. 64–110

more impulse control, better study habits, a greater interest in course areas (particularly those in which he is superior), and a more favorable attitude toward school in general than does the low achiever; he also exhibits a greater degree of achievement motivation, more independence, less test anxiety, and a number of other strengths.[14]

In some studies of noncognitive factors (Tribou, 1958; Lynch, 1960) quantified replies on a sentence-completion test have been used as a measure of reactions to items pertaining to perceptions of parents, remote goals, and relationships to peer groups and teachers. These measures have yielded single-variable scores which correlate as highly with academic achievement as does a single IQ score. The construction of a standard measure of such noncognitive factors, however, presents difficulties which have not yet been successfully overcome; at present no reliable test of noncognitive factors is commercially available.

Measures based on demographic factors, such as family size, ordinal position in the family, and socioeconomic level, have also yielded significant correlations with academic achievement. These variables are not in themselves factors in achievement; rather, they relate to the quality and quantity of empathy and nurturance which the child receives in the home and to the educational and developmental opportunities available in his background. There have also been a great many studies on sex differences in academic achievement which indicate that low achievement is almost twice as prevalent in males as it is in females. Underachievement in boys is reported as early as the first grade and increases by increments from the third to the tenth grade; in girls underachievement appears at about the sixth grade.[15]

For years motivation has been singled out as some unitary trait which differentiates the high achiever from the low achiever. Counselors, teachers, psychologists, and psychiatrists alike have explained poor or mediocre scholastic performance as the student's "lack of motivation." Despite its widespread use in this sense, lack of motivation is not a causal condition; it is, in essence, an abstraction used to denote passive, nonproductive be-

14 Lavin, 1965, pp. 100–101, 106, 110   15 Impellizeri, 1961, p. 11; Meeks, 1961, p. 31

havior in a given area. For that matter, "motive" is in itself an abstraction: "Motive is a term used in conceptualizing psychological phenomena. As such it is for the observer to decide what he will call a motive."[16]

Motivation pertains to all behavior in the sense that any act must be motivated in order to occur; hence it can be described on the same basis as any other factor that governs behavior. To be motivated to an action means to anticipate some form of reward, either tangible or intangible, or to forestall some form of loss, such as the loss of affection or support. Specifically, if a child is not motivated to study, it is probably because he has no anticipation or hope of increasing his self-esteem as result of a higher level of achievement.

The personality traits of social responsibility, achievement motivation, persistence, good cognitive skills, impulse control, and independence have all been noted in the high achiever. Many of these traits have also been found to be correlated with a positive self-image (self-esteem). It therefore seems logical to find that a close relationship between a child's self-image and his academic performance has been demonstrated at all educational levels, from elementary school to graduate school. The self-concept of the high achiever consists of a positive attitude not only toward himself, but also toward the world, the future, and life in general. Moreover, because of his high level of self-acceptance, the typical high achiever is much freer to focus on problems outside himself than is the low achiever, who generally views himself as inadequate, powerless, and threatened by all the external forces that seem to control his life.[17]

The largest proportion of research on the relationship between achievement and self-concept appears to deal with the junior high and high school age group, which suggests that achievement problems are more acute at this uncertain age. Studies of our highest-ranking students, however, such as finalists in the National Merit Scholarship tests, show them to be conspicuous for their high self-esteem (Stalnaker, 1961; Holland, 1963), and studies conducted at all levels of high school have consistently shown a significant correlation between academic

16 Schafer, 1968, p. 53

17 Shatkin, 1966, p. 15; M. Gilmore, 1964, pp. 17–21

achievement and self-esteem (Reiss, 1966; Davids, 1966; Jones, 1966; Quimby, 1967; Bachman, 1970).

Experiments with eighth- and ninth-graders demonstrate that a student's concept of his own ability is a better predictor of his classroom achievement than his measured IQ (Morse, 1963; Haarer, 1964; Harding, 1966). In one interesting experiment Gibby and Gibby (1967) administered a test of word fluency to two groups of high-ability seventh-graders and then gave them the same test three days later. Immediately before this retest, however, they told the students in one group that they had failed the test the first time. These students not only performed more poorly on the second test than they had on the first one, but manifested their lowered self-esteem in generally lowered intellectual productivity.[18]

In a study of ninth-grade black students Blair (1967) found that intelligence scores as well as academic achievement were related to self-concept and noted that academic achievement tended to correspond with self-concept, level of independence, and degree of inner control.[19] An investigation by Caplin (1966) of children in a racially mixed school indicates that the self-concepts of black and white children alike are adversely affected by de facto school segregation; in students of both races self-concepts, levels of aspiration for academic achievement, and achievement itself were significantly related.[20]

Studies at the elementary school level show a similar relationship between achievement and self-esteem (Campbell, 1965; Coopersmith, 1967), and the same pattern appears at the college and graduate levels. Silverman (1964) grouped college students according to four levels of self-esteem and found that their cognitive input corresponded directly to their own self-images. He suggests that persons with low self-esteem require themselves to maintain a low self-evaluation; hence they take in less information and maintain an academic achievement level in keeping with this evaluation.[21] In an investigation of sex differences Barker (1968) noted that among female college students higher self-concept of ability corresponded to higher college grades and persistence in college; among male students, although high self-

18 See Purkey, 1970, pp. 24–26   20 Caplin, 1966 (1966A), pp. 979–980
19 Blair, 1967 (1968A), p. 3013   21 Silverman, 1964, pp. 116–118

concept of ability was not a consistent predictor, the lowest self-concepts were found in chronic nonpersisters.[22] Keefer (1966) found self-predictions of academic achievement to be better predictors of actual scholastic performance than either high school grades or American College Test scores; moreover, these self-predictions continued to be more accurate after the freshman year than the traditional measures of grades and test scores.[23]

In three other important studies at the college or graduate level academic achievement as such was not the specific variable, but it is implied in the characteristics of the groups investigated. In a study reported by Sutherland et al. (1962) female students at the University of Texas School of Education were classified according to three levels of mental health.[24] The students in the low group were characterized by low self-esteem, conflicting feelings about life, self-centered desires, guilt about their need for affection, and a tendency to antagonize and alienate people of their own age. As students they were disorganized and ill-directed and needed help in working out a more productive life style. Those in the average group were characterized by dependence, conformity, and a tendency to learn classwork by rote. Their academic work was also average. Members of the group rated high in mental health were strongly motivated to learn and took a keen pleasure in the process of achieving understanding. They demonstrated firmly entrenched habits of initiative, clear thinking, objectivity and foresight and were characterized as relaxed, outgoing, optimistic, and self-confident, with a generally good attitude toward themselves and a high degree of self-acceptance. The low group was dependent and indecisive, and in general both the medium and low groups had fewer of the qualities which could be classified as high self-esteem than did the high group.

In a study conducted by Barron (1968) at the University of California, Berkeley, graduate students in their last year of doctorate work were rated on personal soundness (here equivalent to self-esteem) by members of the Institute of Personality Assessment and Research and the Department of Psychology.[25] The study was designed to compare the detailed personality characteristics of the high- and low-soundness groups in terms of certain

22 Barker, 1968 (1968A), p. 1100

23 See Purkey, 1970, p. 24

24 Sutherland, Holtzman, Koile, and
     Smith, 1962, pp. 183–192

25 Barron, 1968, pp. 37–65

aspects of their life histories rather than in terms of a single inter-vening variable. One of the characteristics which differentiated high and low personal soundness was self-confidence. The high-soundness students were stable, unaffected, self-assured, and possessed of a kind of self-confidence which enabled them to assert themselves. Those who scored low in personal soundness were characteristically anxious, awkward, immature, defensive, and evasive; they also expressed feelings of unworthiness and were somewhat given to deceitfulness and lack of frankness.

A third study was conducted at McGill University by West-ley and Epstein (1969), who rated first-year students on the basis of a mental-health scale and selected a group of ninety-six for study over a period of three years.[26] The subjects were the twenty healthiest and the twenty most disturbed, with the remaining fifty-six students as a control. The dependent variable was the family background of these students, with such intervening vari-ables as academic achievement, extracurricular activities, and re-lationships with the opposite sex. All ninety-six students had better-than-average grades, and roughly half of them had an aver-age of 65, which at McGill would give them second-class stand-ing. The students rated as high in mental health were able to give a clear picture of their own feelings, reactions, and role relation-ships to their parents. Those in the low group differed considerably in the quality, quantity, and content of their responses concerning their families, but in general their replies tended to be cliché-ridden, irrelevant, repetitive, and lacking in significance. Self-esteem is not specifically reported as a factor in these findings, but it may be inferred from some of the data.

The foregoing findings on the relationship between self-esteem and academic achievement at all educational levels are further supported by one of the follow-up studies of the famous Terman gifted group. In 1922 approximately 1400 children be-tween ten and eleven were found to have genius-level IQs placing them in the top 1 percent of the population. As they developed, however, there proved to be a wide variation in their actual productivity. In the follow-up surveys of 1940 and 1950 (at which time the subjects were in their thirties and forties), three

25 Barron, 1968, pp. 37–65   26 Westley and Epstein, 1969

factors differentiated the most successful from the least successful groups. These were the personality traits of integration toward goals, perseverance, and self-confidence.[27]

Clearly, academic achievement is far from being determined by IQ alone. There is evidence that the functioning of intelligence and cognitive skills is influenced by such personality traits as persistence, independence, impulse control, orderly study habits, and numerous other variables. Undoubtedly these personality traits play a part in the ability of an individual to utilize his skills effectively; yet underlying all these characteristics—and really fundamental to them—is his self-confidence or self-esteem. It appears that self-esteem is a basic personality characteristic which is prerequisite not only to academic achievement, but to productive behavior in general.

THE CREATIVE PERSON

The creative person has been described (and to some extent idealized), as highly independent, innovative in his approach to problems, and noted for his exceptional sense of the theoretical or the esthetic. He is open to a wide range of experience and is characterized by spontaneity, flexibility, and a complexity of outlook. His independence is reflected in nonconformity, and sometimes in rebelliousness; as a result, his intelligence is not necessarily accompanied by academic achievement. As Trent stresses, creative individuals have different styles of performing and are not all of a type.[28]

Taylor broadly defines other characteristics of creative functioning as intellectual persistence, a fondness for manipulating and toying with ideas, curiosity, the tendency to question, a preference for complexity and its challenges, tolerance of ambiguity, and an ability to solve problems.[29] He also mentions qualities of "divergent thinking," a concept first outlined by Guilford to describe thought processes tending toward exploration, speculation, innovation, risk taking, growth, and discovery. Divergent thinking includes such specific intellectual traits as adaptive flexibility, spontaneous flexibility, fluency of ideas and associations,

27 Oden, 1968, p. 65

28 Trent, 1968, pp. 4–5

29 Taylor, 1963, pp. 236–237

fluency of expression, and abilities of elaboration and redefinition. "Convergent thinking," in contrast, refers to a concern with retaining and conserving what is known, dealing with and conforming to the usual or expected, and the acquisition of facts and information. These two different cognitive styles, or intellective "modes," occur to some extent in all thinking, but in differing proportions.[30]

A general picture of what might be called the creative personality is given by Trezise, who studied twenty-seven rigorously selected creative adolescents of both sexes.[31] These youngsters were found to have ideas on a wide range of subjects which they were eager to share; they were interested in seminar-type classes and more opportunities for independent study instead of drill and recitation. Although they were often more critical of society and its problems, and sometimes even cynical, they were not overtly defiant of rules and laws. They seemed to be searching for positive values. For the most part, they were interested in understanding both themselves and others; they expressed preference for courses dealing with philosophical and ethical issues. One might say that they were good examples of the productive personality in adolescence.

Creativity is widely recognized as a factor of great potential importance in all areas of activity. During the past fifteen or twenty years Guilford's initial investigations at the University of Southern California have been followed by research at the University of Utah under Taylor and Ghiselin, at the University of California, Berkeley, under MacKinnon, Barron, and others, at the University of Minnesota under Torrance, and at a number of other centers.[32] This work has been directed toward the development of some objective measure of creative abilities. The measurable aspects of creativity, however, are for some reason particularly elusive.

There is apparently little relationship between creativity and intelligence, especially in groups where the ability level is high to begin with. This is clearly illustrated by MacKinnon's findings on creative architects, scientists, and mathematicians. In early research on architects and creative scientists at the Institute

30 Getzels and Jackson, 1962, pp. 13–14   32 See Torrance, 1959, pp. 309–310
31 Trezise, 1966 (1967A), pp. 2754–2755

of Personality Assessment and Research he found practically no correlations between creativity and intelligence as measured by the Terman Concept Mastery Test (correlations were, respectively, −.08 for architects and −.07 for scientists). Subsequent investigations with the Wechsler Adult Intelligence Scale pointed in the same direction. When architects were grouped on the basis of three levels of creativity, ranging from the most creative to the least creative, the mean IQ scores of each group were practically identical: 132 for the top group, 131 for the middle group, and 130 for the lowest group. With a similar grouping of research scientists on the basis of creativity, the average IQ was 132 in all three groups. The results were the same in the case of both male and female mathematicians.[33]

Despite these zero correlations between creativity and intelligence, over the whole range of intelligence and creativity there is in fact a positive relationship: as MacKinnon points out, no feebleminded subjects were found in any of the groups studied. He explains that a certain level of intelligence (about 120) is probably prerequisite for careers in demanding professions such as architecture, mathematics, and research science, but beyond this point greater intelligence does not guarantee greater success. In fact even the small variations at this higher level can probably be accounted for by factors such as persistence, self-confidence, independence, and motivation.

A number of other studies of the relationship between intelligence and creativity substantiate MacKinnon's findings. Reported correlations between creativity and intelligence have ranged (depending on the size and heterogeneity of the sample and the measures used) from as low as .18 to .55. However, creativity does not appear to be a predictor of academic achievement; Cline, Richards, and Abe (1962) report that intelligence and creativity combined predict academic success no more accurately than either trait alone.[34] Correlations between the Minnesota Test of Creative Thinking and such intelligence tests as the Stanford-Binet, California Mental Maturity, Kuhlmann-Anderson, and Otis Quick Scoring Test have been positive but not very high (from .16 to .32). Moreover, correlations tend to be lower for girls than for

33 MacKinnon, 1968, pp. 106–108   34 See Wade, 1968, pp. 97–98

boys, lower for selected talented groups, and lower for cases in which tests are administered individually and orally.[35]

Tests of both creativity and intelligence place a high premium on verbal ability, and in both cases some role is undoubtedly played by such factors as persistence and motivation. Also, since creativity implies original thinking, in a broad sense it entails an ability to deal with symbolic concepts in order to solve problems, as well as an ability to record and communicate information. Such skills are similar to those measured by tests of intelligence. Scales of these traits have not been consistently predictive of creative performance, however, and self-ratings of adolescents and adults have proved only moderately reliable.

Nevertheless, there remains a cluster of elusive personality attributes and elements of cognitive functioning which seem to belong to a special domain of human behavior that can be designated as "creative personality functioning" on the one hand and "creative process" on the other.[36] Moreover, most authorities on creativity make a distinction between artistic creativity and scientific creativity. MacKinnon (1962) has given a clear definition of these two creative processes. He points out that in artistic creativity (including both the fine arts and literature) the results or products are[37]

> . . . clearly expressions of the creator's inner states, his needs, perceptions, motivations, and the like. In this type of creativity, the creator externalizes something of himself into the public field. . . .

In scientific creativity (physical science, engineering, industrial research, etc.) the creative product is

> . . . unrelated to the creator as a person, who in his creative work acts largely as a mediator between externally defined needs and goals. In this kind of creativeness, the creator . . . simply operates on some aspect of his environment in such a manner as to produce a novel and appropriate product, but he adds little of himself or of his style as a person to the resultant.

MacKinnon adds that there are additional domains of creative striving which involve both types of creativity, such as the fields

35 See Arasteh, 1969, p. 161   37 MacKinnon, 1962, p. 485
36 Barron, 1968, p. 238

of mathematics and architecture, in which the creator is at once scientific and artistic in his approach and outlook.

Other important investigations of the personality factors associated with creativity are Barron's research on the artistic dimension of the creative writer and Roe's pioneer work on the characteristics of the creative scientist. In his report on the characteristics of creative writers Barron (1968) emphasized their high scores on the Barron-Welsh Art Scale (although they score slightly lower than painters and architects) and noted a marked preference for figures that are free-flowing, asymmetrical, and visually arresting. He also found evidence of superior intelligence, with high ratings on scales of originality, flexibility, and independence. The creative writers scored very high on the Symbol Equivalence Test, which might be said to measure imaginative qualities.[38] Barron made some reference to their being somewhat more "troubled psychologically" than others, but at the same time indicated that they seem to have greater resources for dealing with their troubles. On other scales he reported them as generally more introverted than extraverted, more feeling than thinking, and more intuitive than oriented to sense experience. He also refers to their rich fantasy life and to a deeply felt "cosmological" commitment to their calling as writers.

According to Roe, whose *The Making of a Scientist* and other publications in the early 1950s exerted considerable influence on professional thinking, scientific creativity requires certain personality traits and strengths. Among the most important of these are a sense of curiosity, marked independence and autonomy, persistence, a fairly high level of intelligence (not necessarily in the genius category), and a relatively high energy level.[39] Other writers are essentially in agreement on these characteristics. Holland (1964) refers to the creative scientist's lack of sociability, and Hughes (1969) mentions his rather remarkable memory, often limited, however, to areas which are of particular interest to him (he characteristically dislikes enforced rote learning).[40] McClelland (1962) stresses his intense "masculinity," and comments that a strong interest in analysis and in the "structure of things" has marked outstanding scientists in many fields.[41]

38 Barron, 1968, pp. 240–247

39 Roe, 1960, pp. 66–67

40 Holland, 1964, p. 301; Hughes, 1969, pp. 74ff

41 McClelland, 1962, pp. 149–150

MacKinnon describes the creative architect as a personality type midway between the artist and the scientist, with some traits of both. Like the artist and the creative writer, he is intuitive in his thinking and perceptive rather than judgmental in his attitudes. However, he scores somewhat higher in the esthetic than in the theoretical areas on the Allport-Vernon-Lindzey Study of Values test, whereas the reverse is true for the scientist.[42] Like the writer, he prefers complex and asymmetrical configurations and shows evidence of a sensitive intellect and wide-ranging interests.

In an interesting study of 400 high school boys Schaefer (1967) found that creative adolescents in both artistic and scientific areas had certain common qualities. Both showed intense devotion to their own field of interest and strong desire for achievement and independence, as well as a need for novelty, complexity, and change.[43] It appeared that their parents, who were well educated and culturally active, had done much to stimulate them. The scientifically creative students were reported as masculine, serious-minded, and persistent; the artistic ones seemed to prefer complexity and asymmetrical stimuli and were also reported as being more "spontaneous and gregarious" than the scientific students.

Creativity in younger children has been studied extensively at the University of Minnesota, where the Minnesota Tests of Creative Thinking have been administered to several thousand children. The tests measure such factors as unusual uses of everyday objects, improvements on available products, and imagination in telling stories; scores are given on fluency, flexibility, originality, and inventiveness. Torrance, who has directed a large part of this work, observes that the creative child is likely to become markedly less so at certain periods in his development: at five, when he emerges from the home environment and encounters demands for conformity to outside authority standards; at about the fourth grade, when he encounters the pressure of peer-group demands; at the beginning of adolescence, with the onset of biological pressures; and at about age seventeen, when he begins to reevaluate himself as an adult.[44]

42 MacKinnon, 1962, pp. 489–490   44 See Arasteh, 1969, pp. 159–160
43 Schaefer, 1967 (1967B), pp. 1173–1174

There has been some disagreement on the sociability of the creative person, particularly the scientist (this will be discussed more fully in Chapter Four). In spite of some tendency to remain aloof from "cocktail party" sociability, however, there is no evidence that the creative scientist is lacking in genuine social concern or that he is in any way lacking in emotional security. On the contrary, White (1968) has demonstrated that a low level of anxiety is an important factor in divergent thinking, long recognized as a characteristic of creativity. He concludes:[45]

> The best evidence is that persons high on divergent thinking ability are not interpersonal recluses as some popular literature might lead one to believe, nor are they shy, apprehensive, and generally anxious.

There is increasing evidence that all genuinely creative persons have a basic quality of self-confidence, or self-esteem. It is difficult to explain their possession of such traits as persistence, independence, tolerance for complexity and challenge, and sensitivity to the environment without the speculation that they have (or have had) someone close to them who has believed in them and in whom they have had complete trust and confidence. Without the assurance that someone, either in reality or in fantasy, believes implicitly in their uniqueness as individuals, such persons would not be able to accomplish their objectives. Self-esteem, then, appears to be an essential element in the creative personality.

Rogers has suggested that the conditions which foster constructive creativity are psychological safety and psychological freedom, and that an "internal locus of evaluation"—confidence in one's perceptions and judgments—is one of three traits consistently associated with creativity (he defines the other two as openness to experience and pleasure in toying with elements and concepts).[46] Psychological safety stems from an environment in which the individual is accepted as being of "unconditional worth," with empathic understanding and a minimum of restrictive evaluation by others. Psychological freedom is fostered by

45 K. White, 1968, pp. 124–126   46 See Wade, 1968, p. 99

opportunities for "symbolic expression." In other words, it is a home rich in opportunities for intellectual and artistic expansion that gives rise to the creative spirit.

As in the studies on academic achievement, there are many references to the trait of self-esteem in the literature on creative individuals. MacKinnon reported the most creative group of architects as more poised, more self-confident, and more self-assured than either of the other groups.[47] Similar findings were obtained by Domino (1971) in a study of men working in the field of cinematography.[48] In a study of faculty members in university psychology departments, Drevdahl (1964) classified his subjects as creative productive, noncreative productive, and noncreative nonproductive. Although self-esteem was not mentioned specifically, the data suggest that the creative productive psychologists were more emotionally secure than those in the noncreative nonproductive group; more signs of emotional disturbance, insecurity, and inferior feelings were noted in the latter group, not only at the time, but also in reports of their early life.[49]

Maslow (1954) found all self-actualizing persons to be creative in one sense or another; these people also had no doubts about their self-worth and did not seem to feel it necessary to play any kind of a role in their relationships with others.[50] Creative scientists rate themselves high in professional self-confidence.[51] Barron notes that mature professional writers report high aspiration levels and wide-ranging interests and concerns, while the less mature student writers seem more anxious about their adequacy as persons.[52] The findings in other studies (Garwood, 1964; Helson, 1967; Sisk, 1966; and Lett, 1968) have been essentially the same.

There have also been a few studies of children which contradict the traditional picture of the creative child as lonely, withdrawn, and isolated. In a study of seventh-grade children Reid, King, and Wickwire (1959) found the creative pupils "more sociable, easy-going, and warm-hearted" than their peers. Weisberg and Springer (1961) reported that the creative fourth-graders in their investigations demonstrated significantly stronger self-image and greater ease of recall than the control-group children, although certain other characteristics suggested "oedipal anxiety

47 MacKinnon, 1962, p. 487
48 Domino, 1971, pp. 413–414
49 Drevdahl, 1964, p. 174

50 Maslow, 1954, pp. 208–209
51 Holland, 1964, p. 301
52 Barron, 1968, pp. 237–240

and uneven ego development."[53] Thus, although some studies have depicted the creative child as less well adjusted than his peers, there is other evidence that he is actually better adjusted, less anxious, less rigid in attitudes, and more self-confident and persistent in working toward goals than the less creative child.[54]

On the whole, self-esteem appears to be an important attribute for the creative individual to possess. According to Coopersmith:[55]

> An essential component of the creative process, whether it be analysis, synthesis, or the development of a new perspective or a more comprehensive theory, is the conviction that one's judgment in interpreting the events is to be trusted.

It is only with the possession of complete emotional security that an individual can function with the degree of independence which is a requisite to any kind of creative expression.

THE LEADER

Leadership occurs in many different situations and takes a variety of forms. In many cases a person becomes a leader by virtue of his position in some authority structure. Individuals may also become leaders because of their exceptional achievement in some area—or even by expressing some conviction or taking a moral stand which provides a model for others. Another aspect of leadership is constructive leadership, the role of the leader in some group or enterprise which facilitates the productive functioning of its members.

Some basic assumptions underlie the concept of constructive leadership in any group.[56] To begin with, a group must be productive in order to survive—that is, the contributions of its members must lead to some common goal or objective. In a collective enterprise, therefore, regardless of the productivity of the individual members, the productivity of the group itself depends on the quality of its leadership. Leadership, however, is a reciprocal relationship: one is a leader only if he is followed. Hence, for the group to be productive, the leader must meet the needs of its

53 See Arasteh, 1969, p. 167
54 Maslow, 1954, pp. 208–209; Kurtzman, 1967, p. 162
55 Coopersmith, 1967, p. 59
56 Petrullo, in Petrullo and Bass, 1961, pp. xv–xviii

members. Even Napoleon is said to have observed: "There go the people; I must hurry and catch up with them, for I am their leader."

A leader, in other words, is the individual whom the group chooses to enable its members to fulfill their own objectives. The leader of any group, whether he is selected on a formal or an informal basis, is a person who is viewed as competent with respect to the central tasks of that group. He must also have belonged to the group long enough for other members to evaluate his potential contribution to their goals and to develop both trust and esteem for him. Not only must he be competent, but others must have confidence in his judgment and the fairness of his decisions. In general, groups choose as leaders those persons who represent their own superegos, or ideal selves; the leader is selected as a model with whom they wish to identify.

These observations are supported by a neatly designed experiment by Chowdhry and Newcomb (1952), which showed that the person chosen as a leader is one whom the group perceives as having the ability to judge their own opinions on the particular issues which are relevant to them.[57] In other words, leaders are chosen partly because of their recognized quality of empathy, or sensitivity to the feelings of the others in the group. The findings also indicated that, in addition to a sense of fairness and good judgment, the leader must demonstrate a specific ability to deal with the problems of that particular group; thus his knowledge or competence must be in the area that is central to its concerns. The leader, if he is to lead effectively, must be able to communicate his ideas clearly and easily to others. Jennings (1943) observed that leaders seem able to establish rapport quickly and effectively with a wide range of other personalities. Another characteristic of leaders, then, is friendliness, which is also an expression of empathy.

The studies on adult leadership suggest that leaders are chosen not because of some unitary trait of leadership, but because of personal characteristics of empathy, friendliness, self-esteem, a sense of responsibility to others, independence of judgment, and skill in communication. In fact, the qualities of potential leader-

57 Chowdhry and Newcomb, 1952, pp. 56–57

ship are apparently the same qualities expected of good followers. Holland and Webb (1955), in a study of 187 aviation cadets at Pensacola, asked each of their subjects (1) whom they would select as leaders of a hypothetical military mission of which they were members and (2) whom they would select as followers on the same expedition if they were the leader. The answers indicated clearly that the person chosen as a leader would also be the one chosen as the best follower.[58]

A survey of leadership studies of children indicates that the same personal qualities are found in both the young and the adult leader. Hartup (1970) observes that leadership in children is related to peer acceptance, which in turn is related to friendliness, acceptance of others, social participation, assurance (self-esteem), good moral judgment, social sensitivity, and a willingness both to give and to receive friendly overtures.[59] A University of Michigan study of "socially powerful" children—those who are not necessarily leaders but are influential in peer groups—also reveals a small but significant correlation between social power and IQ. These children were perceived by their peers as capable in school, camp situations, and athletics. They were more inclined to participate socially and had relatively fewer emotional problems than their less influential peers.[60]

Studies of adolescents indicate a relationship between social acceptance and conformity to the mores of the peer group, as well as to "good moral judgment" as perceived by peers and to empathic sensitivity toward others' feelings. Although popularity appears to be associated with behavior in accordance with peer values, the evidence does not suggest that the popular person is excessively conforming or compliant in social situations. Leaders are, in fact, more likely to have positive self-concepts and to be more "socioempathic" than nonleaders. Hartup points out a low but significant correlation between peer acceptance and self-esteem.[61]

It appears that leaders have some of the same characteristics that are common to the academic achiever and the creative person. In a study at Purdue University Karasick et al. (1968) evaluated questionnaires returned by 12,000 high school students and

58 See Hollander, 1961, p. 36

59 Hartup, 1970, pp. 388–389

60 See Hartup, 1970, p. 401

61 See Hartup, 1970, pp. 390, 402

found that 57 percent of the high leadership group had above-average or excellent grades, whereas only 35 percent of the low-leadership group had grades of the same quality. The high-leadership group also perceived themselves as having more friends than their classmates.[62] In another study of leadership and achievement Holland (1963) examined teacher ratings on a random sample of National Merit Scholarship finalists consisting of 649 boys and 345 girls. He found that both boys and girls who were high in academic performance were also rated high on citizenship, popularity, and social leadership, as well as on self-assurance and perseverance.[63]

Further evidence of the same basic personality qualities in both academic achievers and leaders comes from a study by Sorrentino (1971). He postulated that the motivational factors found in high academic achievers, such as self-confidence, range of interests, and quantity and quality of verbal interaction, were also associated with potential leadership factors. From his results Sorrentino concludes that achievement-related motives may represent possible sources of leadership qualities, but only in conjunction with "the affiliation motive and present versus future goal orientations."[64]

Studies of leadership in children indicate that peer-group leaders in nearly all cases exhibit a constellation of attributes which include intellectual ability, active and appropriate sociability, and in the case of boys, assertiveness and aggressiveness. Moreover, factors which are correlated with popularity in children, and with leadership positions in elementary and high school, are probably also predictive of later social power or leadership.[65]

The research on self-esteem and peer acceptance in children strongly suggests that those with high self-esteem tend to be more powerful in social relations, that they attempt to influence others, and that they are less susceptible to others' attempts to influence them; in contrast, those with low self-esteem tend to seek the acceptance and support of others.[66] Studies of leadership at the adolescent and adult levels show a similar relationship. In fact, self-esteem appears to be as basic a quality in leaders as it is in the academic or the creative achiever.

62 Karasick, Leidy, and Smart, 1968, pp. 4–8

63 Holland, 1963, p. 517

64 Sorrentino, 1971 (1971A), p. 1625

65 Hartup, 1970, p. 402; Florestano, 1970 (1971A), p. 173

66 Gergen, 1971, p. 76

One of the earlier studies of leadership was an investigation by Gardner (1948) of executives.[67] The upward-mobile executive who was successful in progressing to higher positions was marked by a clear sense of identity; he knew who he was and what he wanted and had devised means for getting what he wanted. In contrast, his less successful colleagues, those who did not seem to get their share of promotions, believed that they were not as admirable or worthy as they should be.

An important longitudinal study related to leadership is reported by Cox (1970), who examined sixty-three men and women ten years after their graduation from three outstanding colleges.[68] As undergraduates all had been elected to leadership (student council) positions and were studied intensively at that time by Bond. Cox rated the same group ten years later on a mental health scale and found most of them (77 percent) unimpaired in mental health. The distinguishing characteristic was not specifically labeled "self-esteem," but the highest-rated members of the group were described in such terms as "well above average in adjustment and work," having a "positive outlook," or "no problems visible or sensed by the investigator." Cox also noted their outstanding purposefulness, their satisfaction in their work, and their ability to love wholeheartedly. Even in those who were lower down on the mental-health scale (category B), the work and love relationships were moderately satisfactory, although the subjects were somewhat less efficient in work. The group designated as impaired in mental health showed characteristics of low self-esteem: chronic irritability, a sense of injury, and unrewarding love relationships between spouses and within families.

Cox noted further that the ego strength (self-esteem) characteristic of the higher-rated subjects had enabled them to cope with a number of stresses in the period following college which were not typical of the entire group. Over half of them had obtained advanced or professional degrees and had dealt with difficulties of a real nature over the years, whereas the stresses of the low, or impaired, group were at least to some degree self-created.

Brewster Smith (1966) conducted another interesting investigation of the personality traits of Peace Corps teachers who had

67 Gardner, 1948   68 Cox, 1970, chap. 8

served in Ghana.[69] At the end of the first and second years of service, items selected from tape-recorded job-focused interviews were distributed by a Q-sort technique as traits ranging from "saliently characteristic" to "saliently uncharacteristic" of the group as a whole. When the items were intercorrelated, the most characteristic trait was found to be self-confidence and the least characteristic was low self-esteem.

In a study of the relationship between social mobility and self-esteem Douvan and Adelson (1966) classified 518 adolescent They found that 54 percent were upward mobile—aspiring to an occupation higher than that of their fathers—while 32 percent had the same aspirations as their fathers and 14 percent were downward mobile. There were marked personality contrasts between the upward- and downward-mobile groups which were related to differences in self-esteem. Those in the upward-mobile group were more poised, more self-confident, more self-accepting, and more objective about themselves than the downward-mobile boys. Those in the downward-mobile group, in contrast, were listless, physically awkward, and unattractive in appearance, with indications of social immaturity, low energy level, lack of self-confidence, and feelings of alienation.

The Harvard School of Business Administration has also published some important investigations of leadership characteristics of business personnel. Moment and Zaleznik (1963) studied men in relatively responsible positions in middle and upper management—people who were committed to a working career and to the responsibilities of marriage, parenthood, and community participation.[71] The subjects were rated by their fellow-workers on the ability to present ideas and guide a discussion, on qualities of friendliness and leadership, and on their desirability as a colleague and/or a friend. Those who rated high on ideas and congeniality were designated as "stars," those high in ideas and low in congeniality were classified as "technical specialists," and those low on ideas but high on congeniality were termed "social specialists"; a fourth, low-ranked group was called "underchosen."

69 Brewster Smith, 1968, pp. 283–284
70 Douvan and Adelson, 1966, pp. 63–69
71 Moment and Zaleznik, 1963, pp. 120–125

Among the detailed findings reported by Moment and Zaleznik, it should be noted that high self-esteem was conspicuous in the stars, who were found to be spontaneous, integrated, and varied in their communication with others; they had confidence in themselves, could defend a position while remaining flexible in attitude, and could relate well in general to others. They were viewed by their associates as leaders. Those in the technical-specialist group had excellent ideas, but were somewhat mediocre in dealings with committees, groups, and individuals; as a rule they were task-involved and inclined to "talk shop," while being short on social amenities. They tended to be evasive in expressing their feelings about people, and even in expressing their own ideas, and maintained a certain distance between themselves and others. The social specialists, although involved with people, displayed somewhat dependent modes of behavior; they appeared to need other people and to value social relationships more than career success. The underchosen had markedly low self-esteem and were reported as characteristically defensive, bitter, cynical, critical, and competitive.

In another study sponsored by the Harvard Business School Zaleznik, Dalton, and Barnes (1970) classified the managers and specialists of a large firm as "oriented" or "conflicted" regarding their future vocational plans and aspirations.[72] All subjects were tested for personality characteristics on the Thematic Apperception Test (selected cards), and they were then grouped on the basis of the Allport-Vernon-Lindzey Study of Values test; the oriented group consisted of those whose aspirations and values were congruent or consistent, and the conflicted group consisted of those whose level of aspiration did not correspond to their answers on the values test. Apparently the factor which differentiated the oriented and conflicted subjects was not training or ability, but self-esteem. Those in the oriented group exhibited self-confidence, a basic trust in their environment, low anxiety, and an ability to concentrate on intellectual endeavor; they were found to be creative, receptive, and relatively independent in their relationships with others. The conflicted subjects, however,

72 Zaleznik, Dalton, and Barnes, 1970, pp. 167–169

were characterized by low self-esteem. They required rather extensive ego gratification and demanded sympathy or reward for their efforts; impulsivity was also evident.

Zaleznik et al. state that aspiration level is also a good measure of self-esteem, since it indicates the individual's degree of confidence in anticipating success or failure in the future. Those who were oriented anticipated success in their chosen careers and preferred activities. In contrast, members of the conflicted group were struggling with anxiety regarding their identities, reflecting uncertainty over their self-esteem. The conflicted managers appeared to be overcommitted, and the conflicted specialists were withdrawn.[73]

A recent study by Baker (1971) on the successful investor is pertinent here because leadership emerged as one of the dependent variables differentiating the successful from the unsuccessful. After a pilot study of sixty-four introductory psychology students at the University of Oklahoma, the California Psychological Inventory was used in a more intensive investigation of the personality traits of sixty stockbrokers working with six large firms.[74] The successful broker was found to be extremely confident in his social interaction and to have a high sense of personal worth; he was not plagued by self-doubt or disillusionment and was able to coordinate and direct other persons. The scores of the less successful brokers suggested a person who is shy and withdrawn, indifferent, undependable, and aloof and distrustful of others.

Two extensive studies of self-esteem in children and adolescents also deal with the question of vocational aspiration. In a study of fifth- and sixth-graders Coopersmith (1967) found that children with high self-esteem not only expect more of themselves, but are also more likely to meet their own expectations.[75] They have higher self-ideals than children with lower appraisals of their worthiness. They also set higher achievement goals for themselves and increase their self-esteem still further by meeting their expectations rather than lowering their goals. As a result, the gap between aspiration and fulfillment is less, despite the fact that their aspirations are higher. In contrast to his less secure counter-

73 Zaleznik, Dalton, and Barnes, 1970, pp. 60, 61, 75

74 Baker, 1971, p. 86

75 Coopersmith, 1967, p. 147

part, the self-confident student experiences a continuing spiral of academic success, more respectful treatment from others, greater competence—and hence further success. Such a person not only aspires to be successful; he has every expectation of being successful.

Rosenberg (1965), who studied self-esteem in high school students, has come to similar conclusions.[76] He found that although adolescents with high self-esteem do not particularly seek leadership, those with low self-esteem actively reject leadership situations. They have just as much wish to get ahead, but they do not *expect* to get ahead. Of the 5000 adolescents of both sexes in Rosenberg's study, more than three-fourths (78 percent) of the low self-esteem group doubted that they would ever advance in life as far as they would like, whereas almost the same proportion (71 percent) of those with high self-esteem felt confident that they could go as far in life as they wanted. Replies on the questionnaires also reflected a striking parallel between self-confidence and involvement in school affairs. Nearly half (49 percent) the adolescents in the high-self-esteem group—but only 15 percent of those in the low group—were participating to any great extent in extracurricular activities. This difference also extended to leadership roles; those with high self-esteem were usually the ones chosen as leaders, both as elected officers of school organizations and as informal leaders of peer groups. In short, there was a marked parallel between self-esteem and the potential for leadership in this large adolescent population.

dynamics of productive functioning

It is apparent from descriptions of the three types of productive personality that self-esteem plays a key role in their functioning. In the area of academic achievement there is a consistent relationship between the level of a student's self-esteem and the level of his performance. Moreover, his performance can be predicted more accurately from his own self-concept than from such objective measures of ability as IQ tests; in other words, it

76   Rosenberg, 1965, pp. 193–201, 234–235

appears that his self-esteem is a determinant of his productivity. Obviously it is not the only determinant; however, it accounts for the basic attitude of hope which, along with other cognitive skills and personality attributes, is part of the essential equipment for coping and mastery, as discussed in Chapter Five.

The pictures of the creative person vary. Creativity in both the artistic and the theoretical realms, however, is characterized by a flexibility of perceptual and cognitive processes which in itself necessitates the fundamental self-belief to stand alone. Similarly, the qualities of leadership reflect a basic sense of personal worth to which others seem to respond. To understand the productive personality, then, we must consider the origins of this positive self-image and the basis on which it affects productive functioning.

The productive person is singular not only in terms of his contribution, but also in terms of himself. He appears to have a unified personality organization which enables him to function productively both in his relationships with others and in his own areas of accomplishment. He does not hesitate to stand alone in his values, ideas, commitments, or the nature of his product. He may be interested in the opinions of others, but he seeks them as additional information, not as advice. He may also be deeply concerned about the effect of his decisions on others; but he makes his own decisions.

The internal strength that enables the productive individual to function independently stems from a sure knowledge of himself. He perceives himself clearly as an entity separate and distinct from others—and he knows who he is. In short, he has a clear sense of identity. The process through which he develops this

the formation
of identity

CHAPTER THREE

sense of himself, however, stems from empathy—a sense of one-ness with another. Paradoxically, unless an individual can feel at one with another person, he cannot feel at one with himself.

identity

Identity is a vital aspect of the productive personality. However, the term itself has taken on such a wide and confusing variety of connotations, that we cannot discuss identity without first clari-fying the precise meaning and nature of the concept. Schafer (1968) has been particularly critical of the ambiguities in current usage. He points out that the boundary line between identity and such personality factors such as the self, the ego, and character is not clear. The concept of identity has, since its introduction by Erikson, acquired a number of inexact connotations, as well as becoming fashionable, especially among psychoanalysts. Thus it has taken on the aura of an "answer" to many behavior problems and has often been employed to gloss over incomplete data or an inadequate analysis of issues.[1] Leites (1971) also rather aptly de-scribes the confusion and contradictions that surround the term in recent literature.[2] As a label, it may have become, in effect, a convenient catch-all for describing personality characteristics without a full understanding of their causes. Among diagnosti-cians, for example, especially in clinical psychology, "identity" too frequently means sex-role identity—often in a negative sense. Malfunctioning individuals are often described as "lacking sex identity" or having "confused sex-role identification."

There is little doubt that identity, or some concept akin to it, is a vital aspect of personality development. This is apparent from the research on identity not only by Erikson, who has repeatedly emphasized its importance, but by such authorities as Robert White (1952), Lichtenstein (1961, 1963), Henry Murray, Greenacre (1958), Mahler (1957), and Eissler (1957). There appears to be general agreement with Erikson's view that identity pertains more to maturity than to childhood. It is the result of a long develop-mental process which, at some point in late adolescence, crystal-

1 Schafer, 1968, pp. 39–40   2 Leites, 1971, pp. 109–141

lizes an accumulation of preadolescent experiences and identifications with many persons and objects.[3]

Both lexicographers and theorists seem to agree in two respects on the definition of identity, which derives from the Latin word *idem*, meaning "the same." Indirectly or directly, they refer to the characteristic of sameness and to the element of continuity. In general usage the term connotes unity and persistence of personality. One psychoanalytic definition by Lichtenstein refers to "the capacity to remain the same in the midst of change."[4] Since 1950 Erikson has contributed a series of wide-ranging and influential discussions of identity, which he prefers to call "ego identity."[5] Specifically, he defines ego identity as that sense which "provides the ability to experience one's self as something that has continuity and sameness, and to act accordingly."[6] Schafer summarizes Erikson's various conceptions of identity formation as[7]

> the subject's relatively successful struggle for integrated functional and experiential continuity in a changing biological, familial, cultural, and experiential past, present, and future.

Identity has also been associated with the concept of integration by Greenacre (1958), who refers to an integrated person as one whose parts are "sufficiently well-integrated" for the effect to be "oneness."[8]

In a broad sense, then, identity is the sum of all the parts of the individual; it denotes oneness or wholeness. Conversely, lack of identity indicates that the parts are not functioning as a unified whole. This context provides us with a useful framework for understanding the essential uniqueness and individuality required for productive functioning.

Identity must also have some reference point. One can see himself as separate only in relation to some group of others—that is, only in the sense of "separate from." Each person has some form of group membership, and he perceives himself in relation to that group. Paradoxically, an individual can develop a sure sense of himself only when he is able to find some aspect of others in his social framework with which he can clearly identify.[9] He must

3 Jahoda, 1958, p. 30

4 See Jacobson, 1964, p. 29

5 See Erikson, 1950a; 1950b; 1960; 1968

6 Erikson, 1950a, p. 38

7 Schafer, 1968, p. 41

8 See Leites, 1971, p. 111

9 Lynd, 1958, p. 215

have a sense of belonging to something—before he can have a sense of individuality. People vary with respect to their need to identify with groups; some are content to relate themselves to family, friends, or their immediate community, while others find it essential to identify with a larger community such as a profession, a nation, or even all humankind. As Douvan and Adelson (1966) put it:[10]

> However we define ourselves, whether we imagine ourselves as we are, or were, or will be in the future, the sense of ourselves carries with it some placing of the self in the social system.

Specific references to identity are surprisingly meager in the studies of productive individuals. The most eloquent of the theorists is Maslow, whose famous study of self-actualizing persons included such notables as Eleanor Roosevelt, Jane Addams, William James, and Goethe, as well as outstanding college students and other subjects. Maslow reports that the self-actualizing person has greater self-confidence and seems to be more at home with himself than those he defines as non-self-actualizing. He describes his subjects as "fused" with the world, as having the quality of *Gemeinschaftsgefühl*, a feeling for mankind:[11]

> Our subjects . . . were more completely individualized, more unmistakably themselves, less easily confounded with others than any average control group could possibly be. That is to say, they are simultaneously very much alike and very much unlike each other. They are more completely individual than any group that has ever been described, and yet are also more completely socialized, more identified with humanity than any other group yet described.

Maslow goes on to say that "self-actualization is actualization of a self, and no two selves are altogether alike. There is only one Renoir, one Brahms, one Spinoza."

Specific references to identity appear in a few other studies. McClelland (1962) commented on the strong sex-role identity of creative scientists; male physical scientists score higher than any other group on measures of typically masculine interests and

10 Douvan and Adelson, 1966, p. 18   11 Maslow, 1954, pp. 217, 232

attitudes.[12] In their study of freshmen at McGill University Westley and Epstein (1969) found that in the group classified as mentally healthy "all were capable of demonstrating that they were developing a sense of identity.[13] Gardner (1948) characterized the successful and upward-mobile business executive as distinguished by strong self-identification; these men know who they are and what they want, and they develop techniques for getting what they want. MacKinnon (1963) noted with respect to his highest-ranking sample of creative architects:[14]

> What is most impressive . . . is the degree to which they have actualized their potentialities. They have become in large measure the persons they were capable of becoming.

IDENTITY AND SELF

The concept of self has served for a number of years as a convenient, though nebulous, construct for research on various aspects of growth and personality development, as well as for therapeutic practices. Self may in fact be a valid description of some general area of personality. However, as Coopersmith (1967) points out, there is still insufficient evidence to describe what this complex and multidemensional quality may include.[15]

Like identity, self has been described in a variety of ways. According to Lewis (1971), the self is a perceptual product of the individual's sensory experiences of "body" and "distance." It literally involves a localization of the body as a bounded and separate entity in space, and localization of all experiences as either originating within the body or originating "out there." The self is thus the fundamental reference point for the perception of other experience.[16] According to Jacobson's comprehensive definition, the self includes the individual's image of his physical appearance, as well as the layers of his consciousness, his emotions, and his "physical and mental functions."[17] Horney has defined self as "the whole person—somatic as well as psychic, conscious and unconscious—as he really exists at any point in time."[18]

The definitions above refer primarily to the individual's

12 McClelland, 1962, p. 149

13 Westley and Epstein, 1969, p. 56

14 MacKinnon, 1963, p. 277

15 Coopersmith, 1967, p. 21

16 Lewis, 1971, pp. 31–33

17 Jacobson, 1964, p. 22

18 See Hinsie and Campbell, 1970, p. 690

perception of himself from moment to moment. MacLeod (1962) also views self as a factor in the perceptual process itself:[19]

> The cognitive field includes not only all the things, events, and relations as they are apprehended, but also the self which is the crucial anchorage point of all apprehension. Perceiving is a special kind of relation between self and object. . . . The cognitive conditions for thinking, then, must be sought in certain special self-object relations.

Barron (1964) feels, moreover, that the distinction between self and not-self is "the beginning of perceptual structure and the most primitive achievement of the ego." He contends that the ability to distinguish between what is inside and what is outside us is the first requirement for causal thinking; once this is established,[20]

> . . . we can make discriminations in space and time, we can describe events at specific space-time coordinates, we can give reasons, and we are able to be objective and experience our self as subject, a subject distinct from the world of objects.

The close relationship between self and identity is reflected in the use of circular definitions. For example, "self" is defined as "the identity, character, or essential qualities of any person or thing."[21] References to sameness, which appear in most definitions of identity, are sometimes found in descriptions of self. Erikson makes the following observation:[22]

> Identity in its vaguest sense suggests . . . much of what has been called the self by a variety of workers, be it in the form of a self-concept, a self-system, or in that of fluctuating self-experiences. . . .

He thus appears to consider the experience of self as an aspect of the individual's identity. Fromm (1955) carries this idea further in referring to mental health as characterized by "a sense of identity based on one's experience of self as the subject and agent of one's powers."[23] Identity, then, is a much broader and inclusive concept than self. Whereas self is an early perceptual distinction, identity evolves after many years of experience with self.

48

19 MacLeod, 1962, pp. 190–191

20 Barron, 1964, p. 81

21 Webster's new world dictionary of the American language, college edition, 1962, sv self

22 Erikson, 1968, pp. 208–209

23 Fromm, 1955, p. 69

As a child develops, his perception of himself is altered by his physiological development, by his acquisition of language, and by his experiences with his environment. He also becomes aware of discrepancies between what he is and what others wish he were, and he perceives himself as worthy or unworthy according to the amount of this discrepancy. Thus the accuracy of his self-perception, and hence his ability to perceive his environment accurately, depends on the degree of acceptance and esteem he receives from those who are significant to him, specifically his parents.[24] Moreover, since it is his interactions with his environment that comprise his experiences with self, accuracy of self-perception appears to be a factor in the development of both identity and competence.

The high level of self-acceptance which is characteristic of productive persons thus provides a clue to both their perceptual skills and their general functioning. MacKinnon (1963) writes of the most creative architects in his study:[25]

> One is struck by the accuracy of self-perception, by the degree to which architects "see themselves as they really are. . . .

In another article he observes:[26]

> One of the most valuable nonintellective indicators of creative potential has proved to be a person's concept of himself, that is, his self-image or his self-percept.

IDENTITY AND SELF-ESTEEM

From the vast amount of literature referring to self-esteem in such equivalent terms as self-concept, self-acceptance, self-confidence, self-respect, and self-image, there seems little doubt that a well-developed sense of identity is closely associated with self-esteem. Erikson (1960) points out that a sense of identity indicates the experience of a preconscious sense of psychological well-being:[27]

> . . . a feeling of being at home in one's body, a sense of "knowing where one is going," and an inner assuredness of anticipated recognition from those who count.

24 Arieti, 1970, pp. 101–103

25 MacKinnon, 1963, p. 276

26 MacKinnon, 1968, p. 112

27 Erikson, 1960, p. 51

This is, in effect, the same feeling which Fenichel (1945) describes as the origin of self-esteem in every infant. In the adolescent a sense of identity must be preceded by what Erikson terms a "realistic self-esteem"—a self-concept which reflects his competence not only in meeting the demands of his environment, but also in meeting the demands of his superego, or conscience. According to Fenichel, every feeling of guilt lowers self-esteem.[28] The lowering of self-esteem in turn causes a loss in identity; hence identity and self-esteem both depend on an absence of guilt feelings.

Jacobson (1964) also refers to the superego as a guide for self-esteem.[29] Schafer suggests further that healthy development of the superego "eventuates in a thoroughly internalized regulation of their moral conduct and self-esteem."[30] Barron (1964) extends this concept to the individual's value system as a factor in a clear sense of identity:[31]

> A person is most alive and is functioning in such a way that he knows who he is and you know who he is and he knows who you are when his thoughts and actions are in accord with his moral judgment.

The close relationship between identity and self-esteem has also been emphasized by others. Sullivan notes that both self-identity and self-esteem seem to be related to the evaluation that the child receives from significant adults.[32] Jacobson views self-esteem as implying a sense of identity—a feeling that all is well, that one need not reach out for support and assistance;[33] Gergen writes that "to be without esteem is symbolic of one's basic anguish in an unpredictable and uncontrollable world."[34] Coopersmith observes that in persons with high self-esteem there is less discrepancy between fulfillment (actual self) and aspiration (ideal self), despite the fact that such persons have higher aspirations than those with low self-esteem.[35]

There seems to be general agreement that identity and self-esteem are closely related, and that self-esteem is perhaps the foundation of a sense of identity.[36] It also appears that identity is a much more nebulous concept than self-esteem. Self-esteem is a

28 Fenichel, 1945, p. 41

29 Jacobson, 1964, p. 133

30 Schafer, 1968, p. 157

31 Barron, 1968, p. 145

32 See Arieti, 1970, p. 101

33 Jacobson, 1964, p. 130

34 Gergen, 1971, p. 69

35 Coopersmith, 1967, p. 146

36 Murphy, 1962, p. 374; Coopersmith, 1967, p. 4

more concrete aspect of personality; it is more easily defined, and hence more easily quantified. Nevertheless, there is need for some concept to describe the aspect of personality that constitutes individuality. Since a person's sense of self is a crystallization of all his previous identifications, we can approach the concept of identity by means of process through which it develops. In this connection Lynd (1958) writes:[37]

> Developing a sense of identity [with its combination of inner and outer direction] includes both discovery of the kinds of identifications one may have with the life-style of one's own society and culture, or with wider groups and values, and an idiom of one's own that comprises but is distinct from these identifications.

the identification process

Although the various schools of psychology are essentially in agreement on the general concept of identity, there are differences among the theorists, and between the theorists and experimentalists, concerning the manner in which identity is formed. In general there is an agreement that a process of modeling, imitation, or identification either precedes or is a component of identity. The learning theorists prefer "modeling" or "imitation"; the term "identification" is more favored in psychoanalytic theory.

The infant and young child requires the continuous presence of one or more adults to supply his basic physical requirements, and the affective relationship he develops with such persons has been called "identification." No child acquires the skills that enable him to cope with his environment merely through a process of trial-and-error experimentation. The growth process and the concomitant need for guidance and direction require a continued affective relationship with parents or with others in the child's environment; it is in this identification process that he develops modes of behavior that enable him to function with some effectiveness in the social, academic, and later adult worlds. There is little doubt concerning the existence of this phenomenon

37 Lynd, 1958, p. 210

of affective interaction (positive or aversive), not only between child and parent, but between and among persons of all ages. In general all theorists agree that identification is a lifelong process and does not end with some given stage of development.

Most definitions of identification refer in similar terms to a dynamic interaction between a child and a model. In psychoanalytic theory, however, identification is considered to be largely an unconscious process. Hinsie and Campbell (1970), for example, define it as the process by which a person incorporates within himself a mental picture of an object and then thinks, feels, and acts as he conceives the object to think, feel, and act."[38] On this basis, identification is the most primitive method of recognizing external reality, a form of mental mimicry which the child employs to transform the strange and frightening to the familiar and enjoyable. Thus identification "operates in the interest of and clings to the defense of narcissism."[39] Social learning theorists also view identification as an unconscious process in the sense that it does not stem from direct teaching. Mussen et al. (1969) hypothesize that it is the process by which a young individual seems to acquire spontaneously or to absorb from a parent or other model certain of his personality characteristics, motives, attitudes, or moral standards.[40] Aronfreed (1968) suggests that identification might be a type of "evaluative cognition that supports the child's perception of a broad similarity between itself and an external model."[41]

There is some question, however, about whether imitation results in identification, or whether identification results in imitation. Bandura (1969) contends that if diverse criteria were seriously applied in categorizing modeling outcomes, in most instances of matched behavior, there would be little difference between behavior that in one instance would be labeled as identification and in another as imitation. He therefore prefers the term "modeling" to describe a process which involves a matching type of behavior.[42]

From the viewpoint of behavior modification or social learning theory, the designation "modeling" or "imitation" may adequately explain the dynamics of the interaction between child and

38 Hinsie and Campbell, 1970, p. 373

39 Hinsie and Campbell, p. 374

40 Mussen, Conger, and Kagan, 1969, pp. 356–357

41 Aronfreed, 1968, p. 75

42 Bandura, 1969, p. 119

parents. In terms of the growth and development of the productive personality, however, the concept of identification provides a more complete description of the interaction between the child and significant persons in his environment from infancy through adulthood. Moreover, since there is some evidence of the relative permanency of the early acquired behavior patterns (Maccoby, 1968; Schafer, 1968; Bandura, 1969; Kagan and Moss, 1962), identification appears to be more applicable to the formation of identity, and modeling, or "learning by observation," more applicable to the socialization process, which is discussed in Chapter Four.

One of the most comprehensive definitions of identification is stated by Schafer in his book *Aspects of Internalization*:[43]

> *In its fullest sense, the process of identifying with an object is unconscious, though it may also have prominent and significant preconscious and conscious components; in this process the subject modifies his motives and behavior patterns, and the self representations corresponding to them, in such a way as to experience being like, the same as, and merged with one or more representations of that object; through identification, the subject both represents as his own one or more regulatory influences or characteristics of the object that have become important to him and continues his tie to the object; the subject may wish to bring about this change for various reasons; an identification may acquire relative autonomy from its origins in the subject's relations with dynamically significant objects.*

BASIC ASSUMPTIONS CONCERNING IDENTIFICATION

In order to understand fully the dynamics of the identification process—particularly as it applies to the development of the productive personality—certain basic assumptions should be taken into account. Some of these emerge from Schafer's comprehensive definition above.

It is a basic premise that some identification process, whatever its form, is universal and necessary. No infant can survive without someone to meet his physical requirements; therefore

43 Schafer, 1968, p. 140

some identification is inevitable. Moreover, no child develops the ability to cope with his environment merely by a process of trial-and-error experimentation; by identifying with and imitating another person or model, he gradually acquires modes of behavior that enable him to function in his progressively complex social, academic, and adult worlds. A reciprocal relationship of empathy and nurturance gives him the confidence to act independently. Freud pointed out that a significant part of every personality is crystallized around identifications and that they are necessary for the maintenance of significant personal relationships.

Another basic premise is that identification is one means of transmitting culture from one generation to the next. Cultural values, mores, and socioeconomic patterns could hardly have continued over the years without the existance of models in each generation. No newborn infant can acquire through the processes of direct learning all the factual, social, physical, and emotional information that he needs in order to function in society. The vicarious learning he experiences through the process of identification with both live and symbolic models is fundamental to the whole learning process.[44]

We must also assume that the earliest forms of identification are those involved with the physiological needs of the newborn infant. The newborn infant brings to his interpersonal relationships his first and most obvious need—hunger—and it is the mother's alleviation of his hunger pangs that becomes the primary basis for the development of self-esteem. These early infant identifications set directions and limits for the child's ultimate social development. It follows, of course, that the basis of the infant's identifications lies in his own endowment of neurological, physiological, and affectual equipment. It is this basic equipment which determines his capacity to respond; but it is the identification process which determines the forms of this response in the child's social and physical milieu. The specific form of expression thus depends both on maturation of processes and on the manner in which these processes are influenced by environment.[45]

Identification must also be a selective process; one cannot absorb all possible identifications in his milieu and combine them

44 Bandura, 1969, p. 145   45 Schafer, 1968, p. 147

to form his own identity. A large number of models are available to most children in their early years. The models they select, however, are those who are significant to their self-esteem.[46] Bandura (1969) claims:[47]

> *People tend to be selective in what they reproduce, suggesting that imitative performance is primarily governed by its utilitarian value. . . . Performance is primarily a function of anticipated outcomes. . . .*

Even the infant selects on this basis. During the first weeks of life, it is the mother's feeding which relieves the infant's tension and contributes to his self-esteem. The father contributes little to his physiological needs, and hence little to his self-esteem in these early weeks. Later, as the child's horizon expands to include other needs, other identifications become critical to his self-esteem. At any stage, however:[48]

> *. . . the selection and performance of matching responses is mainly governed by anticipated outcomes based on previous consequences that were directly encountered, vicariously experienced, or self-administered.*

Identifications based on immediate physical safety and security needs are most readily acquired. It is much easier to model one's behavior on that of a person who is directly providing for such needs than on that of someone who is not available for help. In other words, a young child is (or should be) able to identify more easily with his mother or father than with other persons. Moreover, since the child's basic physical safety needs are repeatedly met in the same environment for many years, these early identifications tend to be relatively permanent. This permanence is apparent from the fact that adults and adolescents who reject their early experiences are able to dispense with their early identifications with only partial or intermittent success.

At any given time the individual identifies with the particular aspect of the model behavior which will meet his immediate needs. In early infancy identification is actually diffuse, or "global," in nature. At later stages, however, identification is

46 Aronfreed, 1968, p. 17; Lynd, 1958, p. 218

47 Bandura, 1969, p. 126

48 Bandura, 1969, p. 132

more specific. A child may need as a model someone who has power, charisma, a particular method of communicating, or social skills. The model with whom he identifies is not just important to him, but "impressive" and "emotionally significant." Whether this identification is temporary or permanent, direct or subtle, conscious or repressed, it is based on the model's significance at a given time.[49] This process of selection relates not only to the model, but also to representations of that person such as his selection of friends, books, hobbies, reading interests, and a multitude of unimportant matters (which are, nevertheless, important to the child). Included in such identifications are facial expressions, patterns of speech, gestures, and other means of expression. Those representations with which the child identifies depend on his own needs at the moment, his level of maturation, his previous experience, and his own perception of the model.[50]

Studies in behavior modification have shown that the influence of the model on the child's behavior continues even after the model is no longer physically present.[51] Once the model's behavior has been adopted, the child will continue to apply this behavior in situations that he perceives as related to the original modeling situation. The aspect of behavior with which a child identifies, however, is not necessarily that behavior which the model intended. Children are quite perceptive in identifying with their parents' actual methods of dealing with problems, and parents are sometimes astonished to find behavioral characteristics in their children that they may not even have considered apparent in themselves. This is especially the case with ethical and moral behavior. Freud notes that the child's superego is not built on the model of the parents' overt behavior, but rather on the model he perceives in their superegos.

Identifications are not limited to human models. Behavioral identification with pets, wild animals, and machines is frequently observed in children, and adolescents and young adults commonly identify with representations of persons no longer living, with fictional characters, or with significant historical or legendary figures.[52]

Although early identifications have an aspect of perma-

49 Schafer, 1968, p. 159
50 Schafer, 1968, p. 142
51 Bandura, 1969, p. 83
52 Schafer, 1968, p. 142

nence, they are not necessarily static. Once they are established, they may, as Schafer has observed, be "generalized, pruned, tempered, revised in their details, and coordinated with other identifications."[53] Not all identifications are intended to endure; some are an aspect of the developmental process or are abandoned for various reasons as the individual matures or as his life style changes.[54]

EARLY FORMS OF IDENTIFICATION

infantile identification In the view of numerous theorists the identification process begins at or shortly after birth. This primary, or "anaclitic," form of identification is an interaction between the infant's physiological needs and the affectional response of the parents. Thus the mother's degree of empathy and the manner in which she expresses her response are critical factors in this initial symbiotic relationship. At this time the foundation is laid for what Erikson terms the "sense of basic trust" in those who are interpreters of the external world.[55] In theory it is this first identification that influences all subsequent identifications in the individual's life.

Immediately after birth the infant must cope in some manner with the realities of the external environment. The first disturbing threat to his existence is the hunger pangs which upset his homeostasis, create a state of anxiety, and cause him to resort to such physical responses as crying as devices for coping with his problem. Fenichel (1945) claims that satisfaction of the infant's hunger forms the basis of his first identification. In a state of complete helplessness and temporary discomfort, in a world he perceives only as a place of either threat or pleasure, this tiny individual does have at his command a social relationship with someone in his surroundings who can minister to his hunger cravings. In his perception, the first reality is, literally, what he can swallow.[56] The first person who attends to his needs becomes the object of his first identification; between the reality of hunger and the satisfaction of being fed there has occurred a relationship with another person.

---

53 Schafer, 1968, p. 142

54 Schafer, 1968, pp. 142, 176

55 See Lynd, 1958, p. 207

56 Fenichel, 1945, p. 37

The infantile feeling of satisfaction after being fed is described by Fenichel as a "return of narcissistic feelings," or an "oceanic feeling"—the infant's awareness of closeness to his original feelings of omnipotence. Since he does not yet have any real awareness of outside objects, the gratification of his hunger needs has removed the only threat he is capable of perceiving; hence all is now well both with himself and with the world. Fenichel considers this infantile sense of gratification as the beginning of self-esteem. The person who supplies the satisfaction of nourishment—usually the mother—thus becomes the first regulator of the infant's self-esteem, and the primary method by which self-esteem is enhanced is through his relationship with and longing for the person who can relieve his disturbing displeasure. Upon being fed, the infant first realizes that he is dependent on the outside world; he is no longer omnipotent. He must now regard the surrounding persons as omnipotent, and henceforth:[57]

> Every token of love from the more powerful adult . . . has the same effect as the supply of milk had on the infant. The small child loses self-esteem when he loses love and attains it when he regains love. That is what makes children educable. They need supplies of affection so badly that they are ready to renounce other satisfactions if rewards of affection are promised or if withdrawal of affection is threatened.

Schafer has referred to this initial primitive identification process as "merging," a largely unconscious phenomenon in which the infant "condenses representations of the total subjective self and the object," so that he experiences himself and his mother as if they were one person.[58] Since the infant perceives no separation between himself and his mother, this rudimentary form of identification is incomplete.

As the infant gradually develops awareness of his surroundings, and his perceptions of persons around him become more discriminating, the forms of identification change. Murphy (1962) points to evidence of the infant's early coping in what she calls

57 Fenichel, 1945, p. 41   58 Schafer, 1968, pp. 151–152

his "selective looking" as an attempt to control the environmental stimuli to which he is exposed. He looks at, looks for, or looks away from outside objects; he constantly shifts attention from threatening (nonempathic) objects and persons to safe ones, and in some cases returns his gaze to a threatening object in order to master it.[59] Spitz (1959) has noted that the normal child shows signs of awareness of other people at about three months, and extensive research has been conducted on this stage of child development in recent years. Murphy adds further that the early coping attempts of the two- or three-month-old infant are the precursors of both defense mechanisms and coping styles in later life. The child's first motor responses to external stimuli accompany his real perception of another person in his environment, and his identification with that person will depend upon the latter's acceptance of him; this person (usually the mother) becomes the object of the expression of his feelings.

There seems to be some disagreement as to the length of time during which these early, dependent forms of identification persist. Some authorities feel that they continue until about the age of four; others claim that they last only until the end of the second year.

During the first few weeks the infant's feelings of merging during feeding time are usually global. Later he begins to sense degrees of acceptance or rejection from the mother. If he perceives complete acceptance, a continuing, reciprocal empathic relationship develops between them. In such a relationship the child has the security to become gradually more and more independent of his mother. However, if his mother's responses and gestures convey a lack of empathy, he experiences a feeling of emptiness and loss. The child of a perfunctory mother often has this sense of loss, and as a defense against it, he may incorporate an image of his mother into his own psyche and imitate her behavior and mannerisms in the hope of being accepted in reward for the resemblance.[60] This behavior, termed "introjection," is a common response when there are ambivalent feelings toward the model.

Introjection differs from identification in that identification

59 Murphy, 1962, pp. 300–301   60 Schafer, 1968, p. 151

is directed toward the development of a separate sense of self or identity. Thus it is essentially a growth process:[61]

> In introjection, one imagines having what one lacks or may lose; in identification, one becomes what one needs to be.

Freud has referred to this form of identification as a regressive stage in which there is only a libidinal tie with the object (mother). Such behavior is sometimes referred to as overidentification with the mother, perhaps more descriptively labeled the "too-much-alike" syndrome.[62] In such a situation the child spends excessive energy and time trying to be like his mother at the expense of his own growth. The result is a type of retarded development often described as immature or irresponsible, or as paradoxical. This pattern is apparent in the adolescent who describes his behavior in terms of the conduct expected of him even though his actual behavior belies his verbal description. He has introjected the terms, but is still acting out against a nonempathic environment.

generative empathy Empathy, from the Greek word empatheia, meaning "affection and passion," refers in general to:[63]

> the imaginative projection of a subjective state . . . into an object so that the object appears to be infused with it . . . ; the capacity for participating in or a vicarious experiencing of another's feelings, volitions, or ideas. . . .

Aronfreed (1968) describes empathy more explicitly in terms of identification; he defines it as:[64]

> an individual's affective experience when it is elicited by cues of a corresponding affective state in the expressive behavior of another person. . . .

that is, by facial or gestural cues that are the direct expression of pleasure or distress.

When the parent is wholly accepting, nurturing, and concerned with the child, an intense affective relationship develops

60

61 Schafer, 1968, p. 154

62 Gilmore, 1967, p. 58

63 Webster's third new international dictionary, 1971, sv empathy

64 Aronfreed, 1968, p. 115

between them which can be termed "generative empathy." Schafer (1959) defines generative empathy as:[65]

> the inner experience of sharing in and comprehending the momentary psychological state of another person . . . a sublimated creative act in personal relationships which combines the gratifications of intimate union with the recognition and enhancement of personal development of both persons involved.

Generative empathy is sometimes employed in therapy situations to enable the therapist to embrace his patient's sense of conflict. However, it is also applicable to the ideal parent-child relationship. As in merging, the child experiences the feeling of being at one with another person. However, in this more articulate and sophisticated form of identification the child maintains his own perspective as an individual. Schafer points out that such a relationship provides a maximum opportunity for the individual to develop competence and independence in a supportive situation which provides him with security and at the same time enables him to maintain his own individuality.[66]

Freud referred essentially to this same concept in describing identification as a common quality shared with another person which is not strictly libidinal. Generative empathy also encompasses the sense of basic trust which Erikson considers the foundation of development in the healthy child. Aronfreed defines empathy in similar terms—as a relationship in which the subject feels that he is one with another, but experiences this feeling from his own perspective as an individual. It is this type of relationship which forms the basis for the child's self-esteem and his future development as a creative and productive individual.

As the mother relates to her child, certain aspects of her behavior help to establish his empathic relationship with her. For example, her smile, her outstretched arms, and her direct and loving gaze all indicate a form of openness and acceptance. Her affectionate vocalizations symbolize recognition, and her firm embrace conveys to the child a form of protection. These behavioral cues are perceived by the child as evidence that he has

65 Schafer, 1959, pp. 345, 370   66 Schafer, 1968, p. 153   **61**

evoked her pleasure; hence they contribute to his self-esteem, and his own response of pleasure creates an exchange of feelings between them. Aronfreed notes experimental evidence that:[67]

> The nurturance of a potential model [the mother] toward a child does enhance the child's disposition to imitate the model's expressive behavior.

facial expression Genuine empathic interaction between infant and mother does not seem to develop until the child himself begins to look and smile, usually around the third month. After interviewing mothers of newborn infants, Robson and Moss (1969) reported that the mothers evidenced no strong, personal, affective bonds until the infant appeared to be "looking at" its mother or "smiling at" her.[68] Moss (1967) also noted an increase in the mother's affectionate behavior at about the third month, when the child's rates of looking at its mother, smiling, and vocalization increased. Bell (1971) comments on the importance of the infant's eye-to-eye contact and smiles at this stage in the feeling of a reciprocal relationship between child and mother.[69]

The empathic experiences between infant and mother, and later between child and father, are obviously directly related to the positive expressive cues which the child perceives in his parents. From expressive cues such as a smile, pleasant verbal recognition, and various verbal and nonverbal expressions of approval, encouragement, and physical affection he acquires a feeling of self-esteem which allows him to gain a feeling of individuality in this relationship. These early empathic responses may be reinforced by many other relationships as the child's world expands to include other adults and his peers.

Parents are more likely to respond to their children with expressions of affection and approval when their own behavior is "under the control of positive affect"—when they feel happy or their self-esteem is high.[70] Moreover, when pleasurable events are directly and simultaneously experienced by child and parent—as when both enjoy and laugh at the same thing—the child's affectivity becomes conditioned by the parent's responses. From the evi-

62

67 Aronfreed, 1968, p. 307

68 See Harper, 1971, p. 79

69 R. Bell, 1971, p. 68

70 Aronfreed, 1968, p. 118

dence of experimental psychology, Bandura (1967) contends that:[71]

> *Affective expressions of a model are most likely to elicit high self-arousal in observers under conditions where participants have experienced similar pleasurable or painful experiences.*

A study by Kagan (1968) provides some interesting validation of the theoretical explanations of the early identification process in infants.[72] Kagan studied four-month-old infants from lower-middle-class, middle-class, and upper-middle-class homes, (classified on the basis of educational level and occupation of the parents). He presented four pictures of faces to the infants—one showing a regular three-dimensional representation, one with the features scrambled, one with no eyes, and one with only the outline of a face. To isolate the infants' emotional reactions from their motor ability at this age, a cardiac response (slowing of the heartbeat) was used as the indicator of emotional reaction to each picture. Infants in the middle- and upper-middle-class groups registered more cardiac deceleration in response to all four pictures than those in the lower-middle-class group, indicating that they were better able to discriminate the distinguishing characteristics of a face. Kagan suggests that there is probably more frequent face-to-face contact between parents and their children in families at higher socioeconomic levels.

In another phase of this study Kagan also found that more infants from better-educated families smiled at the collage of an achromatic photograph than did infants from poorly educated families.[73] Since a smile at four months of age can be regarded as an index of recognition, the smile and the deceleration data are in agreement. Kagan concludes from the differences in this smile response that better-educated parents tend to engage not only in more frequent, but also in more distinctive face-to-face contact with their children. Apart from the other socioeconomic factors involved, this study helps to explain the empathic and identification processes between the child and the mother.

The importance of the face as a visual stimulus is also indicated by studies conducted with older children. Messick and

71 Bandura, 1969, p. 202

72 Kagan, 1968, pp. 211–250

73 Kagan, 1968, p. 234

Damarin (1964) reported that field-dependent children showed greater incidental learning than field-independent subjects when the incidental material consisted of human faces. They also observed that children with a "global cognitive style" (an undifferentiated, immature cognitive style) looked up at the face of the examiner twice as often during a test performance as children with an "articulated cognitive style," indicating that the former were more dependent. In another study Crutchfield et al. (1958) found that children with a global cognitive style were somewhat better at recognizing and remembering the faces of people they had been with earlier.[74]

verbal communication Another factor in the child's early identification experiences, of course, is verbal communication. In this case it appears that there are differences related not only to socioeconomic level, but also to the sex of the child. For example, Kagan (1968) found that the ways in which mothers exchanged vocalizations with their male infants did not differ from one group to another. With female infants, however, there was a difference. The best-educated mothers generally responded more distinctively to the vocalizations of their female infants and were less likely to ignore them.[75] This finding indicates not only that the mother who is better educated may have more empathy, but also that she may have a distinct preference for girls over boys. Kagan suggests that this greater vocal interchange between educated mothers and their girl babies may explain the more advanced development of language skills in girls at the higher socioeconomic levels.

Other investigators report similar differences in parental treatment of girls and boys. In a study of babbling Moss (1967) observed that mothers of infant daughters imitate their infants' vocalizations more than do the mothers of infant sons. In an earlier study (1964) he noted that when mothers and fathers were requested to get their seven-week-old infants to smile, they spent more time with female babies than with males, although the infant girls responded no better than the boys.[76]

64

74 See Lewis, 1971, pp. 142–143   76 See Harper, 1971, p. 77

75 Kagan, 1968, p. 238

LATER FORMS OF IDENTIFICATION

As a child begins to walk and talk, he acquires new skills for coping with the physical requirements of his environment, and each new experience of mastery contributes to his self-esteem. Thus his sense of identity develops through his own vocal and motor expressions. Erikson has observed that when a child learns to speak, he is acquiring one of the prime functions supporting a sense of individual autonomy.[77]

judgment   As his language skills and physical activities expand, the child is exposed to an increasing number of objects and persons to which he can react. If he is to organize his behavior in some manner, he must select among many objects and persons those cues to which he will react at a given time. This selectivity involves the cognitive skill of judgment, which enables him to evaluate the object or person in terms of its effect on his self-esteem. The greater his feeling of empathic identification with his parents, the more easily he can discriminate the objects around him; he can stand alone in relation to his surroundings, without the need to feel himself a part of many persons or objects all at once.

Another aspect of judgment depends on language—the symbols or labels which the child associates with objects, persons, and actions, enabling him to identify and anticipate events and to remember the consequences of certain actions. To evaluate or appraise actions in terms of future consequences, however, the child must also be able to interpose the element of time between his perception of the stimulus and his own behavioral response. The ability to postpone an immediate response in favor of a future action that promises to be more rewarding is an essential factor in being able to master one's environment, and hence in developing a sense of identity. However, the child must be able not only to evaluate the consequences of his behavior; he must also be able to tolerate the tension of postponing his reaction to an immediate stimulus. Thus the control of impulse depends at least in part on

77   Erikson, 1960, p. 48

the security produced by a nurturing and empathic environment. The secure child is able to control his impulses and examine the possible consequences of his acts, tolerate the tensions of necessary postponement, and—provided that his cognitive skills are sufficiently developed—choose a course of action which is most likely to enhance his self-esteem.

superego identification   A child can predict the consequences of his behavior with respect to his self-esteem only if he perceives his environment as fundamentally predictable. Unless his interactions with others proceed according to some established code of behavior, he has no basis for developing the judgment, self-control, and cognitive skills necessary for him to function in his social environment. Moreover, at a very fundamental level, he has no means of coping with his physical environment; if his social behavior is not approved, the supply of his simple physical needs is jeopardized. The child is dependent, therefore, on a stable and consistent environment in which he can learn to predict the behaviors that are expected of him and test the outcomes of behavioral alternatives in terms of his self-esteem.

This important aspect of the identification process is termed "superego identification," or the development of conscience. In general, parental practices are relatively constant throughout most of the child's growth period.[78] Hence his early identifications receive constant reinforcement through the repetition of activities involving explicit reciprocal behaviors on the part of parent and child. In the course of frequent mutual interactions he learns to anticipate the customary responses to behavioral alternatives, and in an empathic and nurturing environment he develops confidence that the accepted behaviors will contribute to his self-esteem. In this respect the power of the model or models over the desired outcome is an important factor in predictability. To assure himself of the help or approval of the "power model," the child may rehearse different courses of action, either overtly or in fantasy, in order to test his perception of the model's probable response.[79]

78 Maccoby, 1968, pp. 229–269, esp. 253   79 See Bandura, 1969, pp. 139–140

sex identity

Sex identity—or, more appropriately, identification with one's own gender—warrants separate consideration because of the extensive research which appears in psychological and psychiatric literature. An understanding of this aspect of identity is vital, since it appears to be closely linked with different degrees of productivity. The term "sex identity," however, is greatly in need of redefinition and clarification. Part of the confusion stems from the vagueness of the term "identity" itself, but the problem has been compounded by the ambiguous reference to sex. Especially in Western societies, the distinction of biological sex functions has been extended to a corresponding polarization of social, economic, and vocational roles. As a result, the term "sex identity" is applied to behaviors that are unrelated to any biological distinction. Unfortunately, it is also employed as a diagnostic label more on the basis of stereotypes than evidence.

As noted by Simon and Gagnon (1971), masculinity and femininity are complex and widely misunderstood concepts which require much further explanation. Gershman (1968) suggests "gender identity" as a more accurate designation for what is, in essence, a social concept rather than a biological distinction. Whereas biological sex is fixed by chromosomes and established at conception, gender identity, really one aspect of personal identity, is "the individual's capacity to experience himself or herself as a man or woman" in a multiple number of situations involving social relationships with both sexes.[80] Unfortunately, the term "gender identity" has not come into wide use, and the more ambiguous label "sex-role identity" remains predominant.

When we speak of sex-role or gender identity, we are, therefore, actually describing a social role (a role determined by society), and not a sex role as such. In the past it was convenient to describe masculinity and femininity in terms of distinctive behavioral characteristics. The male was perceived as strong, aggressive, rational, and instrumental and the female as compliant,

80 Gershman, 1968, pp. 80ff

intuitive, and nurturing. In our culture the traditional male role has involved protection, responsibility for the economic welfare of the family, and the authority to make and enforce decisions; these functions—essentially active ones—have constituted the father's role in the family structure. The female role, perceived as more passive, has been to care for and nurture the members of the family.

These roles evolved in an environment in which protection of the family and mastery of the environment depended on the exercise of physical skills. As mastery of the environment has come increasingly to depend on cognitive skills, however, there has been a change in the perception of what is strictly masculine or feminine behavior. The perception of what is appropriate sex-role behavior varies in different socioeconomic groups. An emphasis on traditional sex-role characteristics is typical, for example, at the lower socioeconomic levels, possibly as a displacement of financial, educational, or other problems. It is likely that concern over sex role is symptomatic of the general social and economic insecurity experienced in these groups; the traditionally "masculine" vocations, dependent on physical stamina and skill, are the least rewarding economically. In contrast, in the middle- and upper-class groups there is less emphasis on the traditional masculine-feminine traits. As men and women acquire more education, they acquire similar interests; thus education is also a factor in minimizing differences between the sexes. The traditional cultural interests, more intellectual and less physically active than those of males, were in the past the prerogative of women, but these activities are now shared. Similarly, women are now participating in active sports.

Sex roles are, then, undergoing noticeable changes, and perceived differences between "masculine" and "feminine" traits are diminishing. Even though an overconcern about sex-role characteristics may be symptomatic of other identity needs— —particularly at the lower socioeconomic levels and adolescence—there is nevertheless a need for some structure in sex roles for clarity of communication, proper socialization, and

68

productive effort. In interpersonal relationships individuals are not comfortable with ambiguity; they want to know not so much whether the two sex groups have the same or different interests, but rather whether members of these groups are biologically male or female. Such a "knowledgeable" classification makes them predictable. Within this dichotomy, however, there is apparently developing a growing similarity in traits of behavior, interests, and skills which appear to be appropriate to both sex groups.

The vagueness which surrounds the concept of sex identity has made it difficult to conduct adequate research in this area. Investigators appear to have defined masculinity or femininity as they themselves perceive it; some studies have also used the somewhat questionable procedures leaving the definition to the judgment of teachers and peers. Moreover, as Vroegh (1971) points out, the test items on measures of gender-role identity have generally represented "between-sex" differences rather than "within-sex" differences; in other words, it has been assumed that masculinity and femininity are bipolar concepts.[81]

In one study of sex-role identity Vroegh (1971) investigated concepts of masculinity and femininity in a population consisting of 209 boys and 201 girls in grades 1 through 8 in a white upper-middle-class suburb.[82] She found that students in grades 4 to 6 described as feminine the traditional characteristics of patience and naïveté, but they also included the same characteristics of competence (outgoingness, confidence, and abstract thinking) that they attributed to boys. In grades 7 and 8 differences between traits common to one sex or the other were temporarily blurred. No clear picture of femininity emerged at this age, although boys were viewed as venturesome, assertive, and group-dependent. Vroegh explains this finding as a need on the part of both boys and girls to make themselves attractive to the opposite sex. The situation changes, however, with adults: Jenkin and Vroegh (1969) and Vroegh et al. (1967) report that adult males and females "share similar qualities of appropriate identity," and that there is a moderate agreement ($r = .42$) on the characteristics of ideal masculinity and femininity.[83]

81 Vroegh, 1971b, pp. 407–408, 411   83 Vroegh, 1971a, p. 260

82 Vroegh, 1971a, pp. 254–261

A study of sex-role concepts at the community college level also shows that young adults perceive less difference between ideal male and female roles than is evidenced by their own sex-role behavior. Elman et al. (1970) found that both male and female students rated themselves closer to the stereotypes for their sex than to what they viewed as ideal sex-appropriate behavior.[84] The investigators concluded that members of both sexes perceive "ideal men and women and ideal self as possessing many of the characteristics presently valued for the opposite sex, in addition to the same-sex-valued traits."

A further indication that people may feel less need to differentiate each other solely on the basis of sex group is provided by a long-term study of three different populations aged sixteen to forty. An analysis of the responses to two Rorschach test items which usually elicit information on sex identity showed that there had been a marked shift over a period of nearly twenty years in the imagery of both men and women in the direction of less frequent designation of specific sex associations.[85]

Anxiety or confusion over sex identity is prevalent at all levels of society and often comes to the fore during periods of physical illness or with the influence of alcohol or drugs. It is more frequent in men than in women, and as Jacobson points out, it is usually the basis of identity problems in disturbed personalities.[86] In the diagnosis of behavior, however, sharply defined dichotomies—such as active-passive, independent-dependent, competitive-noncompetitive, or empathic-hostile—are sometimes used to characterize "good" sex identity, as opposed to "poor," or confused sex identity. Theoretically, those behavior traits which, in package form, constitute good sex-role identity include independence, activity, coping skills, social competence, empathy, and ego strength. Thus, in terms of general productivity, all these traits indicate confidence in the environment. The label "poor sex identity" has been somewhat inappropriately used in a generic sense to describe what is actually low self-esteem, expressed in general social irresponsibility. Diagnosticians have frequently labeled an individual as having poor sex

84 Elman, Press, and Rosenkrantz, 1970, pp. 455–456

85 Roche report, 1971, pp. 5, 8

86 Jacobson, 1964, p. 198

identity when they are actually referring to behavioral characteristics—such as passivity, lack of confidence, overconcern about the body, or aggressive demands for attention and affection—which may or may not be related to gender. Thus the criteria for both "good" and "poor" sex identity could conceivably apply equally to either sex.

The influence on subsequent adult behavior of the sex-role identity acquired in the early years has been verified by a number of studies. In a longitudinal study at the Fels Institute Kagan and Moss (1962) reported that sex identity was one of the more stable characteristics from childhood to adulthood. For example, adult traits of passive withdrawal, dependency on family, ease of anger, intellectual mastery, social interaction anxiety, sex-role identification, and patterns of sexual behavior were each related to somewhat analogous behavior which had appeared in early school years.[87] The researchers concluded that aggression, dependency, and sex identity are the three areas of conflict in our culture, and that the forms in which an individual expresses aggression, dependency, and sexuality are partly related to his concept of his sex identity:[88]

> The construct of sex-role identification [is] in a central position in directing the selective adoption and maintenance of several behavior domains.

On this basis sex identity appears to reflect a basic personality characteristic, like ego strength or self-esteem.

SEX IDENTITY AND PRODUCTIVITY

The clear sex-identity status of productive persons seems to reveal itself in two areas of their lives. One is interest, and in the case of males active involvement, in strenuous physical activities and sports; the other is their heterosexual relationships.

Barron (1968) found that in male graduate students, the three characteristics significantly correlated with personal soundness were intellectual competence, self-assurance, and

87 Kagan and Moss, 1962, p. 266   88 Kagan and Moss, 1962, p. 271

masculinity. Moreover, he noted that several of those in the high-soundness group were in competitive sports; some had been outstanding college athletes and their activities in graduate school included mountain climbing, tennis, swimming, and some contact sports.[89] McClelland (1962) noted that high masculinity scores on the Strong Vocational Interest Blank and other measures were typical of male physical scientists and that they too revealed a liking for nature and outdoor sports; he comments further that such persons are likely to express their masculinity through the pursuit of scientific analysis.[90] The group of business leaders ranked as most oriented by Zaleznik et al. (1970) were unusually consistent in their interest and participation in athletics at all periods in their lives. They had played sandlot baseball as little boys and varsity sports in high school; they were members of intramural teams in college, and were actively pursuing their interest in athletics through such sports as golf and tennis. This consistency of interest in athletics significantly differentiated the oriented managers from all of the other groups (.02 level).[91] In the follow-up study of Terman's gifted group, Oden (1968) found that sports were popular with both the A (successful) and the C (unsuccessful) groups, but the As showed "considerably more interest in active sports and games," whereas the Cs were interested more as spectators.[92]

Not unexpectedly, an individual's sex identity is also reflected in his heterosexual relationships. The security and stability of relationships between members of the opposite sex are to a considerable extent dependent on the confident sense of identity of the partners involved. Information on the marital status of productive individuals is somewhat sparse, but from the available evidence, they are generally as successful in this area of their lives as in their other endeavors. In her ten-year follow-up study of outstanding male and female undergraduate students Cox (1970) found that the rate of successful marriages was far higher in the healthy group (one divorce out of 22 marriages) than in the impaired group (one divorce in 8.5 marriages).[93] More than 80 percent of the married healthy subjects reported that their marriages "get better all the time," and Cox concluded that their

89 Barron, 1968, pp. 47, 61

90 McClelland, 1962, pp. 149, 167

91 Zaleznik, Dalton, and Barnes, 1970, p. 258

92 Oden, 1968, p. 70

93 Cox, 1970, pp. 171, 167

marriages seemed to be giving them warmth and contentment and "providing an unquestioned base of emotional security for their lives and the lives of their children." Barron (1968) also noted stable heterosexual relationships in his high-soundness subjects; 90 percent of them were married or involved in a long-term relationship (more than a year) with a member of the opposite sex.[94]

In her follow-up study of the Terman group Oden (1968) found a marked difference in marital stability between the successful and the unsuccessful groups. All of the A group were or had been married, and only 16 percent had been divorced. Nearly all were parents, and nearly all reported that marriage was their greatest source of happiness aside from their vocations or professions.[95] It is interesting to note in this connection that although the three unmarried women in Cox's unimpaired group stated that if the right man came along, "the job could go hang," the three who had gone directly into marriage without ever having proved their competence in a career also had the lowest mental-health scores in the group.[96]

Maslow (1954) has written eloquently about love in self-actualizing persons. He found his subjects so confident in their sex identity that they seemed to have no need to protest it; they were completely untroubled by conflict over the masculine-feminine or active-passive dichotomies.[97] Maslow describes marriage among self-actualizing persons as a supremely happy physical and psychological union in which husband-wife competition is nonexistent, defenses and role playing are at a minimum, and there is an abundance of respect as well as a spontaneous sharing of love, caring, and tenderness.

Roe (1953) and McClelland (1962) present a somewhat different picture with respect to the creative physical scientist. Although they score higher than any other group in masculine interests and attitudes, young male scientists are apparently so deeply absorbed in their work that they tend to be fairly late in developing an interest in women. McClelland reports that they are "typically not very interested in girls, date for the first time late in college, marry the first girl they date, and thereafter appear to show a rather low level of heterosexual drive."[98] Drevdahl

94 Barron, 1968, p. 61

95 Oden, 1968, p. 68

96 Cox, 1970, pp. 50–51
Rutherford, 1966, pp. 167–178

97 Maslow, 1954, pp. 235ff

98 McClelland, 1962, p. 154

(1964) gives essentially the same picture of creative psychologists. He reports that his subjects showed little concern over the masculine-feminine dichotomy, but also little concern over matters of sexuality in general.[99] The McGill University study of college freshmen suggests, however, that these findings do not represent a lack of sexuality. Westley and Epstein (1969) observed that the subjects in the mentally healthy group reported their sexual feelings as disturbing, and at times even frightening; however, they were able to recognize and accept them, and chose to postpone acting on them until a later, more appropriate time.[100] Although their attitudes toward sex were conservative, they evidenced little of the anxiety and guilt that was observed in the less healthy group.

Most of the studies of productive persons have dealt with male subjects or mixed groups, but there a few findings on women which are particularly interesting in terms of the changing attitudes toward masculine and feminine role behavior. In a study conducted at Vassar Webster (1956) used both verbal and nonverbal measures to rate senior girls in masculinity-femininity. On the basis of these measures, the senior girls tended to be more "masculine" than freshmen, in the sense that they were less conventional and less passive; at the same time, however, they were more feminine in their inner life than girls at the lower undergradate levels. In discussing these findings, Sanford (1956) points out that the discrepancy is related to educational level, rather than to any confusion over sex identity; the characteristics which have been construed as typically "feminine" may not pertain to the educated woman of today.[101]

Cox (1970) found further evidence of clear, positive sex identity in college-educated women. Of the twenty-seven productive wome graduates in her follow-up study, the eight who had left their jobs to raise children reported that they were doing exactly what they wanted to do and expressed very little feeling that they had "given up a career."[102] Haan (1963) found that adolescent girls who had increased their verbal ability over the years became quite feminine in their later life (those who increased their mathematical skills, however, became less feminine).[103]

99 Drevdahl, 1964, pp. 174–175
100 Westley and Epstein, 1969, p. 54
101 See M. Stein, 1963, p. 38
102 Cox, 1970, pp. 50–51
103 Haan, 1963, pp. 18–19

Other studies demonstrate that the female college students who are most certain of their gender identity do not hesitate to compete with males for academic grades, whereas as those who are uncertain are more reluctant to compete with men for fear of losing favor with them.[104] Simon and Gagnon (1969) report that women who have graduate degrees experience practically no love-relationship problems in marriage, suggesting a good sense of identity and acceptance of themselves as members of their own gender.

The clearcut sex identity of the productive person is a marked contrast to the findings for less productive groups. Barron's low-soundness subjects were reported as far less masculine and physically competitive, and also as far lower in good sexual adjustments. In addition to cases of overt homosexuality, effeminate but sexually quiescent behavior, and overcompensated masculinity with promiscuous heterosexuality, less than half of those in the low group had established stable heterosexual ties, whereas 90 percent of the highs had formed such ties.[105] In the Terman group, although all the A (successful) subjects were married, nearly one-fifth of the Cs had remained single, and a considerably higher percentage of the C marriages had ended in divorce. Furthermore, nearly one-third of the C marriages were childless, while only 8 percent of the As had no children.[106] In Drevdahl's (1964) study of creative psychologists those in the lowest-ranked group (noncreative nonproductive) evidenced more concern over relationships with the opposite sex or their sex life in general than the other groups. This group also showed signs of neuroticism and reported childhood feelings of social inferiority.[107]

THE SEX-IDENTIFICATION PERIOD

Most psychologists agree that sex-role identity is established very early in life, but they differ on the age at which it begins. Some, including Erikson, consider the age of about four to six as the critical period. Others contend that sex roles are learned much earlier: Kohlberg (1966) claims that a child learns to classify himself by sex as early as the second year, and Gershman (1968) feels

104 See M. Gilmore, 1964, p. 13

105 Barron, 1968, pp. 61–62

106 Oden, 1968, pp. 68–69

107 Drevdahl, 1964, pp. 174–175

that gender identity is established by age three.[108] Vener and Snyder (1966) found that children as young as two and one-half years could associate their own genders with certain sex-linked artifacts. Both boys and girls did better with female-linked artifacts. The boys showed a slight preference for female items at this age, but this association was completely corrected by the age of five. According to Hetherington (1965), girls develop a preference for their own sex role at a somewhat later age than boys.[109]

There appears to be a significant increase in the number of sex-role preferences between the ages of three and four, as revealed by an experiment with the It Scale for Children, a projective test. This study (Hartup and Zook, 1960) also showed that the acquisition of sex-role preferences appears to be a less complicated developmental process for the male than for the female.[110]

By the age of five, sex-role preferences seem well established in both boys and girls. In an analysis of the process of sex-role development in thirty-two children in kindergarten through second-grade, Ward (1969) also suggests that preferences precede role adoption in both sexes, and that role identification occurs earlier in girls than in boys, since adoption and identification coincide for girls but occur in sequence for boys.[111]

Although the child is aware of sex differences from a very early age, he is usually relatively free to assume various mixed roles in his social and play relationships until he is about six. By this age, however, he is expected to behave in the manner that society perceives as fitting for his particular gender. In accepting this reduction of freedom by internalizing the appropriate sex role, the child develops a structured behavior which will be met with approval, and hence enable him to maintain his self-esteem. In most societies the boy's sex role requires that he identify himself with what is appropriate to the male; therefore he must extricate himself from the infantile role he has played opposite the mother and develop those characteristics which his parents perceive as masculine—independence, the ability to protect himself physically, competitiveness in his relationships with others.

In psychoanalytic theory the sex-identification period has frequently been called the "oedipal stage," a term used by Freud

108 See May, 1971, p. 484; Gershman, 1968, p. 82
109 See Harrington, 1970, p. 14
110 Hartup and Zook, 1960, p. 426
111 W. D. Ward, 1969, pp. 163–168

to designate the conflict in the male child somewhere between the ages of three and six, when he perceives himself as his father's rival for his mother's love. At this time, he becomes aware not only of the physiological differences between himself and his mother, and of the expected role behaviors associated with each sex, but also of his own sexual feelings. This conflict, sometimes labeled the "phallic stage," is also associated with the female child's rivalry with her mother.

In either case, the child is uncertain over which role behavior to adopt. The male child has greater difficulty in this respect, since he spends more time with his mother than with his father during the early years. In a normal environment this difficulty is offset by the need for his father as a model as he becomes more independent and achievement-oriented and is at the same time subjected to increasing environmental pressure to acquire socially approved behavioral traits. Thus, although he retains some identification with his mother, it is his father's values and coping style which he adopts as appropriate male behavior.[112]

The challenge to the child at this period is to develop an awareness of behavior values sufficient to offset his sexual and aggressive drives. This is a difficulty often taken too lightly by parents. Freud postulated, in fact, that the child's social and emotional development cannot proceed normally until the conflict over sex-role identification has been resolved. Schafer observed that a child coping with the demands of sex identification needs considerable ego resources to reach, sustain, and transcend the oedipal situation and must have the skills, perception, and motivation to organize his identity relationships with his parents.[113]

Since sex-role identification entails the acquisition of behavioral values considered socially appropriate to one's gender, the development of moral values constitutes a part of this socialization process. Apparently moral development takes place through the same process as sex-role identification, or sex typing. According to Mussen et al. (1970), the conditions which enhance healthy "developmental identification" also encourage the development of high levels of moral behavior consistent with the child's own sex role.[114] Jacobson (1964) contends that the child's

112 Schafer, 1968, pp. 182ff; Fenichel, 1945, chap. 5

113 Schafer, 1968, p. 207

114 Mussen, Rutherford, Harris, and Keasey, 1970, p. 190

emerging conscience may even be a more important influence on his sex-identity development than the resolution of his oedipal conflict.[115]

According to Kohlberg (1964), one factor in moral development is ego strength, which he associates with the individual's general intelligence, his capacity to anticipate future events and to forego immediate gratification for remote but more rewarding outcomes or goals, his ability to maintain "stable, focused attention," his control over his "unsocialized fantasies" (his aggression), and his self-esteem.[116] Perhaps one of the most important of these traits in terms of sex identification is the child's capacity for postponement in anticipation of future outcomes. Schafer (1968) points out that before the sex-identification age the child has already gone through an extensive period during which he has learned to build up inner controls (as in toilet training, for example); thus he has gradually acquired the necessary capacity for delay, testing of reality, and "relatively neutralized interests."[117]

It is generally agreed that certain conditions are important for the child's normal development sex-role identification. These include a general atmosphere in the home of "affection, nurturance, respect, intimacy, and warmth"; parental models who are rewarding and consistent; a father who plays a distinct role as a strong and effective model, for children of both sexes, particularly boys; and the child's own level of self-esteem.[118]

Both theorists and researchers agree that the father represents a particularly important psychological model to children of both sexes. According to Fromm (1956), he represents to the child "the world of thought, of man-made things, of law and order, of discipline, of travel and adventure."[119] Moreover, he serves as a model for the conscience or superego development of the child of either sex, since it is the father who "interprets the outer world to the family."[120] With the gradual depolarization of the sex roles, the increase in urbanization, and other sociological changes, the father's role in the identification process has increased in recent years. No longer is he the harsh authoritarian in all cases, and despite the fact that he spends less time with the children he may

115 Jacobson, 1964, p. 131

116 Kohlberg, 1964, pp. 390–391

117 Schafer, 1968, p. 207

118 Mussen, Rutherford, Harris, and Keasey, 1970, p. 190; Mussen and Rutherford, 1966, pp. ???–???

119 Fromm, 1956, p. 42

120 See Rogers, 1969, p. 205

have a greater influence than the mother on the sex identity of both his sons and his daughters.[121]

the father-son relationship The father's relationship with his son is of special significance in superego identification, or sensitivity to the codes and rules of society. Barron (1968) noted that his high-soundness group of graduate students had identified with a strong father figure and that this identification carried over into their adult moral behavior.[122] There is evidence that maternal affection alone, without strong psychological ties with the father, actually has adverse effects, especially upon boys. Researches which have been conducted over a period of more than two decades have demonstrated that a boy's warm relationship with a father who is himself masculine plays a very significant part in his sex-role development.[123]

Not only do studies show masculinity in boys and men to be associated with a warm, nurturing, and rewarding father-son relationship; there is also evidence that boys with highly masculine interests are higher in self-esteem than those with relatively feminine interests. Mussen (1961) found adolescent boys with high masculine interests to be "more carefree, more contented, more relaxed, more exuberant, happier, calmer, and smoother in social functioning" than boys who were more inclined to feminine interests.[124] Further evidence of the relationship of clear sex-role identification and self-esteem is provided by Biller and Barry (1971), who studied sex-role patterns in 104 lower-middle-class and middle-class male college freshmen.[125] The subjects were grouped according to four different patterns on the basis of "sex-role orientation" (masculinity-femininity) and "sex-role preference" (attitudes and activities). Subjects with both masculine orientation and masculine preferences appeared to be more like their fathers and to be better adjusted than those in the other groups. The masculine-preference group had higher self-esteem scores (defined as more favorable self-attitudes, greater self-confidence, and better personal adjustment) than the feminine-oriented group.

121 Rogers, 1969, pp. 204–205; Bronfenbrenner, 1969, p. 201

122 Barron, 1968, pp. 59–60

123 Nash, 1965, pp. 261–297; Biller, 1970,
pp. 181–196

124 See Mussen, Conger, and Kagan,
1969, p. 691

125 Biller and Barry, 1971, p. 107

There are also a number of studies testifying to the detrimental effects of the father's absence from home. The problem of the "father-absent boy" has received much attention in recent years. In general, it has been established that "early" father absence (absence before the child is four) is likely to result in the development of a boy who by the age of nine is[126]

> . . . more dependent, less aggressive, less adequate in peer relations, less masculine and less competitive in games than boys whose fathers are present in the home continuously or whose fathers are absent after the child has reached the age of six.

Research on the effects of father absence has proved extremely complex, partly because of the difficulty of defining father absence itself.[127] Herzog and Sudia (1970) cite the great difference in potential impact of an absence which is temporary, planned, and socially approved and one which is permanent and socially deplored or condemned.[128] The research problem is also complicated by the necessity of considering the possible influence on each situation of many other factors beside the father's absence—such as socioeconomic and cultural level, the size of the family, the mother's response to the father's absence (especially her ego strength and coping ability), and community influences. Other potential influences are the length of the absence itself, the "type" of absence (whether or not it is intermittent), and the possible availability of male surrogate models such as uncles, Boy Scout leaders, and male teachers. There has even been some evidence that in two-child father-absent families, the sex of the sibling may be a factor; boys with brothers are less likely to suffer than those with sisters.[129]

It appears that father absence is most detrimental at the lower socioeconomic levels. The sons of middle-class mothers left alone through death or divorce seem to have fewer identity problems. Other tentative findings suggest that such factors as ordinal position and the presence in the family of an older sister may have some influence on the boy's identity. Cohen (1970) has found that the presence of an older sister has apparently been oversimplified; he also found that boys from father-absent families did not show

80

126 National Institute of Child Health, 1968, p. 16

127 Biller, 1970, pp. 181–201; Herzog and Sudia, 1970

128 Herzog and Sudia, 1970, p. 6

129 Biller, 1970, p. 186

any greater confusion over sex identity than those whose fathers were present, except that boys in lower-class homes tended to be more antisocial. (The antisocial behavior was not defined as related to concern over sex identity.)[130] Other research indicates that while father absence undoubtedly affects sex-role typing of preschool-age boys, influences outside the family may, in later years, either correct sex-role identification or else produce compensatory masculinity.[131]

In any case, masculinity is not the only personality trait in boys which may be adversely affected by father absence. Bronfenbrenner comments on low achievement motivation, inability to defer immediate gratification for the sake of later (and greater) rewards, low self-esteem, susceptibility to influence of groups, and even tendencies toward juvenile delinquency—all of which effects are much more marked in boys than in girls.[132] Coopersmith (1967) also notes the detrimental effects of intermittent father absence on a boy's self-esteem.[133] One conspicuous result of severe deprivation of the father's influence is impulsivity.

Two of the many variables which have interested investigators of the father-absent boy are the age of onset of the father's absence and the relationship between the boy and his mother afterward. In agreement with other findings, Biller and Bahm (1971) noted in a study of forty junior high school boys that father absence which occurred before the boy was five was most likely to affect the masculinity of his self-concept, but that after that age the absence seemed to be less injurious.[134] It was also found that the mother's behavior toward the son was especially critical if the father left the family during the preschool years. The mother of a father-absent boy is normally somewhat concerned about his masculinity and tends to encourage him in aggression. Biller and Bahm reported that in preschool boys the effects of "perceived maternal encouragement of aggression" were indeed associated with a higher self-concept of masculinity; the relationship, however, was not found among father-present or late-father-absent boys. This finding would suggest that it is in the impressionable preschool boy that the effects of both the father's absence and the mother's attitudes are most clearly marked.

130   Cohen, 1970, pp. 120 et passim

131   Hetherington, 1972, p. 323

132   Bronfenbrenner, 1969, p. 210

133   Coopersmith, 1967, p. 90

134   Biller and Bahm, 1971, pp. 178–181
         see also Rogers, 1969, pp. 226, 228

The effects of father absence on cognition have also been observed, especially the influence which father absence may exert on differences between girls and boys in verbal (versus mathematical) skills. Problem-solving ability and skill in conceptual and analytical tasks have been generally associated with masculine rather than feminine personalities. Reflecting this trend, high school students' verbal and mathematical scores on the Scholastic Aptitude Test generally differ according to sex; girls tend to have higher scores in the verbal area, while boys are higher in mathematical aptitude.

Several investigators have suggested that the masculine analytical approach is probably acquired through a close and harmonious father-son relationship. Carlsmith (1964) investigated Harvard freshmen from the classes of 1963 and 1964, many of whose fathers had served overseas during World War II, as well as senior high school girls and boys from nearby suburbs.[135] Comparing carefully matched groups, she found that early father absence was markedly associated in both sexes with a reverse trend in SAT scores (father-absent boys' verbal scores were higher than their math scores). Moreover, if the father had left home early (before the son was twelve months old) and if he had been away for more than one year, the son's later SAT verbal-aptitude score was higher than his math score. If the father's separation had been late and brief, there was some increase in the boy's mathematical aptitude; if there was no separation, however, the relative increase was greater. The effects on cognitive development were generally the same for girls as for boys.

The studies by Carlsmith and others suggest that early close and positive father-son relationships may well be a prerequisite for development in a boy of a masculine conceptual approach to problem solving. The same results were reported in an earlier study by Maccoby (1961), who related college board aptitude scores of male students at Stanford University with certain reported childhood experiences.[136] Boys whose mathematical aptitude was lower than their verbal aptitude reported that during childhood their fathers had been absent for a period of one to five years, that they almost never discussed personal problems with

135 Carlsmith, 1964, pp. 16–19   136 See Carlsmith, 1964, p. 19

their fathers; that they feared their fathers; and that they were punished exclusively by their mothers. The precise nature of this apparent relationship between early father-son identification and the development of masculine conceptual thinking is still not fully understood. Also, the social perception of mathematics as a "male" skill may be changing; the three fields currently attracting the largest number of women at one Ivy League college are science, premedical studies, and psychology, all of which require some mathematical skill.

the father-daughter relationship   There is also recent research showing that the father plays an important, although slightly different, role in the sex identification of his daughter; in this case he serves as a mature male model to whom she can relate, and hence he influences her later relationship to men in general.[137] A father who is both highly masculine and warmly affectionate toward his daughter reinforces her in the development of feminine behavior by actively encouraging her participation in feminine activities. Moreover, he tends to reward her for femininity by maintaining an attitude of approval not merely because she is "good," but because she is "pretty." According to Mussen and Rutherford (1966), in such a relationship the girl becomes "motivated by the positive desire to get love by giving love, which . . . is the defining attribute of femininity."[138]

Some studies suggest that the father's role is particularly critical in the daughter's sex identification because the feminine role is in itself somewhat ambiguous. Female children are allowed greater latitude in sex-appropriate social and play behavior than boys; the tomboy is indulged, but the noncompetitive boy is condemned. The father may therefore be a vital factor in differentiating the adult gender roles for his daughter.[139]

Mussen and Rutherford (1966) also point out that the feminization of girls is a more complex process than the masculinization of boys. In middle-class American culture male behavior has tended not only to be more clearcut and well-defined, but also more highly valued and rewarded than female behavior; as a result, it may be necessary for a girl's family to play a more

137   See Rogers, 1969, p. 205

138   Mussen and Rutherford, 1966, p. 175; Johnson, in Rogers, 1969, pp. 226, 228

139   See Fitzgerald, 1970, p. 3

direct role in encouraging her to identify as a female than is necessary in the sex-role development of the boy.[140]

Father absence, especially early absence, has been found to affect the personality development of the daughter as well as that of the son, although in a somewhat different manner and generally at a later stage of growth. Father absence during adolescence apparently does not affect feminine sex typing as such, but it does affect the later ability to interact appropriately with males.[141] Moreover, Hetherington (1972) found marked differences between the heterosexual attitudes of daughters whose fathers had died and those whose fathers were absent because of divorce.[142] The daughters of divorcees were fairly aggressive in their attitudes toward men, whereas the daughters of deceased fathers tended to be more withdrawn and retiring. Both groups of girls, in their tense and inadequate heterosexual behavior, reflected a basic anxiety caused by the "lack of opportunity for constructive interaction with a loving, attentive father."

the role of the mother The mother, whose importance is paramount during infancy and the earliest stages of childhood, is also significant in the later sex-identification process. Pable (1965) notes that in the boy's development she plays a subtle role in relation to her husband by supporting the boy's identification with his father, "while herself avoiding an intrusive, demanding kind of orientation" to her son.[143] Her relationship to her daughter is also critical. Doll-play studies have demonstrated the importance to young girls of maternal warmth, affection, and nurturance, as well as intense and warm mother-daughter interactions. By adolescence a girl's healthy ego identity seems critically dependent on her previous identification with her mother. In a study by Block and Turula (1963) girls who identified highly with their mothers ascribed to themselves such personality attributes as calmness, self-control, confidence, and wisdom, whereas those low in maternal identification referred to their fickleness, impulsivity, rebelliousness, restlessness, and other traits of weakness. The former group also perceived their actual and ideal selves as more closely similar and consistent.[144]

140 Mussen and Rutherford, 1966, pp. 176–178

141 Biller, 1970, p. 195; National Institute of Child Health, 1968, p. 16

142 Hetherington, 1972, pp. 313–316

143 See Mussen, Conger, and Kagan, 1969, p. 690

144 See Mussen, Conger, and Kagan, 1969, pp. 362, 691

the effect of parental models Research findings are complex concerning the relative influence of each parent on the child's sex identification. Investigations have focused since Freud's time on the role of the father. Moreover, since anxiety over sex identity appears to be more frequent in boys than in girls, the research for a number of years has concentrated more on the father-son relationship (usually involving the mother as well) than on the father and daughter. More recent investigations have explored the influence of the "cross-sex parent" with respect to both the father and the mother. Some findings indicate that the father exerts a positive influence on his daughter's femininity even in infancy. For example, researchers at McGill University found that the sex identification of their subjects, particularly the girls, was more secure when the father had participated in their care as infants.[145]

Mischel (1970) suggests that perhaps a parent is more tolerant and empathic toward an opposite-sex child. Although there appears to be some empirical support for the identification theory (father-son, mother-daughter), as Mischel points out, sex-typing behavior is affected by a number of factors in the whole social learning situation.[146] Theoretically, sex typing is dependent on the same circumstances that apply to other forms of social behavior. It is the interaction with the family structure, and not simply identification with the same-sex parent, which influences the child's sex typing.[147] Mussen et al. (1969) note that when a child perceives both parents as nurturing, powerful, and competent, he will identify to some extent with both of them; later he identifies with the same-sex parent (provided, of course, that he perceives sufficient empathy in that parent to do so).[148] Hoffman suggests that in moral development (which is part of sex identification) the father may play a more important role in the child's development of resistance to temptation, while the mother's early discipline contributes more to feelings of guilt.[149] However, Mussen et al. feel that "both acceptance of one's own sex role and the adoption of high levels of moral behavior" are associated with the child's social adjustment and his level of ego strength, which in turn depend on a warm, positive relationship with his parents and rewarding interactions with his peers.[150]

145 Westley and Epstein, 1969, p. 164

146 See Mussen, Rutherford, Harris, and Keasey, 1970, pp. 56–60

147 Weisbroth, 1970, p. 401

148 Mussen, Conger, and Kagan, 1969, p. 359

149 Hoffman, 1969, p. 182

150 Mussen, Rutherford, Harris, and Keasey, 1970, p. 190

CONFUSED SEX IDENTITY

If an empathic and nurturant family milieu is essential for the development of clear sex identity and moral values, it should not be surprising to find that a lack of empathy, warmth, and support is related to problems of confused sex identity and immoral conduct. The failure of the child's environment to meet his self-esteem needs frequently results in some forms of acting-out sexual behavior as an expression of aggression.

One of the better studies on the relationship between aggression and sexual behavior was conducted by Bandura and Walters (1959), who compared teen-age boys identified as socially aggressive by court or police records with another group from the same socioeconomic level who were classified as non-aggressive.[151] A study of the families of the aggressive boys revealed that the fathers had spent little time with their sons in early childhood and were more lacking in warmth, more hostile, and more rejecting and generally uncommunicative than the fathers in the control group. The mothers, although warmer than their husbands, at the same time tended to reject and punish dependent behavior in their sons. This combination of a rejecting father and an inconsistent mother was undoubtedly a factor in the aggressive behavior evidenced by this group. Moreover, their sexual behavior appeared to be an outlet for their aggressive feelings. Two-thirds of the aggressive boys who were sixteen or older, but none of the nonaggressive boys—had had sex relations. In the aggressive group measures of physical, verbal, and direct aggression were correlated significantly with sexual behavior, whereas in the nonaggressive group the correlations were practically zero. In the aggressive group guilt over sex behavior was significantly correlated with aggression against parents, indicating that overt sex activities may be one method of displacing aggression toward parents, particularly toward the father.

Masturbatory activities in the aggressive group were correlated significantly with feelings of rejection by parents, hostility toward both father and mother, and anxiety about dependency on them; masturbation was also associated with rejection by peers.

151 Bandura and Walters, 1959, pp. 85, 301

Conversely, ample warmth and acceptance from both father and mother in the nonaggressive group were associated with an absence of masturbation. In both groups the withdrawal of love as a disciplinary technique was associated with masturbation.

More recent studies by the Kinsey Institute also suggest a relationship between the incidence of masturbation and a nonempathic environment. Masturbation in children of both sexes was more frequent in blue-collar than in white-collar groups (particularly between the ages of eight and ten), and almost twice as frequent in boys as in girls.[152] This may be partly because the parents at this socioeconomic level are typically more authoritarian, less empathic, and less affectionate than those of middle-class families, and in particular treat male children with less empathy than females.

In general, if the father is weak, both boys and girls tend to resent or reject the same-sex parent as a model. In a home with a weak father there may also be a dominant mother, and the children have been shown to have more difficulty with their own peers, especially those of the opposite sex, than do children from homes in which both parents are competent. Other researchers have noted that the weak, irresponsible father repeatedly appears as a factor in cases of confused sex identity (Wyden and Wyden, 1968; Gebhard, Gagnon, Pomeroy, and Christenson, 1965). Bieber (1962) describes the "classical" homosexual triangle as a situation in which the mother is "close-binding-intimate" with respect to her son and "dominant and minimizing toward a husband who is a detached father, particularly a hostile-detached one."[153] Overt homosexuality is less frequent in girls than in boys, but it is also associated with a sterility of affect and a weak father.[154]

Langner and Michael point out that the control and channeling of the sex drive is nearly always associated with upward mobility.[155] Gebhard et al. observe that all groups of sex offenders show a downward mobility trend—in some cases quite marked—and Kinsey contends that the sexual history of an individual invariably predicts where he will end up in the status system.[156]

In light of the reported evidence, it seems logical to conclude that an individual's sex identity is primarily related to the

152 See Bonime, 1969, p. 32

153 Beiber et al., 1962, p. 172

154 Wyden and Wyden, 1968, pp. 79–80, 107

155 Langner and Michael, 1963, p. 451

156 Gebhard, Gagnon, Pomeroy, and Christenson, 1965, p. 44

amount of empathy within his environment. Sex identity, as one aspect of general identity, is fundamentally associated with one's feelings of acceptance.

identity and the productive personality

The productive individual's security in his own identity, including his sex identity, appears to be a factor in several aspects of his functioning. His ability to trust his perception of himself enables him to trust his perception of his environment, and thus to cope with it realistically. Also, because he knows who he is, he can afford to see others as they are, rather than in terms of confused or conflicting self-images. This is apparent in the stable marriage relationships that characterize productive persons.

Both identity and self-esteem develop through empathic experiences which can be traced in theory to the infant's earliest awareness of himself in relation to the crucial person in his environment. It is the degree of empathy in these experiences that determines the individual's perception of himself, and hence the identifications from which his sense of identity evolves. In a warm and empathic environment in which he perceives himself as a person of worth, he adopts those identifications which will enable him to sustain this perception. In an environment lacking in empathy, he is deprived of the primary basis for developing a clear sense of who and what he is.

The empathic relationships that form the basis of individual identity also constitute the basis for another important aspect of the productive personality—a sense of social responsibility, in which empathy and altruism are essential elements.

We have defined the productive person as an individual who, through some expression of himself, produces a recognizable contribution to the world around him; we may therefore assume that he has some fundamental sense of responsibility to others. This social responsibility is expressed in two basic dimensions of social behavior. One relates to skills of social interaction or interpersonal competence, the qualities of spontaneity, friendliness, tolerance, fair-mindedness, tact, and consideration that enable the productive individual to maintain a direct, open relationship with another person. This dimension of social responsibility generally implies the expectation of some reciprocal response; one person reaches out to another on the assumption that the recognition will be returned.

A second, and much broader, dimension of social responsibility relates to the productive individual's own value structure. Studies of mature productive persons reveal that one basic attribute is a highly developed internal value system based on a deep empathy and concern for others, a respect for the intrinsic worth of their fellow man. This aspect of social responsibility is independent of direct reward or recognition by others. The conduct of

CHAPTER FOUR **social**
responsibility 89

the courageous statesmen portrayed in Kennedy's *Profiles in Courage* and the single-minded dedication of a Harriet Tubman, an Albert Schweitzer, or a Solzhenitsyn are clear examples of behavior governed solely by the inner dictates of conscience.

social responsibility in productive persons

Although productive individuals vary to some extent in the level of their skills in interpersonal competence, the hallmark of the productive person—and of the mature and emotionally healthy individual in general—is an inner strength that enables such a person to function independently on the basis of his own personal convictions. Thus, in a broad frame of reference, the characteristics of mature social responsibility encompass not only the specific qualities and skills which reflect a basic empathy with those in one's social milieu, but also a sense of personal commitment to those ethical and moral standards that stem from an underlying concern, altruism, and sympathy for other human beings in general.

The formation of this inner system of values, which is the fundamental goal of the socialization process, is referred to as "internalization," the replacement of regulations that have arisen in interaction with the outside world by inner regulations.[1] Schafer (1968) formulates a more complete and inclusive definition of internalization as[2]

> . . . all those processes by which the subject transforms real or imagined regulatory interactions with his environment, and real or imagined characteristics of his environment, into inner regulations and characteristics.

The core of such inner regulations, according to Schafer, is a well-developed conscience, or superego—a relatively stable and structured inner monitor which operates, for the most part unconsciously, to govern the individual's behavior independently of the external environment.[3] Aronfreed (1968) also describes internalized behavior as autonomous; it is independent of external

1 See Schafer, 1968, p. 8
2 Schafer, 1968, p. 9
3 Schafer, 1968, p. 13

outcomes, in the sense that right and wrong are no longer dictated directly by the evaluations of others, but by the individual's own value system.[4] The "value" of a given behavior to the individual is the extent to which it would increase or lower his own self-esteem:[5]

> It is the quality and magnitude of the affectivity that becomes associated with particular classifications which permit the [evaluative] structure to enter into the operations of value and to exercise some control over behavior.

In the context of social relations the term "values" designates a behavioral structure based on recognition of the rules, codes, and regulations which govern the relationships of individuals with one another. From an objective standpoint value refers to:[6]

> relative worth, utility, or importance: degree of excellence; status in a scale of preferences. . . .

Other definitions deal with the conceptual or symbolic aspects of values with respect to the relevance, desirability, or utility of some aspect of behavior as the basis for its selection from alternative forms of behavior. Although these definitions are helpful in outlining the concept of a value structure, they provide no reference point with respect to the personality factors which determine an individual's inner evaluation of a set of alternative behaviors.

A person with a well-developed sense of values can describe his feelings about various kinds of behaviors without reference to immediate, concrete acts or events. His evaluations are based on his experiences with both the causes and consequences of acts in terms of his self-esteem. An act which he judges as good or morally right enhances his self-esteem and an act which he judges as bad or morally wrong threatens his self-esteem. Although there are behaviors to which he may have a neutral affective reaction, a unified behavioral structure requires that he be able to differentiate and classify all behaviors on this continuum. It is this classification which becomes his system of values.

---

4 Aronfreed, 1968, p. 31

5 Aronfreed, 1968, p. 278

6 Webster's third new international dictionary, 1971, sv value

The internalization of a value system thus entails more than a cognitive awareness of the desirability of certain acts over others. It entails the ability to apply value judgments to the consequences of behavior, rather than to the behavior itself. If the consequences of an act contribute to happiness or the relief of distress, the act is "good"; if its consequences contribute to pain or unhappiness, it is "bad." For example, drunkenness is associated with physical deterioration and with automobile fatalities, and infideltiy is associated with the breakdown of family relationships. Acts are neither good nor bad in themselves; rather, they are good or bad only in so far as they have positive or negative consequences.

The value system of the productive person, however, extends beyond the consequences of his behavior to himself. It encompasses a sense of social responsibility based on an underlying concern, respect, and esteem for others. According to Barron (1968), these qualities are also the hallmark of the mature and emotionally healthy individual:[7]

> Psychologically healthy people do what they think is right, and what they think is right is that people should not lie to one another or to themselves, that they should not steal, slander, persecute, intrude, do damage willfully, go back on their word, fail a friend, or do any of the things that put them on the side of death as against life.

In other words, the person with a mature value system is committed to a highly developed sense of personal ethics and a code of behavior which reflects not only a respect for human dignity, but an active concern for the welfare of others—that is, the quality of altruism.

Social responsibility in this sense may be expressed over a wide range of social behaviors, from the capacity for friendly, spontaneous, and open interaction with others to an unswerving devotion to the standards of one's profession. In some cases the expression of altruism and sympathy for those in distress lies not so much in the dimension of interpersonal skills as in a deep compassion for the problems and needs of all human beings, both

7 Barron, 1968, p. 145

seen and unseen. A person such as Einstein, for example, who was extraordinarily shy, might be called socially concerned, rather than sociable.[8] The truly altruistic person may, in fact, devote much of his life to acts of unselfish concern for and devotion to others for which he expects no reciprocity even in the form of recognition.

THE ACADEMIC ACHIEVER

Studies on productivity have dealt with a variety of personality traits, such as self-confidence, achievement motivation, persistence, originality, and cognitive patterns. Apparently, however, researchers have viewed the area of interpersonal relationships as secondary, despite the frequent association of academic achievement with leadership activities. Nevertheless, incidental observations in some of the research on outstanding academic achievers refer to their social competence and effectiveness in interpersonal relationships, as well as to their altruistic concern for others and their adherence to a well-defined sense of values. In one study Stalnaker (1961) reported that National Merit Scholars typically had greater social presence, greater social skills, and a greater interest in people in general than non-scholarship winners. Lavin (1965), in summarizing the multivariate research on achievement and personality variables, concluded that social maturity in the student role was associated with high academic performance, as indicated by such references as "greater social presence," "greater social maturity," "greater socialization," responsibility, and restraint in social behavior.[9] High achievers were also reported by Durr and Schmatz (1964) as significantly higher on personal adjustment measures, more mature, more emotionally stable, and less anxious than low achievers.[10]

Kennedy (1960) reported on forty mathematically gifted adolescents who had been rigorously selected from a population of 5000 for special summer training. These young persons, although somewhat anxious and competitive, seemed to be maturing much more rapidly than their high school peers, were uniformly well adjusted, and showed few signs of egocentricity.

8 See Hughes, 1969, p. 75   10 See Shatkin, 1966, p. 6
9 Lavin, 1965, pp. 106–107

They were also much concerned with ethical problems, had a marked tendency toward abstract beliefs, and were faithful church attenders.[11] There appears to be a relationship between mental health and social responsibility among university students. In his study of personal soundness of graduate students Barron (1968) described the high-soundness group as appreciative, sociable, tolerant, fair-minded, and responsible.[12] In contrast, he noted that the students who were lower in personal soundness were characteristically self-centered, egotistical, and defensive; they were also rated as dull, immature, unstable, self-punishing, withdrawn, and tense. In the McGill University study Westley and Epstein (1969) found that the students who were rated as lower in mental health tended to be more out of touch with certain kinds of affect and were not overconcerned about the values of others in their social milieu.[13]

A decrease in cognitive skills also seems to be accompanied by lack of social effectiveness. Haan (1963) compared two groups of men whose IQ scores had changed over a period of years and found that those whose IQs had gone down were in general more deliberate, less empathic, and more defensive than those whose IQs had increased.[14]

A study of dropouts from the classes of 1940, 1951, and 1960 at Princeton University suggests that self-esteem is a factor in interpersonal relationships as well as academic achievement.[15] Apparently these students had low self-esteem to begin with and felt a sense of alienation from their peers. Needing the moral support which a larger circle of friends might have provided, they suffered further deterioration of self-image when this support was lacking; and consequently they eventually withdrew from school. It was also found that there was subsequently a higher divorce rate among the dropouts than among those students who remained in college. Other reports refer to the low achiever as immature, socially inadequate, and lacking in adaptability, independence, and responsibility. He has been found "defensively rigid" and anxious and guilty about his aggression toward others. These characteristics suggest a strong desire to be accepted by the group, as well as a fear of hostility from peers.[16]

11 Kennedy, 1960, p. 665

12 Barron, 1968, p. 46

13 Westley and Epstein, 1969, p. 53

14 Haan, 1964

15 Pervin, Reik, and Dalrymple, 1966, pp. 42–43, 52

16 See M. Gilmore, 1964, pp. 20–21

Thus the high achiever appears, at least in the context of the limited reports, to be friendly and outgoing as well as unselfish and ethically concerned, whereas the low achiever tends to be self-centered, withdrawn, defensive, and dependent.

THE CREATIVE PERSON

The picture of social characteristics is slightly less clear in the studies on creativity, especially with regard to the creative scientist. There seems to be general agreement that the creative scientist is not a gregarious person. Holland (1964) noted that the student with scientific aptitude is not particularly given to social graces and seems more concerned with things and ideas than with interpersonal relationships.[17] Roe (1969) comments that the scientist's interpersonal relations are typically of low intensity, and that he dislikes both interpersonal controversy and interpersonal aggression.[18] McClelland (1962) reported similar findings, adding that this characteristic unsociability may be evident as early as age ten.[19] Drevdahl (1964) found that the highly creative psychologists in his study were more likely to derive satisfaction from professional groups than from purely social ones and also tended to be relatively unconcerned with relationships with the opposite sex.[20] A number of other investigations from the 1950s and 1960s point in the same direction. In a study of highly creative psychologists and chemists, for example, Chambers (1964) noted that his subjects showed little interest in civic or community affairs and typically directed all their energies to their own particular areas of research.[21]

It appears, however, that this general lack of sociability and gregariousness in the creative scientist may be primarily a function of his intense preoccupation with his own creative projects; it is far different from the self-absorption and self-centeredness of the low achiever. Moreover, there is other evidence that the creative scientist is deeply concerned with the broader aspects of social responsibility.[22] The creative adolescent has been found to be humanistically oriented and empathic; there are references to his social maturity, liberalism, and lack of authoritarianism, as well

17 Holland, 1964, p. 301

18 Roe, 1969, p. 99

19 McClelland, 1962, p. 145

20 Drevdahl, 1964, p. 175

21 Chambers, 1964, p. 6

22 Hughes, 1969, p. 75

as to his social confidence and popularity among peers (Drews, 1961; Burkhart, 1960; Green, 1957). Such typical attributes of creativity as independence and initiative are found side by side with cooperation, socialization, friendliness, and a lack of inner hostility (Watson, 1960), and tolerance for ambiguity, another characteristic of creative persons, seems to be associated with love and acceptance of others (Frenkel-Brunswick, 1950).[23] Drevdahl (1964) points to the creative psychologist's significantly greater degree of adherence to some orthodox religion—though not necessarily religious orthodoxy—as an indication of his general acceptance of his social, religious, moral, political, and other responsibilities.[24]

One interesting aspect of the personality of the creative scientist is his love of music. McClelland (1962) notes that in listening to music the scientist experiences a sense of "melting" into his environment and feeling of oneness with it.[25] Whether he is participating as a listener or as a performer (many scientists are members of amateur music groups), music appears to provide a strong emotional release. Since Fisher and Cleveland (1958) have also cited the extraordinarily low body boundaries of the scientist as measured by the Rorschach test, McClelland concludes that the creative scientist's openness to his environment may indicate a frame of reference that extends beyond the immediacy of day-to-day concerns and social contacts to larger, broader, and more abstract issues. Another aspect of the social concern of creative persons is touched on by MacKinnon (1963), who reported that highly creative architects are quite socially responsible within the context of their profession.[26] They possess strong inner ethical and artistic standards; they also feel that they can influence and help their colleagues to be more creative. Such an attitude is fundamentally one of altruism.

In some cases professional persons who are highly competent but lower in creativity are described as somewhat more socially aware and concerned for other people and less totally involved in their own creative endeavors than their more innovative associates. However, this finding seems to pertain more to the area of social competence or skills than to the more abstract

23 See Foster, 1958, pp. 112–114   25 McClelland, 1962, pp. 168–169
24 Drevdahl, 1964, pp. 175–177   26 MacKinnon, 1963, pp. 262–278

realm of altruistic social concern. In MacKinnon's study of creative architects, for instance, those in the lower-ranked creative groups (groups II and III) tended to describe themselves in terms of such traits as sincerity, dependability, tolerance, sensitivity, good nature, practicality, and moderation. The highly creative architects (group I) instead stressed their inventiveness, determination, independence, and enthusiasm.[27] Similarly, Drevdahl noted that the middle group ("noncreative productive") of psychologists in his study seemed to differ from highly creative ones largely in their greater concern with people and social relationships.[28] This group also evidenced a certain amount of dependency and irresponsibility, as well as greater competitiveness and rebelliousness, characteristics which are associated with feelings of insecurity and inferiority.

It appears that the most highly creative individuals are markedly independent; having complete confidence in their environment, they do not feel the need to rank themselves in terms of qualities of social competence. It also appears that creative endeavor at the highest levels must preclude the pursuit of most types of social activities; in fact, the creatively productive person who also undertakes many social commitments and responsibilities probably does so somewhat at the expense of his creative endeavors. Nonetheless, a broad concern with the larger social and ethical issues seems to characterize all highly creative individuals.

THE LEADER

There are a number of references to the interpersonal relations and social concern of persons who have been outstanding and influential in various fields of human endeavor. Maslow's (1954) study of self-actualizing persons included great statesmen, such as Jefferson and Lincoln, as well as noted humanitarians, such as Eleanor Roosevelt and Jane Addams, all of whom could qualify as outstanding leaders within their sphere of activity. Regarding the interpersonal relationships of his self-actualizing subjects, Maslow took special note of their spontaneity and naturalness. He also

---

27 MacKinnon, 1963, p. 255   28 Drevdahl, 1964, pp. 177–178

remarked on their deep feelings of identification, sympathy, and affection for all human beings (*Gemeinschaftsgefühl*) and their genuine desire to help the human race; he describes them as capable of "more fusion, greater love, more perfect identification, more obliteration of the ego boundaries than other people would consider possible."[29] At the same time, he notes that such persons generally have a small circle of close friends, rather than a large group of casual acquaintances. The self-actualizer also has a firm sense of values; he is a highly ethical individual, thoroughly confident of the differences between right and wrong and much concerned about the rights of others. The famous personages cited by Maslow could be said to represent social responsibility in its highest form.

Other leadership studies illustrate the general effectiveness of good leaders in all dimensions of socially responsible behavior. Moment and Zaleznik (1963) reported that the highest-ranked businessmen in their study (designated "stars") were relatively low in anxiety in group situations and could express their feelings to other people openly, honestly, and directly; thus they were able to let others know their positions and could engage in a fairly direct and aggressive (but apparently not hostile) give-and-take.[30] Karasick et al. found that leaders in high school perceive themselves as having more friends than do their classmates, and Westley and Epstein reported a statistically significant association between the emotional health of college freshmen and their previous involvement in high school activities.[31] In Oden's follow-up study of the Terman group one of the factors differentiating the A group (the most successful) from the C group (the least successful) was community service. Nearly one-third of the As, but only 6 percent of the Cs (difference was significant at the .001 level), listed participation in at least three activities connected with community health, civic, educational, or church-related programs.[32] Douvan and Adelson noted that the upward-aspiring boys in their study mentioned more often than the downward-mobile ones that they would never break a rule involving a "responsibility to others." These boys showed advanced, and even precocious, social maturity.[33]

29 Maslow, 1954, pp. 208, 217–218

30 Moment and Zaleznik, 1963, p. 68

31 Westley and Epstein, 1969, p. 53

32 Oden, 1968, p. 70

33 Douvan and Adelson, 1966, pp. 60, 63

Cox's (1970) ten-year follow-up study of persons who had been leaders in college describes the healthy (unimpaired) subjects as greatly concerned about ethical standards, integrity of character, and high moral concern for others, particularly with regard to sexual relationships; their "sternest moral imperative" was the obligation to value and protect the individual.[34] These highly productive persons were altruistic in the best sense of the term. They were deeply concerned with civil rights issues as well as with the great international issues of peace and justice. Above all, they placed overriding importance on honesty in all its forms. Applying the strictest standards both to their own behavior and to that of their children, they were wholly preoccupied with the task of living a life of excellence and quality.

formation of basic values

How does an individual acquire a mature value system? How, in other words, does he develop the social-interaction skills, the altruistic concern for others, and the internalized standards of ethics which are characteristic of true social responsibility? This question relates to the entire process of socialization, which begins with the identification processes discussed in Chapter Three. The two processes are not unique and separate, but interrelated and interdependent. As Lynd (1958) points out, an open relatedness to other persons and the search for self-identity are actually one dialectical process. The more a person relates to others, the more he discovers of himself; conversely, the more clearly and firmly rooted his identity, the more he is able (and thus inclined) to reach out to others.[35] Socialization enlarges on identification; it is therefore more inclusive. It is more definitive and structured, and hence more easily labeled and researched.

The ultimate goal of the socialization process is the adoption of behavior which will enable an individual to act with independence and responsibility and to deal effectively with persons in his social and professional life. Findings from the theoretical and research literature support the observation that early child-

34 Cox, 1970, pp. 280–281   35 Lynd, 1958, p. 241

hood environment has a marked, if not a permanent, influence on a person's behavior as an adult. Since the highly productive adult relates to people in a different manner from the low-productive one, we may surmise that his early childhood must have been of a different quality. Unfortunately most investigations of adult productivity fail to report its possible antecedents in early childhood experiences.

As Bandura (1969) has noted, social behavior is a highly discriminative function, and the basic variables in this selection process have not always been fully taken into account by theorists and researchers. To understand all aspects of the social responsibility of the productive person would require a detailed examination of his childhood background, including his interpersonal relations, not only within his family, but also with other persons who may have acted as his socializing agents—peers, relatives, teachers, and all who served as models or exercised leadership and responsibility for situations in which, at various times in his life, he may have been involved. No retrospective research of this magnitude, depth, or detail has yet been attempted.

Nevertheless, the literature on child development provides us with a good picture of the processes by which an individual acquires the particular value system that characterizes the highly productive person. The values that a child acquires usually reflect those of his immediate family and cultural milieu, but in a larger sense they also reflect the broader-based values that are deeply rooted in Judaeo-Christian tradition. All laws, codes, and mores in our society are predicated on the extent to which an individual's actions may injure or benefit another person. Thus the most highly internalized values are altruism—from the Latin *alter*, meaning "other"—and sympathy, the relief of distress in others; by the same token, the most highly internalized monitor of behavior is guilt. Since guilt is one of the most crippling deterrants to productivity, and is at the same time associated with some of the very personality characteristics that characterize the productive individual, it is particularly important to understand the nature of guilt and the conditions in which it arises.

100

ALTRUISM

Altruism is one of the most important and highly valued civilizing traits in our culture. Like other forms of behavior, it cannot exist without some reciprocal benefit to the giver; however, altruism is so high on the value scale that it carries a tremendous reward in self-esteem. As a result, the benefits of an altruistic act even to the recipient need not be directly observable. The individual is cognizant, either from his own direct experience or from his observation of others, that his act will benefit someone else, and his anticipation that it will be highly approved by those who are important to him contributes to his affective security.

The age at which altruism begins to appear in children has been subject to some investigation. Borke (1971) studied 200 upper-middle-class white children, ranging in age from three to eight, and found that even the youngest in the group showed an awareness of others' feelings and could identify the specific situations which evoke different kinds of affective responses.[36] Recognition of happiness occurred at an earlier age (three to three-and-a-half) than did recognition of fear (which occurred at three to three-and-a-half with no greater than chance expectancy, but increased significantly by four-and-a-half to five). Empathic response to and differentiation between feelings of sadness or anger showed the "least consistent trends with age," possibly reflecting the greater complexity of these emotions from the young child's standpoint. One interesting point was that there were no differences in empathic response between boys and girls, indicating that, at least in the population studied, parents were more encouraging of social sensitivity than of aggression in children of both sexes. As Borke observes, these findings challenge Piaget's theory that the child of two to seven is primarily egocentric and unable to empathize with others.

Aronfreed contends that both altruism and sympathy, though different in application, are acquired under similar conditions and are both dependent upon "the prerequisite establishment of the child's capacity for empathy and vicarious

36 Borke, 1971, pp. 263–269

experience."[37] Hoffman also notes that a child's moral development is built on his potential for "prosocial affect" (capacity for empathy) and adds further that socialization practices must integrate empathy with "appropriate cognitive functioning."[38]

He maintains that empathy and awareness of the effects of one's behavior on others can be taught to children by "other-oriented" induction (reasoning) techniques designed to impress upon them the fact that certain forms of behavior may have painful or undesirable consequences for others. Another method he suggests for the learning of empathy is reciprocal role playing, in which the child takes the part of a person who has been hurt by another:[39]

> The result of this experience is a guilt response that is conscious, focused primarily on the victim's inner states rather than on the actor's own impulses; [an experience which encourages] his efforts to be more considerate in the future.

Because situations involving harm to others are emotionally disruptive, there is need for an outside person (usually an adult) who can be objective as well as sympathetic and who can be more effective if he uses "discipline techniques with high inductive components."

Hoffman also indicates that empathy can be acquired through exposure to adults either in real-life situations or portrayed in books or in the mass media, who openly express empathy and compassion, and also through experiences which help the child to understand the motives underlying others' behavior and to recognize that he might behave similarly in their place.[40] Although Hoffman appears to accept identification as a factor in the development of empathy, he provides no experimental evidence demonstrating the effectiveness of either role playing or other-oriented induction as teaching devices. There is serious doubt, in fact, that cognitive methods are even useful in teaching empathy. In a study of 118 college sophomores Dell (1967) found that lectures about empathy and role playing were ineffective in either increasing empathy or projecting it to others.[41] Neither intelligence nor sex was related to ability to empathize, although

37 Aronfreed, 1968, p. 138

38 Hoffman, 1970, p. 346

39 Ibid.

40 Hoffman, 1970, pp. 343, 346, 347

41 Dell, 1967 (1967A), pp. 1447–1448

there was some evidence that the "better-adjusted" individuals possessed this trait to a somewhat greater degree than the less well-adjusted students.

The foundations of altruistic behavior are established through a child's early experiences and observations of others. Because it is so highly rewarded, altruism is especially subject to imitative modeling, even on the basis of one significant experience. Thus a personal interchange involving an expression of altruism has benefits not only for the giver, but also for both recipient and any observer. The power of personal example is strong: a child watching a playmate give half his candy to a younger sibling is benefiting through observational learning. Aronfreed points out that the forerunners of altruism are generosity and honesty.[42] Generosity may be learned by observation in social experiences which involve the sharing of toys and clothes, participation in gift-giving holidays, and recognition for unselfish behavior in daily situations. Early rudiments of honesty can also be supported by positive social reinforcement; for example, the child who can give a truthful report of an incident, or of the day's happenings, is rewarded with approval and affection and thus gradually comes to recognize the consequences of his own and others' truthfulness as one aspect of unselfishness.

One experiment was conducted by Rosenhan and White (1967) to evaluate the effectiveness of teaching altruistic behavior to fourth- and fifth-grade children in the presence of an adult model (who then left the subjects alone). Although Hoffman's report of this study calls attention to certain weaknesses in its design, he notes that the children did "learn in the laboratory setting to donate a valued commodity to charity in the absence of adult authority."[43]

Ordinarily both empathy and altruism are acquired primarily through a child's day-by-day relationship with affectionate parents. In such a relationship the child observes and identifies with his parents' empathic characteristics as they are expressed in attitudes and actions that demonstrate concern for the welfare of others. Thus empathy, as the more fundamental trait, is acquired first.

42 Aronfreed, 1968, pp. 124–125   43 Hoffman, 1970, p. 324

An interesting laboratory experiment performed by Aronfreed and Paskal (1965) demonstrates the teaching of altruism
through a conditioning process which first establishes empathy.[44]
The experiment involved six- to eight-year-old girls and an adult
female socializing agent. The instrument used was a "choice box"
operated by two levers and automated to dispense either a small
candy or a 3-second red light. When the red light flashed the
agent expressed pleasure; she showed indifference to the appearance of the candy. One group of children was given a series of
conditioning sessions which demonstrated to them that pushing
the lever for the light gave pleasure to the agent and therefore was
an "altruistic" act. Empathy was established by a close temporal
association between the agent's expressive cues of pleasure (a
smile and a pleased and excited tone of voice at each appearance
of the red light) and the child's own direct experience of the
agent's physical affection (a firm hug for the child after each red
light). The expressive cues of pleasure and the physical affection
were "dispensed as though they were a spontaneous correlate of
the agent's pleasurable reaction" to the light.

The children who had been exposed to this conditioning
subsequently demonstrated significantly more altruism than did
the control group (who typically chose the candy). Moreover,
those children who had been exposed both to expressive cues (the
agent's smile and her pleased and excited voice) and to physical
affection (her hug) showed more altruism than those who had
been exposed only to the physical affection. Midlarsky and Bryan
(1967) demonstrated further that if a child has already been conditioned by empathy to perform altruistically in one situation, his
altruism tends to be generalized to other situations.[45]

The results of this experiment suggest that affection and
empathy do indeed generate altruism. If an individual's experience with others has been pleasant and reassuring, he should find
it quite easy to empathize with either their joy or their distress. A
child who has enjoyed constant nurturance and support since
infancy will experience an empathic relationship with his mother
in which there is a continual sharing of each other's emotional
states. Such an empathic experience can be generalized to other

44 Aronfreed, 1968, pp. 143–145   45 See Aronfreed, pp. 148–149

persons, both within and beyond the family circle, who are in distress or happiness. Thus empathic experience, which contributes to an individual's self-esteem, enables him from this early experience of nurturance to become more socialized, more socially responsible, and generally outgoing to other people.[46]

Some recent studies of altruism suggest its possible association with certain personality characteristics. Rawlings (1970) has found, for example, that altruism may be heightened in persons who have feelings of guilt. Krebs (1970) reports numerous findings from other research.[47] From a review of various studies he notes that persons who are recipients of altruistic acts are characteristically dependent, and that attractive persons are more likely than unattractive ones to be recipients of altruistic acts. Altruistic behavior in children is apparently not differentiated by sex, but adult men are, on the whole, less altruistic than women toward highly dependent persons. Differences between occupational groups have also been noted: working-class and middle-class entrepreneurial groups tend to use reciprocity as a basis for social behavior, whereas bureaucratic middle-class persons apparently place less emphasis on reciprocity and tend to be more socially responsible in an altruistic sense. There is also some evidence of the important role of observational learning in the acquisition of altruism: it has been found that recipients of altruistic acts become, in turn, more altruistic toward others.

SYMPATHY

Research on productive persons seldom, if ever, covers the trait of sympathy; neither altruism nor sympathy appears specifically in personality tests and rating scales. Studies of sympathetic persons indicate, however, that they have some of the same characteristics as do productive persons. Sympathy is also a form of social responsibility, and in certain respects sympathy and altruism are similar.

Sympathy, described by Aronfreed (1968) as a disposition to relieve the distress of others, has a more restricted affective base than altruism. An individual must be personally and closely

46 Aronfreed, p. 312   47 See Krebs, 1970, pp. 258–302

involved with a specific distressful situation before he can react sympathetically to it, whereas altruism is a more global concern with human welfare in general.[48]

In order to manifest sympathy, one must first react empathically to cues indicating another's distress; then he must perform a specific act with the goal of reducing that distress. Empathy is thus an integral part of sympathy and must be present before sympathy can be genuinely expressed. Sympathy does not consist of a perfunctory effort to relieve distress, nor is it provided when an individual merely reports a distressful situation. The capacity to express sympathy does not depend on previous experience of a similar situation; rather, it depends on a recognition that some behavior of one's own will reduce the other person's distress—or at least its consequences. If no relief can be offered, then empathy alone is involved.

Like altruism, sympathetic behavior is related to the anticipation of some form of psychological reward, either in the form of gratitude from the recipient or through the resulting approval of others. If in reducing the distress of another person the giver also reduces his own empathic feelings of distress, then sympathy becomes combined with altruism. As with altruism, the acquisition of sympathetic behavior depends on the reinforcement of repeated experiences which contribute to self-esteem. Imitative modeling also appears to operate in this learning situation. Lenrow (1965) found that the persons who are most sensitive to overt signs of distress are those who have received verbal reinforcement for sympathetic behavior in past situations.[49]

The successful management of one's own affective life is directly related to one's capacity to act favorably toward others' affective experience. Lenrow notes that direct sympathetic action in adults is related to their sense of past competence and effectiveness in coping with barriers in their own lives.[50] An individual's affective security enables him not only to empathize verbally with others, but also to acquire skills that will enable him to cope with distressful situations. In other words, the individual's confidence in his own competence is itself a resource for sympathetic behavior.

106 48 Aronfreed, 1968, pp. 149–150, 157   50 See Lenrow, 1965, pp. 291–292

49 See Lenrow, 1965, p. 291

Apparently parental respect for the child's autonomy plays a direct role in developing the sense of competence that enables him to be helpful in difficult situations. Whiting and Whiting (1969) found that in cultures in which the mothers customarily delegate important tasks to their children, the children demonstrate a greater degree of sympathetic behavior (they are more likely to offer help, support, and responsible suggestions) than children in cultures which limit all important tasks to adults.[51] In an experiment involving teachers who rated boys on characteristics related to helping behavior, Staub (1971) found that the initiation of cooperative activity, general competence, the expression of affection, and the need for approval were all clearly related to helping behavior (r = .53 to .88, p < .01).[52] However, there were some surprising differences between the sexes: among the girls all four of these characteristics were negatively related to helping behavior, and among the boys all four were positively related. Staub suggests that the negative correlations for girls may be a function of differences in teachers' attitudes toward boys and girls. The highest correlations with helping behavior among the boys were for the variables of initiation of activity and competence.

The fact that sympathy is an attribute of the productive personality does not mean that it can be expressed indiscriminately to all who are in need of it. In order to function productively —indeed, in order to function at all—the empathic person must of necessity be selective of the distress situations in which he can permit himself to become actively and directly involved.

CONSCIENCE

One broad and enduring component of the mature personality is conscience, which plays a particularly important role in the value structure of the productive personality. The development of conscience is an integral part of the socialization process and accompanies the increased demands on the child for control over the bodily processes, task-oriented behavior, and an ability to interact with the peers and adults in his environment.

51 See Staub, 1971, p. 131   52 Staub, 1971, pp. 129–131

Conscience refers to the internalized behavorial controls which govern the individual's choice of response to environmental cues. In psychoanalytic theory the conscience, termed the "superego," performs a somewhat negative function in warning the ego to avoid actions which have painful consequences. The functions of the superego are defined as including approval or disapproval of the ego's actions, "critical self-observation," punishment of self, demands for repentance or reparation of wrongdoing, and enhancement of self-esteem for having done right.[53]

The child's conscience, or superego, develops through his identification with his parents; in adopting their behavior he learns to control and direct his sexual and aggressive actions into socially acceptable channels. The failure to engage in acceptable behavior results in anticipation of the loss of nurturance, which in turn threatens the child's sense of security concerning his physical welfare. This anticipation of loss as a consequence of some transgression against parental expectations and prohibitions is the feeling referred to as guilt. The socialization process is thus directly related to the requirements of the superego. Behaving in a manner that is not subject to criticism or disapproval results in an "easy conscience."

GUILT

In Western culture standards of morality are highly polarized. Altruism, at one extreme, receives almost universal approval; at the other extreme, and subject to equally strong disapproval, are acts which inflict direct or indirect injury on others. Although guilt feelings may result from a minor transgression in interpersonal relations, the greatest amount of guilt is engendered by an act that is actually directed toward another. Both altruism and guilt thus depend on a capacity for empathy: one can feel guilt only through an empathic awareness of the pain for which one has been responsible.

Guilt feelings may be defined as an awareness of having committed a "crime" or "sin" through an act which violates some

53 **Hinsie and Campbell, 1970, p. 728**

moral, ethical, or religious precept. The result of such an act is lowered self-esteem, accompanied by anxiety concerning a potential loss of empathy and support from others. The word "guilt" may have some etymological association with debt, in the sense that one "owes" something to a person for having failed or injured him in some way. Broadly speaking, guilt applies to an aspect of moral behavior which involves the failure to fulfill a personal commitment or the commission of those aggressive acts which have physically or psychologically painful consequences for another.

Ultimately an act is moral or immoral only in terms of its consequences to others. However, "morality," from the Latin *moralis*, meaning "of manners or customs," implies conformity with standards of conduct or character based on society's evaluation of those consequences. Thus moral judgment is applied to an act with respect to the rules and behavioral codes which have been established as a reflection of this evaluation. An act need not be intentional in order to be subject to moral judgment. However, intentional acts are likely to be judged more harshly, since an individual is presumed to have intended the natural consequences of his behavior. As the child gains wider social experience and develops better cognitive equipment, he becomes more aware of the effects of his actions, and hence more attuned to his own responsibility for the results.

According to psychoanalytic theory, no act (at least in the case of adults) is ever entirely unintentional, since all behavior is motivated by the individual's own unconscious. Hence an individual imposes moral judgment on his own behavior whether he "intended" the consequences or not. Moral judgment does not, of course, apply exclusively to one's own behavior, but the repeated observation of harmful consequences to others usually results in some internalization.[54] As a result, neither the conduct nor its consequences need be tangible to be classified as moral or immoral. In most cases, however, an immoral act, whether it is observable or not, brings injury to both parties, although the consequences may be greater for the actor than for the recipient. Even minor violations of an ethical code or transgressions against

54 Aronfreed, 1968, pp. 245–246

social mores can cause self-directed negative affect. The loss of self-esteem, particularly when the act or behavior has been surreptitious or unobserved, is extended to a perceived rejection or retaliation by the recipient, and the guilty individual may react as if the "injured" person actually knew of the act.

The guilt feelings engendered by an immoral act are likely to be intense and crippling, especially for a person who has experienced an empathic milieu. The guilt and its accompanying anxiety may in such cases reach the point of a sense of "annihilation," particularly when there is an awareness of having caused irreparable harm to someone else. Jacobson describes the guilt feelings generated by the conscience as "probably the most insufferable of all unpleasurable experiences."[55] As a result, one of the principal deterrents to productivity is unresolved guilt feelings, since an empathic person spends excessive time and energy in efforts to justify, undo, or compensate for his guilt-producing behavior. In many cases the projected feelings of rejection by others are more painful for an individual than the actual disapproval he receives.

Persons who are overwhelmed by guilt feelings usually require some form of psychological defense in order to maintain a semblance of self-esteem. One such defense is "displacement," the shifting of blame onto someone or something else or onto uncontrollable causes (a defense often observed in children). Another is denial of responsibility for the act itself. A third defense is "isolation of affect," overconcern (or even obsession) with one's guilt. A fourth type of defense is "reaction formation," inappropriate or unwarranted empathy or concern for others as a means of alleviating or compensating for guilt; overt displays of altruism are sometimes expressions of this defense.

An attempt to restore self-esteem which has been lost through a guilt-producing act may also take the form of masochism or self-attack. It has been said that every guilty person becomes his own hangman. Self-inflicted punishment—such as the various psychosomatic conditions, an acquired illness, or accident-proneness—may serve as "penance" or as a distractor.

55 Jacobson, 1964, p. 131

For example, self-punishment for aggressive or hostile feelings commonly takes the form of inappropriate sexual fantasies or overt sexual acts which engender depression or additional guilt feelings that are often more acute than those produced by the original aggression. Freud contended that the control of sexual impulses is more difficult for persons who harbor guilt feelings because the diffusion of energy caused by the threat to self-esteem interferes with the control of the primary drives.

A nurturing, empathic home characterized by praise and affection fosters the qualities of social responsibility that characterize all productive persons. However, the more nurturing and empathic the relationship, the more sensitive the child is to a possible loss of love; hence it is precisely in such a home that he feels even minor transgressions the most keenly. Whiting and Child (1953) found that higher guilt scores were more frequent in cultures where love-oriented disciplinary methods were prevalent.[56] In a study of 236 young adults Allinsmith and Greening (1955) found higher guilt over aggression in those whose mothers had employed psychological discipline than in those whose mothers had used physical punishment.[57] Similarly, in a study of five-year-olds Heinecke (1953) reported that guilt was associated with parental use of praise, infrequent use of physical punishment and isolation, and expressions of affection toward the child.[58]

Guilt is crippling to productivity, however, only when it is unresolved. As long as discipline is based on a close and affectionate parent-child relationship, the child responds to his guilt feelings by accepting responsibility for his behavior, and he is able to restore his self-esteem by confessing, explaining, apologizing, and being forgiven.[59] At the same time, he tends to adopt the approved behavior more readily and therefore has less to feel guilty about.

Maslow (1954) observed that the guilt evidenced by self-actualizers was of a different quality and probably had different antecedents from the overriding guilt and anxiety which hamper the neurotic. He notes that healthy people do feel ashamed, sad,

56   Whiting and Child, 1953, pp. 242–246
57   Allinsmith and Greening, 1955, p. 320
58   See Becker, 1964, p. 182
59   Aronfreed, 1968, p. 40

anxious, or defensive about such matters as improvable shortcomings, remnants of earlier prejudices and jealousies, annoying habits, and the general shortcomings of the species, culture, or group to which they belong; indeed, they should feel distressed about "discrepancies between what is and what . . . ought to be."[60] It appears, in fact, that the productive individual is relatively free of guilt altogether. McClelland (1962) reports very little evidence of personal guilt feelings in the TAT stories of the creative scientists in his study; he concludes that they had little cause to feel guilty. He did find, however, that they became upset about what he called questions of morality, especially violations of honesty in the reporting of scientific data. He also notes that in an earlier study Knapp (1956) had found the TAT stories of science majors significantly low in signs of aggression, guilt, or vindication.[61]

SHAME

Both guilt and shame are reactions to the potential disapproval or negative evaluation of others. However, guilt is the awareness of responsibility for an act that lowers one's self-esteem, whereas shame is the desire to conceal an act that would lower one's esteem in the eyes of others. The word "shame" in fact originated in the Anglo-Saxon word meaning "cover" and is defined as:[62]

> a painful emotion caused by consciousness of guilt, shortcoming, or impropriety in one's own behavior or position or in the behavior or position of a closely associated person or group. . . .

An earlier edition of *Webster* also refers to the emotion caused by "the exposure of that which modesty prompts to conceal." This feeling may range from embarrassment to a sense of deep humiliation, but in general it is associated more with some breach of propriety than with an offense that is personally injurious to others.

As noted by James (1890), shame is often experienced for the behavior of another person who is involved with one's own sense of honor. Thus in a marital situation one partner may feel shame for some act committed by the other, and a parent may feel shame

60 Maslow, 1954, pp. 206–208
61 McClelland, 1962, pp. 148, 165

62 Webster's third new international dictionary, 1971, sv shame

for his child's behavior. Although guilt and shame do not ordinarily occur together, in the parent-child situation the parent may feel guilty for having been the cause of the child's shameful behavior.

There is some experimental evidence that shame is symptomatic of low self-esteem. In a study of hospital patients Lewis (1971) found that those who were "field-dependent" were more prone to feelings of shame, whereas "field-independent" persons were more given to feelings of guilt.[63] Field-dependent persons are also more susceptible to the opinions of others and tend to rely on the defense mechanism of denial, whereas the obsessive thinking typical of isolation and intellectualization is more frequently associated with guilt feelings.

Both dependency and shame are somewhat more common to women than men. Lewis notes that women tend to be more other-directed than men:[64]

> The "self" in women is more vulnerable than in men; the "introjected other" is a more powerful influence over women than over men.

Men's vocational activities usually involve some aggressive competition; hence they may be more prone to guilt feelings.

Shame is often a reaction to sexual behavior motivated by feelings for which one fears exposure. Although expressions of aggression which involve direct contact with another person are more likely to produce feelings of guilt, the indirect expression of aggression through individual sex acts such as masturbation more often result in shame than in guilt.

The association of shame with dependence on the judgments of others, combined with the need either to deny or to conceal the reality of one's own behavior, suggests a lack of confidence in the environment as well as an inability to cope with it. Since shame is often found in conjunction with poor task performance, it is possible that in a nonempathic environment a child is unable either to discriminate or to internalize a value system which would enable him to function effectively in his social environment.

63 Lewis, 1971, pp. 142–143, 173, 196–197, 497   64 Lewis, 1971, p. 148; see also chap. 4

the socialization process

Socialization is the process whereby an individual is prepared, or "trained," to participate in his social environment. In psychoanalytic terms this means a channeling of basic drives and inner impulses to forms of expression that conform with the cultural demands of the environment. Sociologists define socialization from a slightly different viewpoint as "the interactional process by which the individual is taught his place in the social order."[65] Parsons and Bales (1955) refer in more specific terms to identification as the basis of socialization:[66]

> The conditions under which effective socialization can take place . . . will include being placed in a social situation where the more powerful and responsible persons [the parents] are themselves integrated in the cultural value system in question, both in that they constitute with the children an institutionalized social system [the family], and that the patterns have previously been internalized [in meaningful] ways in their own personalities.

The writers emphasize that in all societies, including our own, the family is the "institutionalized system" in question. In the course of the socialization process, the child internalizes the norms of his parents through reactions to reward and punishment (which involve fundamental principles of social learning) and through imitation and identification based on reciprocal love and esteem.

When we speak of effective socialization, we are referring principally to the positive and beneficial consequences of an interaction between two or more individuals which is based fundamentally on an empathic relationship. As pointed out in the discussion of identification, true socialization is generated only when the child's self-esteem needs are consistently met through an affectionate relationship which provides him with a basis for identification with those within the family matrix who represent his particular culture.

A full discussion of the theoretical concepts, basic principles, and the actual research on the cognitive and social learning

65 Hinsie and Campbell, 1970, p. 704   66 Parsons and Bales, 1955, p. 17

processes is beyond our present scope. However, a brief description of the socialization process as it is viewed by such authorities in the field of social learning as Bandura, Aronfreed, Maccoby, and Hoffman will contribute to an understanding of the social behavior of the productive personality.

The developing child's selection and adoption of a given type of behavior depend on his own reaction to the various cues communicated to him by the socializing agents in his environment—parents, siblings, teachers, other adults, and peers. These cues consist of both the verbal and nonverbal means by which the socializing agents convey their pleasure or displeasure with him. The behavior he chooses to express depends on the impact of these symbols on his self-esteem; specifically, he chooses to express behavior which is (or has been) rewarded or approved and avoids disapproved behavior because of the pain (criticism) associated with it. In the early stages of socialization the child's reactions to others are therefore directly dependent on the affective reactions (feelings) which these individuals produce in him. Positive (pleasant) or aversive (negative, painful, or unpleasant) affective reactions may be acquired either through direct experience with reward and punishment or through observation of the consequences of other people's behavior.[67]

In infancy, according to Anna Freud, Murphy, and others, the child's selection of the cues to which he will react becomes a method of coping with his external environment (this is discussed further in Chapter Five). However, the critical factor in determining the degree of pleasant or unpleasant reaction of his self-esteem is the degree of empathy he perceives in his mother. Empathy, the ability to feel with another person, is basic to all forms of effective social interaction. If communication in some form is the basis of social integration, then empathic capacity is an essential component of interpersonal competence.[68]

Since empathy appears to be the basis of identification for the infant, we can assume that the identification processes involved in his socialization also depend on a consistent empathic relationship with his socializing agents. Empathy can be repeatedly reinforced through the many experiences in the growing

67 Aronfreed, 1968, pp. 44–49   68 Foote and Cottrell, 1955, p. 54

child's milieu; but the empathic response obviously cannot be initiated by him or maintained on a unilateral basis. It is entirely dependent on the continued and consistent quality of the affect in the milieu.

Throughout the first two or three years of life, the mother is the child's principal socializing agent, with the father assuming growing significance as the child's development progresses. The personalities and temperaments of both parents determine the degree of their child's emotional security.

THE DYNAMICS OF SOCIALIZATION

The socialization process in its simplest form is an interaction with parents, other adults, and peers within one's sphere of contact. Building on the early identification with his parents, the growing child becomes increasingly dependent on relationships with others in his environment for maintenance of his self-esteem requirements. For this reason one of the most important aspects of the socialization process is the control or channeling of those impulses that would result in lowered self-esteem. Hoffman (1970) calls this a "taming" of the antisocial impulses, and Schafer (1968) refers to it as a "neutralizing" of the sex drives.[69] A state of anxiety (guilt or shame) may be associated not only with the expression of disapproved behavior, but also with its underlying impulses. The two areas in which the control of impulses is considered of primary importance for the welfare of others are sex and aggression. As discussed in Chapter Three, the two drives are related in the sense that inadequately controlled aggression is frequently expressed through sexual behavior, either in fantasy or in reality. As a result moral development is an essential aspect of the socialization process.

According to psychoanalytic theory, moral values are largely unconscious and are based on the need to keep antisocial impulses from conscious awareness. The learning theorists describe the development of these values in terms of specific acts and avoidances learned by techniques of reward and punishment.

116 69 Schafer, 1968, pp. 203–210

The typical laboratory procedure is to use direct or vicarious reinforcement, with little or no accompanying rationale, to elicit "good" behaviors, as defined by culturally shared standards of conduct.[70] Aronfreed defines morality more succinctly in terms of the effect of one's behavior on others: acts which are positive are moral, and those which are injurious to others are immoral.[71]

Social learning theory, which seems to provide the most comprehensive explanation of the acquisition of social behavior, involves approximately three different, but almost simultaneously operative, aspects of interpersonal relations. The first of these may be broadly termed observational learning; the second relates to the role of cognition, and the third is the influence of reward and punishment.

Observational learning begins with the identification process. Almost unconsciously, the child learns from those models who are important to him certain types of behavior which contribute to his feelings of self-esteem; he also learns to avoid those that are not approved. Thus acts are defined as "good" or "bad" according to the favorable or unfavorable response of the socializing agent, and the consequent effect of this response on the child's self-esteem. Initially the parents—particularly the mother—play the most significant role; later the child's peer group and adults outside the family assume significance. Observational learning covers a broad spectrum of experiences in which the child becomes aware of the consequences of others' behavior and then applies his observations and conclusions to himself.

The second aspect of social learning theory concerns the role of cognition as the child develops. The infant perceives his environment as either pleasant or unpleasant. Although various nonverbal cues are always operative, it is primarily through the acquisition of a vocabulary and language structure that the child becomes able to identify an act as good or bad, to understand the basis for this judgment, to articulate his feelings about it, and if necessary to choose some more desirable act for the future.

The importance of language and cognitive skills is apparent in the toddler's behavioral responses to the simple direct verbal or

70 Hoffman, 1970, pp. 261–262   71 Aronfreed, 1968, pp. 245–246

nonverbal commands or prohibitions which enable him to differentiate between acts that will have positive consequences and those that will have negative consequences. He learns not to run into the street or to touch the hot stove because he associates this behavior with reprimand or restraint. This rudimentary cognition is based primarily on the child's internal responses to environmental cues. As his cognitive processes develop, he becomes able to evaluate both his own and others' behavior in terms of their long-range consequences. The more "refined" social behaviors, as Aronfreed terms them, are acquired almost entirely through abstract symbolic cues rather than direct experience. By the time he reaches nursery school or kindergarten age, a child has acquired considerable representational and anticipatory functions; his vocabulary is enlarging and he is learning to utilize his memory processes.[72]

Cognitive skills play an important role in observational learning. Bandura points out that each reaction to a model is "coded" into images or words and then stored in the memory to become a symbol of the original reaction.[73] As he acquires knowledge of more verbal symbols, the child is able to store in symbolic form his reactions to an increasing number of experiences, and this storehouse of information provides him with a basis for differentiating and selecting behaviors in the future. It is through verbal labeling that he learns to categorize social behaviors on a scale according to their consequences both for himself and for others, and thereby develops a scale of values which contributes to his moral and character development.

The third aspect of social learning theory, relating to the reinforcement or punishment of behavior, pertains to nearly all situations involving direct contact or communication between the child and other individuals, particularly those whom he perceives as having some control or power over him. Theoretically it is the parents who are primarily responsible for guiding a child to select socially approved types of behavior and to reject those which are disapproved. Various types of punishment may be employed to discourage or terminate disapproved conduct. The effect of any punishment is to reduce the child's sense of emotional support, to

72 Aronfreed, 1968, p. 45   73 Bandura, 1969, p. 133

threaten his self-esteem, and to create in him a state of anxiety.

In most cases the threat to self-esteem is sufficient to prevent the child from repeating the disapproved act and encourage him to select an approved substitute. Unfortunately, in our present society the young child's physical safety is frequently involved in a given socializing procedure, and as a result, parents are more likely to stress negative controls through a list of "don'ts" than to support positive and rewarding alternatives. Moreover, in Western culture it is traditional and fashionable for parents to control behavior through prohibition and punishment rather than by reward and reinforcement.

There are three forms of direct contact through which a socializing agent either reinforces or punishes a child's behavior. One is the avenue of verbal (and sometimes nonverbal) communication, another is actual physical contact with the child, and the third is removal of contact, either by physical separation or by psychological separation—withdrawal of communication or of visual contact, or simply an attitude of indifference. Each of these methods may constitute either reward or punishment, depending on the degree of empathy which characterizes the overall relationship between child and adult. Differences in empathy may be communicated in subtle ways—through intonation of the voice, through an accompanying gesture or facial expression, through the symbolic emotional implications of rejecting or affectionate body contact (a slap versus a hug), or through the type of separation enforced.

Hoffman (1970) describes these three types of parental discipline in terms of specific methods.[74] "Power assertion" refers to such punitive techniques as physical punishment, deprivation of material objects or privileges, the use of threats, and the like. "Love-withdrawal" techniques may entail verbal expressions of disapproval or anger, cutting off communication, and ignoring or isolating a child. The third method, "induction," utilizes reasoning and pointing out to a child the consequences of his actions, particularly as they affect others.

The particular form of disciplinary contact a parent employs depends largely on the degree of empathy which he or she feels

74 Hoffman, 1970, pp. 285–286

for the child—which depends in turn on the parent's own self-esteem and capacity for empathy. Whether the parent reasons calmly or resorts to harsh, high-pitched, and accusatory language; whether he uses a physical embrace or physical abuse: whether he quietly isolates a child or imposes enforced solitude depends entirely on his own feelings of empathy. The greater the degree of empathy, the less the need for punitive forms of control. Punitiveness almost always implies some hostility, and empathy and hostility are fundamentally antithetical. An empathic and understanding parent does not utilize punitive measures calculated to threaten a child's self-esteem severely; he acts with understanding and attempts to comprehend the situation from the child's point of view.

Parental discipline, even by aversive means, is not necessarily perceived as a threat to self-esteem. Children in highly empathic homes frequently view their parents' prohibitions as evidence of genuine caring which helps them to avoid actions that would almost certainly result in harm or social alienation. Moreover, in an empathic home the child is often given the opportunity to choose between two behavioral outcomes, one of which is rewarded while the other is not. Children from empathic homes frequently imitate their parents' disciplinary behavior in play with peers, indicating their own identification with parental prohibitions.

In a home where there is only a bare minimum of empathy and understanding, and where punishment is frequently severe, painful experiences apparently leave a greater residue in the child's memory than more positive ones. Evidence from many areas of research has demonstrated that behavior acquired under painful circumstances generally persists longer than behavior that has been positively rewarded. One explanation of this persistence may be that exposure to a consistently negative evaluation provides the child with no basis for evaluating his own behavior realistically; hence he tends to cling to the only evaluation that is available to him, particularly with regard to behavior he has acquired at such a young age that he has no verbal or cognitive recognition of it. The effects of painful and threatening punishment in a nonempathic environment may be so severe that the child extends them by association to other situations in which they do not apply. For example, criticism for playing with a toy may cause anxiety concerning all toys. In some cases, severe punishment for an act may be associated with previous acts which have not been punished. Unpleasant and even painful associations may also occur with the fantasy of an act that has never taken place in reality. In a family matrix characterized primarily by critical evaluation, the anticipation of criticism may lead to an "as if" type of behavior, in which the child punishes himself for having merely thought about a deviant act, even though he has not given the fantasy overt expression.

Associated with the principle that empathy is essential for a child's socialization is another basic concept: disciplinary measures can be effective only in situations where the child feels that he has something to lose. The theoretical principle of any punishment is that it poses a threat to the child's self-esteem. Whether this threat is communicated through reasoning, direct contact, or the withdrawal of contact, the intent is to produce sufficient anxiety in the child that he will terminate his deviant or offensive behavior or choose a more acceptable alternative. In homes where punitive measures seem to be ineffective, it can usually be assumed that the parent has not given sufficient empathy and nurturance to the child in the first place. In short, a parent cannot withdraw or take away something which he has not given. As a result the discipline measures become nothing more than supervisory or surveillance devices against which the child rebels, either directly or indirectly. As Aronfreed points out:[75]

> A minimally nurturant base for social attachment is a prerequisite of the child's effective internalization of aversive [unpleasant] control over its conduct.

There are many kinds of evidence to support the premise that disciplinary measures, to be effective, must be based on a firm groundwork of affection. Becker (1964) notes that children with high standards of behavior come from empathic families where love-oriented techniques are used in discipline; he comments that

75 Aronfreed, 1968, p. 310

"love-withdrawing methods seem to be more effective when there is more love to lose."[76] In contrast, investigations of maladjusted children by Levine and Simmons (1962) and Patterson et al. (1964) have shown such children to be unresponsive to social approval, suggesting that because they lacked experience with praise and affection, they simply did not know how to react to it.[77] Psychologists and other family guidance specialists often observe that when parents suddenly change from a punitive attitude to an empathic and nurturing attitude, the child's initial reaction is confusion and anxiety. This is particularly true of malfunctioning adolescents, who often find themselves thrown into turmoil by a totally unfamiliar situation. The younger the child, the less the confusion, and usually the less time required for an adjustment to an empathic, nurturing atmosphere. In brief, as Becker reports, the effectiveness of love withdrawal as a socializing procedure is directly proportional to the amount of nurturance that a child has previously been given.[78]

In an early study Sears et al. (1957) concluded that love withdrawal is effective in moral development only when the parents also freely express enough affection to make it obvious to the child that he has something to lose through deviant behavior.[79] They reported a relationship between the love withdrawal of mothers who were high in warmth and the conscience development of their children. However, similar studies on love withdrawal conducted at the National Institute of Mental Health provide conflicting evidence.[80] Hoffman and Saltzstein (1967) found that love withdrawal does not relate positively to moral indices, although they did find that love withdrawal contributes to an intensification of a child's need for adult approval; hence there may be some relationship "between the parents' love withdrawal and the child's inhibition of hostile impulses" that could be attributed in part to an unconscious identification with the parents.[81]

Contradictions have also been found in the results of laboratory investigations of the relationship between love-withdrawal techniques and such specific moral traits as aggression and resistance to temptation. Nevertheless, there are numerous indications that "love-oriented" homes contribute to several

76 Becker, 1964, p. 185
77 See Patterson, 1971b, p. 174
78 Becker, 1964, p. 185
79 Sears, Maccoby, and Levin, 1957, pp. 388

80 Yarrow, Campbell, and Burton, 1968, pp. 109, 112
81 Hoffman, 1970, p. 302

aspects of socialization. For example, Rutherford and Mussen (1968) found that generosity in nursery school boys was related to a pattern of moral characteristics—which included altruism, kindness, and cooperation.[82] The more generous boys described their fathers as warmer and more sympathetic than the less generous ones. Mussen, Conger, and Kagan (1969) maintain that a child will probably not be particularly threatened by loss of parental love in connection with a specific act, provided the disapproval is confined to the child's behavior and is not extended to the child himself, and also provided the parent's response is not extremely punitive or inappropriate.[83]

There is also experimental evidence that discipline techniques based on induction (reasoning) are associated with internalized standards in children. Hoffman (1970) reports the results of an important study of two groups of white, middle-class, essentially normal seventh-grade children who were classified either "internalizers" or "externalizers."[84] The subjects were rated on the basis of several measures of internalization, subjective judgments by teachers and parents, story-completion data, and observation. Some of the internalizers gave predominantly "conventional-rigid" responses to certain test items, and others gave "humanistic-flexible" responses. However, the parents of both groups of internalizers were reported as higher in induction and affection and lower in power assertion than the parents of the externalized group. Moreover, boys in the humanistic-flexible group of internalizers tended to identify with personal characteristics of their fathers, which included "a relatively direct and visible empathic concern for others." Hoffman concludes that boys may need the combined effects of the maternal discipline pattern and the support of an openly empathic father.

CONDITIONS FOR SOCIALIZATION

As we have seen, the socialization process in general depends on a number of fundamental conditions—a warm and empathic parental attitude, with an optimum degree of communication between parent and child; development of the child's own cognitive

---

82 Rutherford and Mussen, 1968, pp. 755–765

83 Mussen, Conger, and Kagan, 1969, p. 514

84 See Hoffman, 1970, pp. 336–343

skills; and the parents' success in handling discipline problems as they occur, through effective use of praise and punishment. Given these conditions, there are certain other factors which may either aid or impede the normal progress of the child's socialization. These factors are perhaps most relevant to situations which arise fairly often during nursery, kindergarten, and early elementary school years, although they are also applicable to later periods of the child's development.

factors which aid socialization   In general, any form or structure in the child's social environment which helps him to discriminate clearly between acts having positive consequences and those having painful consequences will aid his socialization. Such a classification helps him to learn control, and ultimately enhances the internalization of socially responsible behavior. Social behavior is also more easily acquired if it is dichotomized. It has been demonstrated in experimental studies that when a subject is given the opportunity to choose among positive, unpleasant, or uncertain outcomes, he will choose either the positive or the unpleasant outcome over the uncertain one. An unknown, unpredictable outcome is more threatening than one which is either "good" or "bad."

If a child is given an opportunity to control a reward or punishment through his own choice of behavioral alternatives, he acquires a given social behavior more easily, and probably more permanently. His coping skill is improved, his self-esteem enhanced, and his anxiety correspondingly reduced. The reason or cause for the punishment, however, must be clearly understood. Moreover, a child is more likely to develop the ability to govern his own behavior when rewards or punishments are not in themselves so overwhelming that they interfere with his freedom to make a choice.

Affording a child an opportunity to talk out or to articulate his feelings about an act which has had painful consequences will help him to internalize his own reaction. He thus becomes able to make a conscious choice for a more rewarding act in the future. The language skills with which to identify feelings are thus the primary basis for evaluating behavior in terms of particular outcomes.

A rewarding outcome or consequence of an act is more effective if it follows within a relatively short time. If an act of altruism, for example, is immediately met with spontaneous approval, it is internalized almost at once. Sometimes, of necessity, the outcome is delayed. A child may have prepared with some anxiety for an examination in school, but he may not learn the results of his preparation as indicated by the teacher's evaluation (his test grade) for several days. Even when an outcome cannot be provided immediately, behavior is more effectively reinforced or suppressed when the amount of delay is known or predictable.

The mildness or severity of a punishment does not in itself determine the child's acquisition of a given behavior unless that punishment has some bearing on his self-esteem. Moreover, neither the recall of behavior which has preceded a given act nor a description of future consequences of new behavior has much to do with the acquisition of that behavior. Evidently there is a change in the individual's value system only when a commitment to active behavior is directly related to his self-esteem.[85]

A crisis, an emergency situation, or a new experience may sometimes motivate immediate adoption of a behavioral model that enables the child to cope with a new situation or challenge. New behavior may even be acquired in one observational experience, particularly if it is accompanied by explanations. Behavioral values which have less direct or less immediate significance may take years to acquire, and consequently may require continual reinforcement. For example, the altruistic dimension of social responsibility may not be recognized by a child's peers during middle childhood; hence the reinforcement of peer approval may not be provided until adolescence. In the meantime constant verbal reinforcement must be provided by parents, teachers, older siblings, and other adults.

A situation that is generally nonempathic, arbitrary, and highly critical or punitive impedes the child's socialization because it provides him with an insufficient basis for developing the necessary independence of judgment and social responsibility to

85 Aronfreed, 1968, p. 300

formulate mature behavioral values. There are some further specific factors, however, which hinder social learning. Special learning difficulties, sensory-motor handicaps, and limited or impoverished educational opportunities interfere with the child's ability to communicate with his peers and contribute to a sense of isolation that makes it difficult for him to identify with them. Emotional illness in some other member of the family may distort the environment to which the child is exposed, and may also present him with a confusing model for his own behavioral values.

One personality trait which poses a special problem in socialization is impulsivity. The highly impulsive child does not learn easily from others, since his need to relieve his anxiety through immediate, directionless activity impairs his ability to develop a unified pattern of behavior. As a result, although such children are basically lacking in self-confidence and excessively susceptible to the judgments of others, they are also likely to violate social prohibitions when they are not under direct external constraints.[86] Some further aspects of impulsivity are discussed in Chapter Five.

effectiveness of model   Any or all of the above factors influence the socialization process. One of the most important factors in socialization, however, is the nature of the child's models—his parents, relatives, siblings, peers, and other adults outside the family such as teachers, community leaders, friends and acquaintances, and many other persons. An effective model usually has a number of personality assets, but the most influential characteristics are the traits of nurturance or empathy, competence, and attractiveness.

If a model is nurturing, his or her attributes—especially the "expressive" attributes—are more likely to be acquired by others. Girls are more likely to adopt the expressive behavior of a highly nurturant mother than that of a less nurturant one;[87] findings are similar regarding the relationship of boys to their fathers. The importance of the smile in early parent-child relationships was

86 Lesser and Abelson, in Aronfreed, 1968, p. 40   87 Mussen, Conger, and Kagan, 1969, p. 362

discussed in detail in Chapter Three; even among adults the facial expression and other forms of nonverbal communication convey a much stronger message than an explanation.

Children also tend to identify with models whom they perceive as competent in controlling the outcomes of their own behavior. The average child, in his physical dependence, looks for guidelines to his parents and other adults who are dealing effectively with the stresses of their own environment. A child (or an adolescent) may associate with competence such factors as social power and prestige, professional success, high status, or skill in some special area. In no case, however, will he imitate a model whom he does not hold in esteem; nor will he seek to emulate behavior unless it is both meaningful and perceived as related to his interests.[88]

The model's esthetic qualities are also a factor in observational learning. Details of dress, physical appearance, and behavior are all perceived, and often imitated, as part of the image. Powers of observation are sharpened when attention is focused on a pleasant stimulus. Young children all describe their mothers as "beautiful," and the glamorous television personality is generally more persuasive than the nutrition expert concerning the nutritional value of a breakfast food. Obviously self-esteem is not a function of age. However, very young children, who are limited both in range of experience and in coping skills, are more likely to imitate a model's expressive features than his skills and competencies. Regardless of age, children of low self-esteem more often describe the individual's affective qualities than his skills or competence. Older children, who have more highly developed cognitive skills, more self-confidence, and more independence, are better equipped to discriminate the model's actual skills or knowledge.[89]

Conflicting values among a child's socializing agents can also have a deleterious effect on his development. Parents may reject the values of grandparents; teachers may disagree with the values of parents. In addition to conflicts in values, there are also differences in the degree of approval or disapproval of a given

88 Hartley, 1969, p. 239   89 Aronfreed, 1968, p. 110–111   **127**

behavior. There may be wide variation among a child's teachers from one year to the next regarding trivial standards of behavior or academic-achievement skills. Differences in peer-group values may also reflect differences in the values of parents within a given community.

The characteristics that make a model ineffective are, in essence, incompetence, low self-esteem, and poor communicative ability. Incompetence is perceived in an individual's low vocational, intellectual, and social status; his inability to pursue an occupation affording prestige or advancement; or his poor education. Low self-esteem is manifested in defensiveness, authoritarian and punitive attitudes, and inconsistency. Both these characteristics may be evidenced by verbal communication which is inarticulate, ambiguous, and hostile. For example, parents who do not empathize with their children often exhibit excessively complex behavior with which their children have difficulty in identifying. Their language is intentionally kept at a level which is beyond either the experience or cognitive skills of their children, and they may deliberately exclude the child from conversation that he can understand by spelling out words or items of information which he is not supposed to hear.

FAMILY SOCIALIZATION PATTERNS AND PRACTICES

Although each family is a unique microcosm of society with its own style of intrafamily communication and interpersonal relationships, it is possible to classify families according to their socializing practices. Parents themselves may be differentiated on the empathic-hostile continuum; their basic personality characteristics are also related to such observable factors as their educational, socioeconomic, and cultural backgrounds.

Becker (1964) warns that the consequences of parental disciplinary practices can be properly interpreted only in the context of various other conditions under which a given family may be operating. Chief among these conditions are the warmth of the parent-child relationship, the previous history of the family's disciplinary procedures and emotional relationships, the nature of

128

its role structure, and the social and economic conditions under which it is living.[90]

Nevertheless, some generalizations are possible. Since parents are the leaders of this small but important social unit, it is primarily their own capacity for empathy, basically related to their own self-esteem, which in turn determines their empathic relationships with their children and the forms of discipline they employ. Becker points out that parents who have sufficient personal security to maintain a warm, affectionate relationship with their children are likely to use "love-oriented" techniques of discipline which will promote in their offspring "acceptance of self-responsibility, guilt, and related internalized reactions to transgression." Hostile parents, on the other hand, will employ harsh, power-assertive methods of control which breed in their children further hostility, aggressiveness, and rebellion and discourage the internalization of socially responsible behavior standards.[91]

It is probably safe to say that at or above a certain level of emotional and social security a quality of affection and empathy will be present in the parent-child relationship which should make possible the child's gradual acquisition and internalization of the standards of his parents, principally through the identification process. Hoffman tentatively concludes that affection does play some role in the internalization of moral values, "mainly as part of the larger child-rearing pattern."[92] In any case, an affectionate parent who relates warmly to his child should rarely find it necessary to use either power-assertive or love-withdrawal forms of discipline techniques. Furthermore, the disciplinary measures which parents employ reflect not only their own emotional security, but also their sense of social responsibility and the degree of productivity they envision for themselves and for their children.

Family socialization practices have been classified in various ways. There are no clearcut dividing lines between groups, of course; however, Baumrind (1971) contributes a description of three principal types of what might be called family attitudes and approaches to socialization.[93] In conjunction with the prior investigations of Becker and Hoffman, Baumrind's classification—

90 Becker, 1964, p. 202

91 Becker, 1964, p. 189

92 Hoffman, 1970, p. 303

93 Baumrind, 1971a, pp. 22–23 et passim

based on information obtained from interviews with mothers of 146 white, upper-middle-class preschool children—is useful in relating methods of socialization to future productivity. A critical element differentiating these families is their attitude toward authority.

Baumrind designates one parental type as "authoritarian." Such a parent is basically concerned with shaping, controlling, and evaluating the behavior and the attitudes of his child according to an absolute "set standard of conduct." Implicit in this approach is the value attached to obedience as a virtue in its own right, to be enforced if necessary by punitive measures. According to this type of parent, respect—for authority, for work, and for the preservation of order and tradition—must be inculcated at all costs. The child has little or no say in decision making.

Mothers of the second parental type are defined as "authoritative." Like the authoritarian parent, they try to direct the child's activities, but the approach is rational and issue-oriented, with verbal give and take between parent and child and discussion of reasons for parental policies. Such a parent "values both autonomous self-will and disciplined conformity," and accordingly does not hesitate to take a firm position concerning a matter of importance, yet does not "hem the child in with restrictions." Recognizing both their own and their child's individual rights and interests, they nevertheless set standards and use both reason and power to attain their objectives, without considering themselves either "infallible or divinely inspired." Such a parent probably makes use of induction as a method of handling disciplinary problems.

The third type, the "permissive" parent, is defined as behaving in a "nonpunitive, acceptant, and affirmative manner" toward the impulses, desires, and actions of her child. Consulting with the child about matters of policy and giving explanations of family rules, they make few demands on him, regarding themselves as a "resource" for him to use as he desires and allowing him considerable latitude in regulating his own affairs. Control and obedience are not emphasized; reason is regarded as the proper means for accomplishing all purposes.

Among the other types of parental authority patterns described in Baumrind's study one particularly interesting form is the "harmonious" family. The families in this group were typically unconventional (some were preparing for communal living), but they were distinguished from the other parental types in that the parents appeared to "have control" without "exercising control" over their children. Although there were only six girls and two boys in the group, all of them only children, the parents seemed to be markedly less successful with the boys than with the girls.[94]

Of the three principal types of parental socialization practices, the most successful in terms of facilitating the development of children who are competent, socially responsible, and independent was found to be the authoritative family; the trend was especially well illustrated by the boys.[95] The discipline structure in this type of home appears quite similar to that of the high self-esteem family described by Coopersmith, in which the maintenance of clearly defined and enforced limits makes it unnecessary for parents to use harsh punitive measures and also encourages the development of well functioning, independent, and socially responsible children.[96]

In contrast, the rigid, punitive, and power-assertive methods which characterize the authoritarian family play a consistently negative role in the development of moral values.[97] Neither is social responsibility encouraged in the permissive family, where a general absence of demands tends to produce children who are socially assertive, but who also tend to be unresponsive to external controls, lacking in internal controls, and sometimes have traits of aggressiveness.[98]

It is generally agreed that the foundations of social responsibility are established early in life. Sears et al. (1957) maintain that the learning of internal control takes place mainly before puberty, possibly even during the first six to ten years, and that this early learning process determines the extent to which conscience will operate throughout life.[99] This view is supported by the findings of MacFarlane et al. (1954), which indicate that an individual's average level of moral conformity is the same in early

94 Baumrind, 1971b, pp. 99–102

95 Baumrind, 1971a, p. 100

96 Coopersmith, 1967, pp. 236ff

97 Hoffman, 1970, p. 300

98 Becker, 1964, pp. 191, 197

99 Sears, Maccoby, and Levin, 1957, pp. 367–368

childhood as in later life, suggesting that the basic forces of moral character develop quite early in life.[100]

Although the internalization of values depends on cognitive maturation, the degree of threat or support to the child's affective security is probably a more significant factor.[101] In his study of adolescent behavior Rosenberg (1965) found that the one general motivation behind the selection of self-values was the desire to maintain or enhance self-esteem.[102] Stating the matter from another point of view, Coopersmith (1967) suggests that persons with higher self-esteem are guided by their own value judgments and hence are less threatened by the value judgments of others than the less secure person.[103]

The personality contrasts between internalized and externalized persons have been described by Hoffman (1970) and demonstrated by Douvan and Adelson (1966).[104] They found both boys and girls from the internalized group in close agreement on society's moral code regarding responsibility to self and others. The internalized boys as a group showed a higher level of activity, more self-confidence combined with realistic self-criticism, and more independence of moral judgment than did the externalized boys. Internalized girls, whose sense of morality reflected strong identification with parental values, showed more preference for traditional professions than did the externalized girls and differed from them on "rules they would never break," views of parental regulation, and adherence to parental authority.

It appears, in any event, that parental warmth, trust, firmness, and consistency are a prerequisite for the development of a mature value system. In a nurturing home the child's choice of values develops from a relationship of generative empathy with his parents, as well as through identification with their standards and values, direct experience with reward and punishment, and observation of the consequences of the behavior of others. It is through all these experiences that he becomes able to differentiate behaviors according to their impact on his self-esteem and to select and adopt those behaviors which will produce beneficial results both for himself and for others. The more affectionate and esteeming his environment, the more readily he will adopt paren-

100 See Kohlberg, 1964, pp. 392–394

101 Mussen, Conger, and Kagan, 1969, pp. 363–366; Aronfreed, 1968, p. 272

102 Rosenberg, 1965, p. 249

103 Coopersmith, 1967, p. 142

tal standards and values through positive identification and modeling and the more perceptive he will be in articulating finer and more abstract behavioral values.

In a home deficient in nurturance or inconsistent in discipline the child is deprived of a central quality necessary for his social development. Failure in the identification or modeling process—the means by which he normally absorbs the parental framework of values, behavioral codes, and prohibitions—severely limits his resources for internalization. As a result, since he has little basis for developing his own value system, he becomes dependent on the value judgments of others, such as his peers, for support of his self-esteem. Moreover, his resulting inability to discriminate appropriate behaviors results not only in constant concern over his self-image, but in an inability to cope effectively with interpersonal relationships, which further threatens his self-esteem. In cases of extreme parental rejection, punitiveness, or neglect, the child literally feels that he has nothing to lose. He is more or less incapable of guilt or empathy and is only weakly internalized on "indices of responsibility, control or aggressive behavior, and reactions to transgressions."[105]

social responsibility and productivity

Although there have been no retrospective studies of the socialization processes in productive individuals, the highly internalized system of ethical and moral values, altruistic concern for others, and relative lack of guilt which are conspicuous in all productive persons suggest several common factors in their early childhood environments. One is a warm and empathic parent-child relationship which has enabled them to internalize parental values and develop the emotional security to relate empathically to others. Another concerns the parental values which they internalize; it is likely that the parents, or some other key socializing agent in the child's background, must themselves have had high ethical and moral standards with which the child

104 Aronfreed, 1968, p. 308

105 Douvan and Adelson, 1966, pp. 116–117

106 Lenrow, 1965, pp. 291–292; Aronfreed, 1968, pp. 138–159

107 See Aronfreed, 1968, p. 307

could identify. This factor is also suggested by the family backgrounds of productive persons described in Chapter Six.

As a result of such relationships, the productive individual organizes his values around altruistic behavior which is further reinforced, and hence further internalized, by his experiences with others. Thus on one hand he acquires a system of behavior which provides him with little reason for guilt, and on the other, he expands his empathic identifications—ultimately to the humanitarian feelings of *Gemeinschaftsgefühl* which Maslow has described in the self-actualizing person.

An individual's productivity lies, by definition, in the result of his productive efforts. Hence the manner in which he utilizes his qualities and skills in coping with life situations and the forces in his environment determines his actual productivity. And the extent to which he is able or unable to master the forces that control his own life ultimately determines his perception of himself both as an individual and as a member of society.

The productive person brings to any situation certain basic attributes which are the result of his previous experiences both with himself and with his environment. One of these is a fundamental attitude of hope—the assumption that he is competent to succeed and that his success will be rewarded by the approval of those who are important to him, either specifically or in the abstract. In short, he has the expectation of success, and he therefore proceeds in a manner that will enable him to fulfill his own prophecy. As a result, he increases both his competence and his self-esteem, and therefore his chances of still further success and mastery.

coping
and mastery

CHAPTER FIVE

Effective coping, however, must produce a result. Hence, in addition to the basic assets and skills which the productive individual brings to the problem, he must also have the independence, self-control, and perseverance to arrive at a solution, the judgment to arrive at an effective decision, and the strength and courage to act on it.

coping

Coping is a process, in the same sense that identification and socialization are processes. To cope means:[1]

> to maintain a contest or combat [usually] on even terms or with success; . . . to face or encounter and to find necessary expedients to overcome problems and difficulties. . . .

Coping has also been defined as adjusting, adapting, or successfully meeting a challenge.[2]

The fact that the terms "coping" and "mastery" have been used almost interchangeably in the professional literature has created confusion over the actual meaning of each term. In all probability the background for the concept of coping occurred first in the writings of Anna Freud (Freud, 1946; Freud and Burlingham, 1944). Murphy (1962, 1970) has emphasized coping strategies as a method of mastering the environment, in contrast to defenses as a protection from the environment. Coping involves, among other things, dealing with new situations that challenge one's self-esteem or threaten failure, danger, or loss of physical comfort and security. The underlying basis of coping is a drive toward mastery, and mastery, as the culmination of this process, constitutes a successful meeting, appraisal, and solution of the problem.[3]

According to Murphy, the process of coping begins with the infant's initial utilization of his sensory and motor capacities and extends to include other skills as his physical and psychological structures mature. She contends that coping patterns are most readily apparent when a child or adult is confronted with a new

136

1 Webster's third new international dictionary, 1971, sv cope

2 Hinsie and Campbell, 1970, p. 163

3 Murphy, 1962, pp. 6–7; 1970, pp. 66–82

situation that cannot be handled routinely. Out of this process of dealing with new (and possibly difficult) situations, some form of adaptation is certain to occur. Repeated efforts at coping with difficult situations, particularly those that are similar in context, result in the acquisition of skill or competence.

Defense mechanisms are not necessarily antithetical to coping. Murphy notes that they may be a part of the over-all coping effort, in the sense that they sometimes assist in organizing a complex situation into manageable parts.[4] Anna Freud also commented rather explicitly that not all defense mechanisms are necessarily pathological. She points out that the source of anxiety and danger to the child is his need to avoid pain from the external world and also to avoid danger which may result in pain; thus a defense such as denial represents the child's attempt to deal with the danger by intervening to change surrounding conditions.[5] In this context denial, whether in fantasy, word, or act, and "restriction of the ego" are the primary stages of defense. She also refers to "identification with the aggressor," a combination of projection and identification, as a strategy that applies to normal everyday behavior. Identification with the aggressor, in psychoanalytic terms, is an identification particularly with the mother, and leads to the manner of coping with normal ways of life.

In *Infants without Families* (1944) Freud used the term "coping" a little more directly:[6]

> The first family setting is the framework within which the instincts and emotions of the child grope towards their first objects. The child can never completely possess these objects but in this first display of its feelings [empathy] it learns "to love," to cope with its instinctual forces and thus lay the foundations for its character formation, a process which entails a great deal of discomfort.

In other words, the child attempts to cope with the environment as a means of maintaining his self-esteem. As discussed in Chapter Three, theorists such as Fenichel (1945) view this process as originating in the infant's hunger pangs and the sense of physical and emotional nourishment that results from their gratification in an empathic relationship with the mother.[7] Fenichel's self-esteem

4 Murphy, 1962, p. 7
5 A. Freud, 1946, chaps. 6–10
6 A. Freud and Burlingham, 1944, p. 61
7 Fenichel, 1945, pp. 37–41

construct is borne out by Murphy's experimental research with infants and young children.[8] In children of both sexes oral gratification (self-esteem) in infancy was clearly related to a number of competence-related preschool variables, such as clarity of perception, sense of self-worth, strength of interests, ability to control the impact of the environment, and reality level. Oral gratifications were not related to depreciation of others, loss of perceptual clarity under stress, and a tendency to fatigue. A relationship was also noted between narcissism (which Fenichel equates with self-esteem) and other aspects of self-feeling and the child's capacity to deal with his environment.[9]

Murphy concludes from these findings that it is in an empathic infant-mother relationship that the child first acquires an acceptable way of coping with everyday conflicts.[10] This conclusion is comparable to Erikson's view that a sense of basic trust in infancy is the foundation for adequate growth and development. The methods by which an individual copes with his environment depend, of course, on his capacity to control his surrounding conditions. The vocalizations and squirmings of the newborn are primitive forms of coping; as his perceptual and motor capacities develop, he gains some measure of control in being able to select the stimuli to which he responds. Later, when such cognitive processes as memory become involved, imagery and fantasy enable the child to deal indirectly with an external environment that is beyond his mastery. Another method available to him at this stage is "forgetting," which enables him simply to turn away from a threatening situation; thus forgetting is one form of denial.[11] Coping with one's environment is a fundamental requirement for survival, however, and the child utilizes whatever means are at his disposal to protect himself against threats to his security. Hence such coping strategies constitute more than a mere defense mechanism.

Each person brings to a new environmental situation an accumulation of his previous experiences, both pleasant and unpleasant. If he is secure in the support of others, he is not likely to feel threatened by a strange situation. He is therefore better able to appraise it accurately and deal with it effectively. An insecure

8 Murphy, 1962, pp. 384ff   10 Murphy, 1970, p. 70
9 Murphy, 1962, p. 367   11 Murphy, 1970, pp. 78–79

person may feel too threatened by such a situation to cope with it at all.

Lazarus (1966) has observed that the personality characteristics an individual brings to the situation determine his coping technique. His previous experiences with coping predispose him to certain assumptions or beliefs about whether a situation can or cannot be mastered and how a threatening situation can be overcome. As a result, his coping activities are based in part on certain "coping dispositions," or personality traits, which are then reinforced by subsequent experience. Thus, whether an individual's coping techniques are expressed in perception, learning, memory, or other cognitive activity,[12]

> . . . [his] beliefs about what is morally right or wrong, effective or ineffective, or how the environment will respond to certain kinds of action shape both the coping process and its behavioral expression.

In other words, the nature of an individual's coping activities remains essentially unchanged unless he has some reason to reevaluate the system in which his cognitive processes have developed.

The amount of self-esteem which an individual brings to his various experiences contributes significantly to the degree to which his efforts will produce results. According to Brewster Smith (1968), self-esteem is accompanied by a sense of competence:[13]

> The self is perceived as causally important, as effective in the world . . . as likely to be able to bring about desired effects. . . .

Aronfreed suggests that this presumption of the ability to cope precedes the development of cognitive skills.[14]

Rotter (1966) also places considerable emphasis on the individual's belief that he can control his own destiny as a requirement for dealing effectively with the environment. He observed that the degree of success in an experimental task is significantly higher when the subject believes that the successful outcome on a previous task resulted from his own skill rather than

12 Lazarus, 1966, pp. 242, 245
13 Brewster Smith, 1968, p. 281
14 Aronfreed, 1968, p. 17

from chance.[15] Research with Rotter's Scale of Introversion-Extroversion supports the hypothesis that an individual who strongly believes he can control his own destiny will have certain strengths. He is likely to be more alert to those aspects of the environment which provide useful information for his future behavior and to take steps to improve his environmental position. He also places greater value on skill or achievement reinforcements, is more concerned with his ability level, particularly his failures, and tends to resist subtle attempts to influence his judgment.

In a recent study of the personality characteristics related to "interpersonal trust," Rotter (1971) reports that there is a correlation between an individual's competence and his trust in others $(r = .60)$.[16] People who believe in their environments tend to develop competence, and conversely, more competent persons are more trusting. In addition, Rotter found a relationship between trust and altruism $(r = .63)$, which suggests that the person who believes he will be supported by others is able to reach out to them in some form of empathic relationship and concern. Competence was also found to be related to altruism $(r = .55)$, indicating that the basic characteristics of trust (self-esteem) and altruism (social responsibility) are major factors in an individual's ability to deal effectively with the world in which he lives.

Differences in personalities are sharply revealed by differences in coping styles. The individual who is confident that he is in control of his destiny and is constantly increasing his self-esteem by coping with and mastering all kinds of situations is vastly different from the one who feels constantly threatened and attempts to remove the threat either by acting out against it or by withdrawing from it rather than dealing realistically with it.

Jahoda (1958) reported that among the criteria of positive mental health are integration or unity of the personality (a sense of identity), active mastery of the environment, and accurate perception of reality.[17] It appears that accurate perception both of oneself and of the surroundings is necessary for mastery; one cannot cope effectively with a situation or problem which one cannot perceive accurately. An individual must also trust the en-

15 Rotter, 1966, p. 25   17 Jahoda, 1958, chap. 3
16 Rotter, 1971, p. 450

vironment he perceives before he can relate to it. As Murphy expresses it:[18]

> The child with stable positive self-feeling is apt to be able to maintain and to develop good relationships with others, and to sustain a flexible relation to the environment; this is expressed in perceptual freedom and courage, which together contribute to the capacity to mobilize resources, including substitute gratifications. That is, the child with unassailable positive self-feeling is able to meet threats resourcefully, find solutions, and thus reduce the stimuli to disintegrative reactions.

coping skills

The coping process consists of three essentially distinct stages: in dealing with any situation the individual must first perceive a stimulus or problem; next he must appraise the alternative possibilities for resolving it, and finally he must arrive at some conclusion or decision regarding his own course of action. This process is a constant part of life. In some instances the response, or decision, is almost spontaneous; in others the solution may require hours, or even years. The particular manner in which an individual approaches such situations, however, is fairly consistent and is influenced both by the basic equipment he brings to the situation and by certain aspects of his own personality.

The productive person brings to any situation a fundamental attitude of hope—a conviction, or at least an assumption, that the problem can be solved. He is also equipped with certain cognitive abilities, such as verbal and mathematical skills and memory skills, which depend partly on maturation and partly on the breadth and quality of his previous experience. This combination of a hopeful attitude and a basic level of competence has direct bearing on the manner in which he perceives and appraises a problem. The effectiveness with which he resolves the problem, however, also depends on his independence and reliance on his own judgment, the degree of control he can muster—both over his

18 Murphy, 1962, p. 363

own impulses and over what may be a complex mass of data—and on his persistence and perseverance.

PERCEPTION

The most basic requirement for coping with a situation effectively is the ability to perceive it accurately. As noted in Chapter Three, the accuracy of an individual's self-perception, and hence the accuracy of his perception of his environment, is directly related to his feelings of personal security. The productive individual sees his surroundings clearly and realistically. Maslow says that self-actualizing persons see human nature as it *is* and not as they would prefer it to be.[19] Moreover, such persons do not feel threatened by ambiguity or confusion; rather they appear to relish the challenge of coping with uncertainty in situations and problems.

An anxious, insecure person is more likely to feel threatened by a configuration or stimulus which he perceives as unclear or ambiguous. At the same time, he also tends to see a stimulus as ambiguous because its clarity or reality is even more threatening. As a result, he may maintain the ambiguity to avoid taking a stand or making an independent decision, which further lessens his control over the situation and produces a sense of helplessness.

There is some evidence that a high degree of curiosity is associated with academic performance.[20] There is also some relationship between curiosity and intelligence. In the Fels Institute longitudinal study Kagan et al. (1958) noted that children whose IQs had increased between the ages of six and ten exhibited more achievement imagery and more curiosity about nature than children whose IQs had decreased.[21] Curiosity has been found especially characteristic of the creative person; Taylor (1963) cites the "effective questioning ability" of such persons, and MacKinnon (1963) refers to "strong powers of spatial visualization" in the highly creative architects.[22] Ward (1969) classified fifty-three nursery school children as creative or uncreative and tested both groups in a cue-poor and a cue-rich environment (a room containing objects and pictures).[23] The creative children gave more

19 Maslow, 1954, p. 207
20 See Lavin, 1965, p. 107
21 Kagan, Sontag, Baker, and Nelson, 1966, p. 396
22 Taylor, 1963, p. 237; MacKinnon, 1963, p. 277
23 W. C. Ward, 1969, pp. 543–547

responses in the cue-rich than in the poor-cue environment; however, uncreative children showed no over-all difference in responding to differences in the surroundings. Mendel (1965) found that nursery school children who were low in anxiety preferred a greater degree of "novelty" in an array of toys than did highly anxious children; in other words, they felt freer to express their curiosity.[24] He calls attention to the comment by William James (1904) that anxious persons are more likely to fear and to avoid novelty than less anxious ones.

Sensitivity of perception also appears to be an important attribute of creative persons. Roe (1969) has noted the keen powers of observation of creative physical scientists.[25] In addition to perceptual accuracy and sensitivity, two other traits—intuition and openness to experience—have been noted. Barron (1968) found the quality of intuition a "particularly marked" personality characteristic of creative writers, nearly all of whom (89 percent) were rated as having this trait.[26] MacKinnon (1968) points out that highly creative architects also seem to react intuitively, rather than on just a sensory level, to the environment.[27] They are also open to experience, perceiving deeper meanings and possibilities in their surroundings than other, more matter-of-fact persons. Aware of the "links and bridges between what is present and that which is not yet thought of," they lead lives of spontaneity, flexibility, richness, and variety.

Theoretically speaking, the basis of curiosity is the sense of freedom to reach out to the environment, so that accurate or realistic perception results from an absence of inner conflict or doubt over one's acceptance. Some experimental support for this observation is provided by Gamewell (1967), who attempted to relate the later success of graduate psychology students to scores on the Wechsler Adult Intelligence Scale and the Concept Mastery Test.[28]

A factor closely related to perception is attention, which may be described as conscious application of energy to the perception of a given stimulus.[29] Like curiosity, attention is distinguished by openness or receptivity to the environment, as noted in the highly creative persons described by MacKinnon. Another

24 Mendel, 1965, p. 462
25 Roe, 1969, p. 98
26 Barron, 1968, p. 245
27 MacKinnon, 1968, p. 112
28 Gamewell, 1967 (1967A), pp. 3022–3023
29 Gilmore, 1968, pp. 41–66

distinguishing characteristic is selectivity; an individual tends to tune in on those stimuli which meet his emotional needs and to block out those which do not. The capacity to focus one's attention effectively on a problem (or to give it intense concentration when the situation so warrants) is typical of high achievers; conversely, the tendency to distractibility is typical in the low achiever. In both cases this capacity appears to be directly associated with emotional health or security.

JUDGMENT

At all times, and in all places, each individual is constantly appraising and evaluating the objects, persons, and problems in his environment (that is, his perception of them). The coping strategies he employs and the success with which they are implemented depend directly not only on his perceptual accuracy, but also on his appraisal processes. Coopersmith suggests that the individual goes through certain steps in thinking between his first encounter with a stimulus and his final judgment or decision: he attempts to determine the nature of the stimulus, he organizes and "filters" relevant information, and finally he formulates an opinion.[30] It is the second step of filtering information, or surveying and evaluating alternative courses of action, which constitutes the appraisal process.

Gladwin (1967) enlarges on this definition in describing competence as an "ability to learn or to use a variety of alternative pathways or behavioral responses in order to reach a given goal."[31] In other words, an individual must consider and evaluate the various ways in which he can or will act in the forthcoming solution of a problem situation. Effective appraisal is a most important step in arriving at an effective solution.

HOPE

Studies in all areas of productivity indicate that the productive person is characterized by a high level of aspiration. When one projects himself into the future—as one must in aspiration

30 Coopersmith, 1967, p. 55   31 See Brewster Smith, 1968, p. 274

fantasy—he must have some anticipation of results. The dynamics of aspiration involve hope, faith, and expectancy. In coping with daily problems, an individual must be able to act with the confidence that a solution can ultimately be found for a conflicting, ambivalent, or confronting situation. He must be able to hope that his evaluative procedures and subsequent actions will contribute to an ultimate solution, or that an anticipated goal will be reached and rewarded.

Brewster Smith (1968) contends that the formation of a competent person rests on self-respect, self-esteem, a sense of efficacy, and—especially—an attitude of hope.[32] He suggests that although a minimum of basic trust is essential to personal adequacy, an attitude of hope represents an evaluation of trust in the future. In contrast, fatalism and passivity, which represent a lack of hope, are symptomatic of lack of trust in the environment. Reinforced by positive attitudes toward self (high self-esteem), the person is attracted to challenges having some possibility of success. With each successful experience he develops an active coping orientation, which, in combination with an awareness of increased skills and abilities, translates feelings of efficacy into hopeful expectations.

Very little research has been conducted on hope as a specific attribute. Mowrer (1960) viewed learning to hope as part of the learning process and argued that "hope is a prerequisite for action." Other psychologists have theorized that the individual's expectation of his ability to attain his goals is based on his personality and is a "function only of his perception of the efficacy of his own behavior."[33] In a discussion of productivity, however, we need a definition of hope and a description of the environment in which it occurs, the ego requirements it serves, and the behavioral characteristics which appear to differentiate the hopeful person from one who lacks hope. Some of these parameters are suggested by the brief amount of literature available.

The word "hope" denotes:[34]

> a feeling that what is wanted will happen; desire accompanied by anticipation or expectation.

32 Brewster Smith, 1968, pp. 282ff

33 See Stotland, 1969, pp. 16, 19

34 Webster's new world dictionary of the American language, 1962, sv hope

Thus it differs from expectation—"a considerable degree of confidence that an event will happen . . ."—in that the basis is desire. The experiments of Harvey and Clapp (1965) suggest that students or subjects who refer to hope in connection with themselves are more involved with feelings of affect than those who do not. Hebb (1946) observed from his work with animals that expectancy is somewhat subordinate to hope. Expectancy appears to be related to specific instances, whereas hope is a more general attitude and is laden with more affect.[35]

The importance of an attitude of hope in an achieving person has been underlined by three investigations. In a study of noncognitive factors in the achievement of MIT undergraduates (Gilmore, 1951, 1953), responses to a sentence-completion test revealed more frequent use of the words "hope" and "faith" by the high achievers than by those in the control group. In another study conducted at the junior high level Goff (1969) found that selection of the word "hope" as a multiple-choice test item differentiated the high-achieving and low-achieving groups. An investigation of twelfth-graders (Lynch, 1960) also showed "hope" as a factor differentiating high and low achievers.[36]

Since a sense of hope is essentially an affective response, it depends on contact with another person, either in actuality or in fantasy. A person who feels isolated from his social environment may wish or daydream, but he cannot hope. As Pruyser (1963) points out, one of the consequences of isolation is a sense of hopelessness, which may in the totally isolated person lead to complete personality disintegration.[37] The actual basis for hope is a feeling for others, which in turn is related to the individual's capacity for empathy. Thus the more secure he is in his relationships with others, the greater the likelihood of his maintaining a hopeful attitude. Pruyser argues that hope, by its very language, accentuates the verbs of relationship and receptivity rather than those of action. Hope is something that is given and received; it is an experience which is shared:[38]

> One hopes with, through and sometimes for someone else. Hoping is basically a shared experience. . . . [In the words of William James

35 See Harvey, 1965, p. 255

36 Gilmore, 1951, pp. 221–226; 1953; Goff, 1969, p. 106; M. Lynch. 1960

37 Pruyser, 1963, pp. 94–95

38 See Pruyser, 1963, p. 95

(1890)]: "Just as our courage is so often a reflex of another's courage, so our faith is apt to be . . . a faith in someone else's faith."

Hope may be distinguished from optimism on the basis of relationship. According to Marcell (1944), both the optimist and the pessimist emphasize their separation from others, while the hoping person "remains part of the scheme of things."[39] He is more modest and humble than the self-confident optimist, and also tends to be more patient and forebearing. At the same time his position is unassailable. Expressions of either certainty or doubt regarding some future consequence can be argued by someone with another viewpoint, but the simple statement "I hope" stands above argument. It also represents a more realistic appraisal, since any event that has not yet occurred represents an uncertainty. As Stotland (1969) points out, most situations in life are not so difficult as to be completely hopeless; the future is often more manageable than one thinks possible:[40]

The argument that one needs to be "realistic" (not too hopeful) is literally unsound, since hope refers to the future, which is not yet a reality. It is impossible to be realistic about a non-reality. Hope is a subjective state that can strongly influence the realities-to-come; prophecies are often self-fulfilling.

The person who uses the word "hope" in reference to his actions, or whose actions suggest that he is hopeful of a positive outcome, is bringing to bear on the situation the desire for an outcome that will contribute to his self-esteem. As a result, the probability of his success is increased by his own input into the situation. The lack of a positive effort or a "don't care" attitude in connection with an endeavor may indicate lack of hope, or even an overt denial of hope. If there is nothing to hope for, there is no reason to care, and hence no reason to take action.

This negative expectation may result from the individual's awareness of his own lack of input. Harvey and Clapp (1965) point out that there is a fundamental difference between the student who says he "expects to flunk out of school" and the one who says "he hopes he will not."[41] The individual who expects to

---

39 See Pruyser, 1963, p. 89

40 Stotland, 1969, p. 151

41 See Harvey, 1965, p. 253

fail may be voicing a realistic appraisal of the situation in terms of his lack of sufficient input to prevent failure, indicating possible feelings of low self-esteem. The individual who hopes that he will not fail is also appraising the situation realistically in terms of his known input; however, his concern about the outcome stems from an awareness that his self-esteem will be increased if he succeeds.

Hope, then, is directly related to the individual's trust or lack of trust that his interaction with his environment will contribute to his self-esteem. As a result, an individual's level of hope influences not only the degree of his efforts but also the direction of his response to situations that offset his self-esteem. This is demonstrated by Silverman's study of differential responsiveness to success and failure in four groups of college students classified on the basis of their level of self-esteem.[42] In experimental success-or-failure situations he found that the subjects in both the high and the low groups tended to limit their cognitive input to a level which corresponded to their self-image. He concluded that the individuals with low self-esteem "have made a particular kind of adjustment to their environment which requires that they maintain a low self-evaluation." Feelings of low self-esteem apparently function as a method of justification for dependent behavior; they may also serve to reduce the threat of possible failure by keeping the expectations of need-satisfaction low. In either event, the individual's lack of hope that his self-esteem will be enhanced through acquiring more information deprives him of any inducement to do so.

The degree to which an individual perceives himself to have control over his own fate also influences his interpretation of his actual successes and failures. Stotland notes that those who feel personal responsibility for their destiny may perceive more hopeful implications in a success than will those who do not feel responsible.[43]

The expectations of others also influence an individual's own expectations of his performance; moreover, they can influence his actual performance level and his persistence when faced with failure. It has been demonstrated that when other people

42 Silverman, 1964, p. 118   43 Stotland, 1969, p. 76

communicate to an individual their expectation that he will perform a task at a given level, he will generally do so.[44] These findings also suggest that there is a carryover of these expectations which may affect the individual's performance of other tasks. This hypothesis has important implications for the enhancement of productivity, since, as discussed in Chapter Six, the level of parental expectations has an influence on the child's achievement.

There is further evidence in studies of adults of the relationship between self-esteem and aspiration level (hope). In their study of success in business executives Zaleznik, Dalton, and Barnes (1970) noted that the subjects rated as most successful ("oriented managers") revealed their self-esteem through their confidence in anticipating career advancement, with commensurate increase in salary, whereas those in the conflicted groups, who were marked by low self-esteem, had low monetary aspirations.[45]

Harvey and Clapp's studies (1965) also revealed that when the behavior of their subjects became positive—when they turned toward rather than away from experimental situations involving hope—these individuals expressed significantly more positive feelings toward themselves than those who turned away from hope.[46]

COGNITIVE SKILLS

verbal and mathematical skills Any communication between one person and another takes place through symbols, whether the symbols are the environmental cues which the infant perceives at a rudimentary level or the abstract symbols of thought and language. A knowledge of the verbal symbols labeling persons and objects and of the mathematical concept of quantity is essential to perception and appraisal of the environment. Thus a minimum vocabulary is necessary for dealing with the ordinary problems of living. No problem is open to solution unless it can be identified or labeled, and results of the solution cannot be communicated to others except through symbolic representation, or language. In

44 Stotland, 1969, pp. 100, 106
45 Zaleznik, Dalton, and Barnes, 1970, pp. 75-80

45 Zaleznik, Dalton, and Barnes, 1970, pp. 75-80
46 Harvey, 1965, pp. 253-254

theory, the larger a person's vocabulary, the more effectively he should be able to cope with his environment. Beyond a certain level, however, an increase in vocabulary does not result in greater mastery, nor does a further increase in mathematical skills contribute to greater achievement except in situations that require specialized mathematical skills.

Most tests of general intelligence place a high premium on verbal skills. Studies of highly productive persons, however, indicate that they do not necessarily have outstandingly high IQs. Terman observed years ago that IQ scores above 140 do not differentiate levels of academic achievement or vocational success. In his study of creative architects MacKinnon (1968) found no significant relationship between levels of creativity and scores on a Concept Mastery Test.[47] General intelligence, as measured by current tests, is related at a basic level to the ability to do academic work; no architect in MacKinnon's group had a low IQ. The correlation is not high in many instances, since tests of general intelligence do not measure such factors as memory. Another factor in the low correlations of general intelligence and academic performance at the graduate level is the lack of a wide variation in IQ scores at this stage of education. Roe (1969) reports from her studies of creative physical scientists that the minimum intelligence required for creative production in science is probably considerably higher than average, but that other variables, such as special numerical, spatial, and verbal abilities, play somewhat different roles in different scientific fields.[48]

Some of the noncognitive characteristics which differentiate the highly productive person from others can be measured by individual intelligence tests such as the Wechsler Adult Intelligence Scale (WAIS). Gamewell (1967) found that the postgraduate success of psychology students could not be predicted from intellective measures on either the WAIS or the Concept Mastery Test.[49] However, the noncognitive WAIS variables differentiated both the subjects who were later unsuccessful and those who failed to complete their graduate work. The high-success groups in general exhibited greater strengths in nonintellectual areas

47 MacKinnon, 1968, p. 106
48 Roe, 1969, pp. 97–98
49 Gamewell, 1967 (1967A), pp. 3022–3023

than the low-success and dropout groups. They showed less anxiety, distractability, scatter on the WAIS, and uncertainty; they also had better perceptual organization and memory, greater fluency, more self-control, and more social awareness than the low-success groups. The low-success groups showed more evidence of anxiety, distractibility, scatter, and uncertainty; they were less socially aware and had lower scores on memory, fluency, and self-control than the high-success group.

As discussed in Chapter Two, the individual's own evaluation of his ability is actually a more reliable predictor of his achievement level than his measured IQ. Morse (1963) found that self-concepts of ability predicted classroom performance more accurately than IQ tests among both black and white students, and Haarer (1964) reported essentially the same finding for both ninth-grade public school male students and institutionalized delinquent boys.[50] Haan (1963) found that coping mechanisms are associated with an increase in IQ.[51] Lekarczyk and Hill (1969), in a study of levels of self-esteem as related to test anxiety and stress in verbal learning in fifth- and sixth-grade children, noted that boys with high self-esteem made significantly more correct responses than boys with low self-esteem.[52] Less anxious children of both sexes made fewer errors than those who were highly anxious. The correlation between self-esteem and IQ (Kuhlman-Anderson) in this study was $r = .29$ for boys and $r = .46$ for girls.

memory Another requirement for effective functioning is memory. One must be able to recall what he has perceived and what he has experienced in order to cope with both situational problems and the interpersonal relationships in his environment. Memory is an essential element not only in problem solving, but also in judgment, degree of independence, and many of the skills associated with the coping process. The more information one can bring to bear on any conflicting situation, the more resources he has for arriving at a solution.

Exposure to an abundance of experiences or information does not necessarily guarantee an ability to recall it for use. One

50 See Purkey, 1970, p. 24

51 Haan, 1963, pp. 21–22

52 Lekarczyk and Hill, 1969, pp. 147–154

obvious limitation is the organizing capacity of the individual's memory processes. However, interference with memory may also occur at either the perceptual or the retrieval level as a result of a general or a specific emotional state.

As Joseph (1966) observes, a conflict around affective life may block the imprint of external cues on the memory.[53] For example, the intake of new material may be inhibited by some previously learned prohibition regarding its expression or its application to a given situation. As a result, a highly anxious person usually has difficulty with perception, and his inability to discriminate differences handicaps him still further in dealing with his environment. Forgetting, sometimes termed "defensive forgetting," refers to the retrieval of an experience from the memory store. Freud noted that in a broad sense forgetting was a suppression of information, either active or unconscious, as a defense against conflicting perceptions or as a defense against anxiety. Such a defense may include not only active suppression and unconscious repression, but also denial and isolation.

Forgetting may appear in certain impulsive individuals in whom there is a "short circuit between wish and action." There is little or no time for the intervention of thought and judgment between the cue and the action. The anticipation of pain is so great that the situation must be "gotten rid of" regardless of its solution or of previous experience. According to Joseph, in healthy functioning experiences are stored in the mind as memory, waiting to be summoned to the consciousness by external cues. Energy is required to achieve the transition into consciousness. Memories are always invested with a low level of energy cathexis, since they are either in the preconscious or unconscious. Remembering requires that there be a linkage between the associative ties and the energy which makes free association possible. One requirement for this is a lack of conflict. In many cases the names of certain persons can be recalled only with great effort, since these persons symbolize threat.

A good memory is closely related to perception and also to productivity. The more sensitively an individual perceives his

53 Joseph, 1966, pp. 1–17

environment, the greater is his input to his memory store, and consequently the greater his potential for productivity in any area. Roe (1969) found, for example, that creative physical scientists tended to be highly observant.[54]

Mendelsohn and Griswold (1964) studied 108 undergraduates, using the Remote Associates Test (RAT) and a problem involving thirty anagrams, along with a list of twenty-five words (a test of memory) which were played on a tape recorder.[55] There were no significant differences on rote recall, but the results were interpreted as reflecting a wider deployment of attention and less screening out of irrevelant experiences in problem solving by highly creative persons. The authors offered the suggestion "that one characteristic of highly creative individuals is a greater sensitivity to environmental cues and a greater ability to utilize these cues in problem solving. This does not mean that they have better memories, but rather that they "retain in usable form more of their prior stimulus experience." They may "deploy their attention more widely and thus receive a broader range of information with sufficient strength to influence their subsequent responses."

Although memory is mentioned specifically only in connection with reports of the creative group, its presence is implied in the references to the judgment and lack of impulsivity in academicians and leaders.

Tweedie (1965), who studied the relationships of memory process, environmental stimuli, and the ability to delay gratification, concluded that poor delayers (impulsive persons) do not necessarily have poor memories. Rather, they have particular difficulty in using their memories in demanding situations and when distracting stimuli are present.[56]

In a study of memory Brenner (1971) found in dating couples that the memory recall is greater in the partner who cares more—in other words, who shows greater attention to the other partner.[57] Women tend to have a greater recall than men. Perhaps persons who care most, who empathize most, and who are less concerned with themselves, have better memories than those who are occupied with self or have lower self-esteem.

54 Roe, 1969, p. 98
55 Mendelsohn and Griswold, 1964, pp. 431–436
55 Mendelsohn and Griswold, 1964, pp. 431–436

AGE AND EXPERIENCE

In addition to his cognitive skills, an individual's coping strategies are influenced by his age and the breadth and extent of his previous experiences. Other things being equal, the more information and background he can bring to bear on a complex environmental stimulus or problem, the easier it will be for him to classify different procedures for the solution of a problem. Hence the broader his experiences and education, and the more opportunities he has had to see the results of previous decisions, the more effectively he can appraise and solve a given problem. At the same time, these prior experiences may delimit the range of possibilities he considers.

There should logically be some relationship between age and coping ability. However, the ability to perceive a situation may not be directly related to age, since quality and quantity of experiences may vary within the same age group. Some children are more widely read than others and can utilize their vicarious reading experiences in solving problems. Direct contact with various kinds of people is not necessarily a factor; some people lead a rather cloistered life and may be unable to cope effectively with persons from different cultural or ethnic backgrounds. Extensive travel probably does contribute to one's ability to cope with new situations; and the extent of an individual's formal education, which is not always a function of his age, should enhance his problem-solving ability. In short, the more knowledge, either specialized or general, that the individual brings to a situation, the more skill he is contributing to its solution.

The influence of age on coping skills and cognitive abilities is particularly evident in the case of the young child. Maccoby (1968) and others point out that as he matures, the child's increasing cognitive powers enable him to deal more effectively with his environment—particularly with respect to moral and social behavior.[58] For example, a perception of increasing time span gives him a means of seeing the consequences of his acts, allowing him greater control over his impulses. Increased cognitive skills will also help him to understand rules and directions.

154   56   Tweedie, 1965 (1966B), pp. 618–619   58   Maccoby, 1968, p. 256
         57   Brenner, 1971, pp. 275–276

attributes for effective coping

INDEPENDENCE

One frequently observed characteristic of the highly productive individual is his independence. Independence, or "freedom from the influence, control, or determination of . . . others,"[59] implies an ability to discriminate among objects, persons, or alternatives and to come to one's own appropriate decisions or solutions of problems. The productive person, in order to solve a problem effectively, must not only be able to perceive and appraise all aspects of it accurately, but must then reach an autonomous, unbiased decision based both on his own perceptions and on the information which he can bring to bear. At a fundamental level he must to some extent disturb the status quo, since to contribute anything new to society he must be able to think and act differently from those around him. Hence the productive person must, above all, have confidence in his perception, values, and judgment. He must be prepared to defend his position, often in the face of considerable opposition and criticism; he must be sufficiently free of anxiety to pursue his course despite criticism.

No person is completely independent, since he must function in some way within the framework of his social milieu. An individual who feels confident in himself and his environment, however, usually feels free to choose his preferred style of life. He is often "unconventional" in the sense that he is relatively unconcerned about superficial or temporary ideas and activities. Barron (1968) notes that independent people tend to be more interested in the originality and aptness of an idea than they are in the practical aspects of a problem. They are also relatively unconcerned with superficialities in people; they tend to respond to a person's inward integrity rather than to his "pleasing" characteristics. He notes that the creative writers in his study scored high on the Independence of Judgment Scale.[60] Maslow also pointed to the independence of self-actualizing persons, who do not feel that it is necessary to get along with everyone.[61]

Responsibility is one of the concomitants of true independence. A person cannot be independent and at the same time be

59 Webster's new world dictionary of the American language, 1962, sv independence

60 Barron, 1968, pp. 178–179, 242

61 Maslow, 1954, pp. 213–214

irresponsible, since irresponsible behavior is unpredictable and will therefore be justifiably mistrusted by others. He will also justifiably mistrust himself, and the lowering of his self-esteem will reduce his independence accordingly.

Another aspect of independence is judgment. The ability to discriminate in evaluating problems and human situations has long been associated with the concept of intelligence. Judgment is a cognitive process; because it is involved in decision making, it is related to the ability to do independent thinking. Roe (1969), in reporting the results of a number of previous studies of creative physical scientists, notes that there is a striking agreement on their independence and autonomy with respect to cognition and value judgments.[62]

An independent individual feels sufficiently secure to differentiate between himself and others. He can also differentiate alternatives and courses of action, "good" (valid) and "bad" (invalid) behavior. Judgment is actually based upon concepts of honesty, fairness, and justice; it is also related to the quality of self-esteem. One must choose and judge constantly. In interpersonal relations we view the person who cannot discriminate between valid and invalid behavior as "lacking in judgment." It is more appropriate to say that he is preoccupied with himself because of his low self-esteem. This self-preoccupation interferes with his perceptual and discriminatory abilities; consequently, he cannot make good judgments.

A secure person does not constantly refer to his independence or flaunt it openly, thereby displaying a reaction-formation against dependent feelings. Such pseudo-independent behavior can often be observed in the rebellious high school- or college-age adolescent who tries to emancipate himself abruptly from his parents. He "protests" his independence by acting it out.

The quality of independence has been found particularly characteristic of creative individuals. A person who produces new ideas or products, who presents a drastically different perspective, must also be convinced that his labor is valuable to other members of society. Without such assurance it would be difficult, if not impossible, for him to advocate publicly a point of view

62 Roe, 1969, p. 98

which may be at variance with the popular one. Barron puts the matter very strongly:[63]

> I believe it is literally true that the creative individual is willing to stake his life on the meaning of his work.

Taylor (1963) also stresses the autonomy, self-sufficiency, and independence of judgment of creative persons.[64] MacKinnon (1963), in describing creative architects, also alludes to the great sense of responsibility these men feel not only to their clients, but also to the profession and society.[65] Convinced of the worth of what they are doing, they frequently report a "sense of destiny" in their professions. Moreover, they do not easily accept ideas and/or help from others in the solution of difficult problems. Coopersmith (1967) notes that some creative individuals are characteristically stubborn in resisting outside pressures and influences.[66] Roe (1969) adds that creative physical scientists are not only highly autonomous, but also "Bohemian or radical" and "highly egocentric."[67] Both Drevdahl (1964) and Barron (1955) have reported similar findings. Chambers (1964), who made an extensive biographical and personality study of creative and uncreative chemists and psychologists, found that the creative scientist "emerges as a strongly motivated, dominant person who is not overly concerned with other persons' views or with obtaining approval for the work he is doing.[68]

Coopersmith feels that "an essential component" of the creative process is absolute trust in one's own judgment—in other words, high self-esteem.[69] In administering three tests of creative and related abilities, he found that the groups who were high in self-esteem performed most creatively on all three tests. The groups who were low in self-esteem were consistently less original and innovative. He concludes from these findings that "persons high in their own evaluation are generally more capable of achieving and imposing original solutions" than persons of less self-confidence.

Independence is also characteristic of high achievers. Because these individuals use their own successfully internalized convictions as an authority in decision making, they do not need

63 Barron, 1968, p. 247

64 Taylor, 1963, p. 238

65 MacKinnon, 1963, pp. 273ff

66 Coopersmith, 1967, pp. 58–59

67 Roe, 1969, p. 98

68 Chambers, 1964, p. 14

69 Coopersmith, 1967, pp. 61–63

to rely on the opinions of others. They have both good ego identity and a high level of autonomy. On the other hand, they are not aggressively hostile individuals since aggression might give them possible guilt feelings and therefore lead to less independence.[70] High academic achievers have also been characterized by Lavin (1965) as having originality, independence, a relatively low need for affiliation, and low conformity to peer-group standards.[71] Stalnaker (1961) found National Merit Scholars to be unusually original and imaginative, and furthermore willing to take risks in the field of ideas.[72]

There is also a relationship between independence and intelligence. C. Smith (1969) reports that IQ scores have a high correlation with the dependency-independence continuum.[73] In a study of fourth- and fifth-grade boys, high IQ was found negatively related to dependency ($r = -.29$) and positively to independence ($r = +.55$). On rating scales, highly intelligent boys were rated more independent than boys with low intelligence.

Both independence and responsibility are important characteristics of leadership. According to Karasick et al. (1968), high school leaders seem to agree that being "different" doesn't bother them.[74] Douvan and Adelson (1966) found that one of the traits revealed by the upward-aspiring adolescent boys in their study, as opposed to the downward-mobile ones, was independence—an ability to govern their own behavior according to internal standards.[75]

Whereas independence is associated with high productivity, its absence in low-productive persons is equally apparent. The literature on underachievement reports numerous examples of dependency and related characteristics. The nonachievement syndrome described by Roth and Meyersburg (1965) does not specifically allude to dependency; however, it does suggest that "vulnerability to disparagement by others" is an important characteristic.[76] Lack of responsibility, as already noted, is closely related to the dependence-independence dichotomy. Moreover, adolescent rebellion, an outward protestation of pseudo-independence, is often characteristic of the adolescent underachiever; Green (1963) has observed that such students show

70 M. Gilmore, 1964, p. 22

71 Lavin, 1965, pp. 107–108

72 Stalnaker, 1961, p. 518

73 C. Smith, 1969, p. 123

74 Karasick, Leidy, and Smart, 1968, p. 8

75 Douvan and Adelson, 1966, p. 61

76 Roth and Meyersburg, 1965, pp. 284–285

greater disregard for social customs and conventions than do high-achieving students.[77] The unhappy combination of adolescent irresponsibility and rebellion and what is actually an inner state of dependency is all too characteristic of students at the lowest levels of class standing, particularly in our large inner-city high schools (M. Gilmore, 1964; Roth and Meyersburg, 1965). Dependency can also be found even in persons at the graduate level. Barron (1968) noted that weaker (low-soundness) graduate students tended to be suggestible, gullible, lacking in internal standards of judgment, and somewhat submissive.[78] Drevdahl (1964) also found among his less creative psychologists a greater need for peer and public approval, a greater fear of authority, more concern with social relations, and less independence than in his creative group.[79]

In all these instances of low productivity, it can be inferred that the dependency, vulnerability to others' opinions, and lack of responsibility are associated with what is basically low self-esteem. Support for such a conclusion may be found in the results of research which has been conducted on "affiliation" and "field dependence."

Researchers studying affiliation have demonstrated the influence of self-esteem on independence. Persons who have high affiliative needs do not have sufficient strength to stand alone. Zimbardo and Formica (1963) found that when subjects were faced with threat, and self-esteem was measured by self-ratings, the fearful (low self-esteem) subjects affiliated significantly more than the high self-esteem subjects, who were not fearful. Lazarus (1966), commenting on this experiment, says that the insecure subjects sought social support as "reassurance against threat."[80]

Field-dependent persons have been found to be more susceptible than those who are field-independent to the influence and judgment of others.[81] There is evidence that feelings of insecurity and low self-esteem, which contribute to an individual's dependence and need for social approval, are factors in his inability to make discriminating and objective judgments. Lazarus noted that "feelings of personal inadequacy result in high sensitivity to others' opinions and the tendency to conform to the

77 Green, 1963, p. 204
78 Barron, 1968, pp. 48–49
79 Drevdahl, 1964, p. 174
80 Lazarus, 1966, pp. 249–250
81 Lewis, 1971, p. 143

social pressure rather than take an independent stance."[82] Gergen (1971) also reports that persons low in self-esteem—partly because they are anxious for the acceptance of others and partly because they lack confidence in their own opinions—are not inclined to try to draw others to their position and are more likely to accept what they feel to be "authoritative" opinions.[83] He comments that they have "little to lose by change and may even long to be re-molded for the better." The incessant "joiner" is usually "not so much dissatisfied with the state of the world as he is with himself."

There is some evidence that persons in the middle range of the self-esteem continuum are the most likely to be concerned with conformity to the group. Cox and Bauer (1964) and Gergen and Bauer (1967) found that girls with both low and high levels of self-esteem reject attempts to influence them, whereas those at the medium levels seem to be the most conforming.[84] Coopersmith also noted a greater concern with "group values" in the middle self-esteem group than in either the high or low group.[85] Such persons have less confidence in their own judgment than do high self-esteem individuals, and their sense of worth is less "clearly and definitely anchored." One reason may be that they are trying to stabilize their ambiguous position. Those with low self-esteem have little enthusiasm about conforming to standards which "virtually commit them to judgments of failure."

In a study of the cognitive styles related to defensiveness (an aspect of low self-esteem) Holzman and Gardner (1959) use the terms "leveling" and "sharpening" to describe the perceptual process as it is related to judgment. Subjects in the experiment were asked to make fine discriminations in the sizes of a large number of closely similar squares. Those whose Rorschach responses indicated feelings of depression tended to blur, or "level," the slight differences in the sizes of the squares, whereas the less depressed subjects were able to perceive differences more distinctly. In discussing this experiment Lazarus (1966) suggests that the insecure person may limit the range of information available to him as a defense against having to recognize details or experiences which may be threatening.[86]

82 Lazarus, 1966, pp. 249–250

83 Gergen, 1971, pp. 76–77

84 See Gergen, 1971, p. 77

85 Coopersmith, 1967, p. 142

86 See Lazarus, 1966, pp. 273–274

There is evidence that defensive behavior relates to intelligence as well as to judgment. In a study of defenses and coping devices in relationship to IQ change Haan (1963) alludes to some aspects of judgment.[87] Defensive behavior is described as "rigid, automatized, and stimulus bound" and given to distortion. Coping behavior, in contrast, is marked by flexibility and purpose, by orientation to the reality of a situation, and by a high degree of differentiation in response; it also permits impulse satisfaction "in an open, ordered, and tempered way." Haan found intelligence positively related to coping patterns and negatively related to defenses in both men and women.

IMPULSE CONTROL

The productive person characteristically copes with events, objects, and problems in such a way that the results of his efforts will be commensurate with his purposes and goals. This capacity to maintain control over the outcomes of his own efforts is expressed in two areas. First, he controls his own impulses; he avoids purposeless activity, reduces false beginnings and costly errors to a minimum, and resists the temptation to make hasty decisions. Second, he has the capacity to control the situation by simplifying and organizing masses of disparate information so that the problem or situation is more manageable and amenable to solution. It is this control that enables him both to predict and to determine his own success.

The person who can direct and control his perceptual and cognitive skills, perceive the environment accurately, and make fairly accurate decisions is more likely to be productive than the one whose impulses control his actions. Lack of ego control not only impairs both perception and judgment in coping with problems, but seriously interferes with efficiency, thus adding to the tension. Productivity is further reduced by the additional effort needed to correct errors and deal with the consequences of poor decisions. Kipnis (1971) suggests that impulsive persons are less mature than nonimpulsive ones because they are less accepting of conventions, more exploitive, and less controlled.[88] In a study of

87 Haan, 1963, p. 2   88 Kipnis, 1971, p. 116

high school leaders and nonleaders Karasick et al. (1968) found a marked relationship between ratings on a scale of internal-external control and a scale measuring anomie (alienation from society).[89] They concluded that individuals who feel that they have little control over the events in their lives (that is, who sense a high degree of external control) also show a tendency toward a breakdown in their attachment to society.

Impulsivity has recently become a subject of much research attention. Since it is directly observable as behavior, paper-and-pencil tests are being constructed as a means of measuring it. Preliminary investigations indicate that impulse control may be a trait that differentiates the productive person from less productive ones. Kipnis (1971) reports studies on impulsivity in both college and noncollege subjects which indicate that impulsive persons are poorly restrained and restless.[90] They seem to need and to seek constant stimulation from the environment. Although they are apparently resistant to constructive suggestions from persons who are close to them, their behavior appears to be rather easily influenced by anticipated threats from someone they perceive as a leader, by situations involving sex (an attractive female), and by opportunities to make money rapidly. They reach out to others with the intent of exploitation, rather than for support, and tend to seek friends on the basis of their utility value. In general they are insensitive to behavior that is uncooperative, unfair, or in violation of social norms. They will maximize their monetary returns even at someone else's expense, and on the whole they are less sensitive to the needs of others than nonimpulsive persons.

Impulsivity has been explained as symptomatic of a lack of trust in the environment, accompanied by a feeling of emptiness, alienation, and helplessness. A weak ego (a consequence of low self-esteem) is characterized by a lack of confidence that one's needs will be met, and consequently an inability to postpone an action in anticipation of positive outcomes or consequences. Since low self-esteem is usually accompanied by feelings of depression, the impulsive individual tends to reach out into the environment at random, without proper evaluation and appraisal of the situation or concern for consequences. His need to terminate

89 Karasick, Leidy, and Smart, 1968, p. 7   90 Kipnis, 1971, pp. 36, 54, 58–59, 72, 85–86

an anxiety-producing situation is greater than his need to resolve it successfully.

The characteristic of impulsivity should be clearly distinguished from the quality of spontaneity. Both have an emotional basis, but their origins are antithetical. Impulsive behavior is essentially a defense; spontaneous behavior is a coping mechanism for achieving free and easy communication with others. Spontaneity is based on empathy, impulsivity on fear and hostility. Spontaneity is expressed primarily as verbal behavior whereas impulsivity tends to be motor. Spontaneous actions occur in relation to other persons; impulsive ones tend to occur more in isolation.

A constantly evaluative or critical environment usually leads to chronic impulsiveness. In some cases, however, especially in children, impulsivity is limited to those areas of behavior which have been tinged with critical evaluation. For example, some children are quite impulsive in doing academic work; they can barely wait to get it over with. However, in classes that are not related to pressure for academic performance, such as woodworking, music, or physical education, they are relaxed, deliberate, and persistent.

Impulsivity is characterized by two behavioral traits. One is insecurity. The impulsive person is typically anxious about his concept of himself, about his relationships to others, and about people in general. He mistrusts not only his environment, but also his perception of it. As a result, he finds it difficult to arrive at a clearcut decision. The other principal characteristic of impulsivity is the constant need for a sense of movement. The impulsive individual finds ambiguity intolerable and must have closure of an ambiguous situation to remove the threat. Dittes (1959) studied the effects of experimentally lowering the self-esteem of subjects and observed the influence of the negative evaluations on their impulsivity.[91] He found that those who were negatively evaluated were significantly more impulsive in trying to obtain closure on an ambiguous perceptual task than the comparable control group. Commenting on this experiment, Lewis (1971) suggests that the subjects with low self-esteem were more likely to feel shame and were therefore more inclined to make an impulsive decision, since the need for closure reflects an individual's need for some confirmation of himself such as can be obtained by completion of a task.[92] It is also possible that because of the general anxiety level created by uncertainty over their self-esteem, the need for closure reflects a need to release excess tension through motion.

There appears to be a relationship between impulse control and cognitive skill. Hurwitz (1954) demonstrated that, even among disturbed children, motor activity tends to be low if cognitive development is relatively high, whereas those with low cognitive development are hyperactive.[93] Hurwitz's findings suggest that the higher the cognitive development, the greater the ego control, and hence the less need for motor activity in place of a solution to the problem. In other words, the greater the ego control the greater the problem-solving ability—and this may be reflected as higher IQ. In an investigation of twenty intelligent but underachieving boys and ten boys who were highly successful academically, Davids (1968) found the underachievers to be impulsive in their approach to cognitive tasks, cognitively rigid, and intolerant of ambiguity.[94] Bachman (1970) found the internal control of tenth-grade boys positively correlated with intellectual ability; he also found a modest positive correlation between self-esteem and intelligence.[95]

These findings suggest that impulse control is related to the quality and quantity of self-esteem. This relationship is particularly evident in the value structure of lower socioeconomic groups. Langner and Michael (1963) relate impulse control directly to ego strength and contend that the high level of frustration in low-income groups is likely to produce a poorly internalized superego.[96] As a result the person from a low-income home typically requires immediate gratification; approximately one-fourth of the group interviewed by Langner and Michael agreed that they wanted things "right away." High school dropouts provide another example of the inability of impulsive persons to postpone gratification. As Mussen et al. (1969) pointed out, the dropout feels a more urgent need to escape from frustrations than to work toward long-term goals.[97]

164

92 Lewis, 1971, p. 122

93 See Lazarus, 1966, p. 229

94 Davids, 1968, p. 200

95 Bachman, 1970, pp. 135, 148

96 Langner and Michael, 1963, pp. 459, 461

97 Mussen, Conger, and Kagan, 1969, p. 733

Some other aspects of impulse control have been studied in children. Block and Martin (1955) found that children who were low in "ego control" played more aggressively and less constructively following a frustrating experience than did children who were higher in ego control.[98] In some experiments on reflection versus impulsivity in third-graders Kagan (1966) found that impulsive children made more errors on a serial learning task than reflective ones.[99] There have also been investigations of the possible relationship between impulsivity and sex identity. In a study of 351 children in the fourth, fifth, and sixth grades by Sutton-Smith and Rosenberg (1961) it was reported that highly impulsive boys checked significantly more feminine items and impulsive girls checked significantly more masculine items on a sex-preference test than those who had been identified as low in impulsivity.[100] The writers suggest that the impulsive boys' preference for feminine items may indicate their immaturity. However, the findings can also be explained as symptomatic of emotional insecurity.

Impulsivity has particularly adverse effects on performance in the content-oriented subjects, such as mathematics, science, and languages, where careless errors are inevitably reflected in lower grades. An experiment by Tweedie (1965) demonstrated that "poor delayers" (impulsive persons) made significantly more errors in the presence of a distracting stimulus than did good delayers; they also made significantly more responses to the distracting stimulus. In a study of first-grade reading ability by Kagan (1965) it was found that the children who were impulsive, rather than reflective, made more recognition errors in reading English words which were presented either singly or in a prose selection.[101] The errors made in the first grade were also correlated with the types of reading errors made one year later.

Impulse control appears to be an important variable in problem-solving ability. Banta (1970) notes that "impulse-control training" seems to have little effect in improving analytic perceptual skills; however, there is a relationship between innovative behavior and intentional learning, and impulse control is related to intentional learning.[102]

98 See Lazarus, 1966, pp. 230–231

99 Kagan, 1966, pp. 17, 24

100 Sutton-Smith and Rosenberg, 1961, pp. 187–192

101 Kagan, 1965, pp. 609–628

102 Banta, 1970, pp. 475–476

Scales of impulsivity have revealed significant differences between high and low academic achievers. Kipnis (1971) found that underachievement in bright college students could be predicted from measures of impulsivity, particularly from scores in restlessness and sensation-seeking behavior.[103] Lavin (1965) reports from his survey that students who show high academic performance exhibit a lower degree of impulsivity, and Davids et al. (1962) found high achievers better able to control impulsivity than low achievers.[104]

Still further evidence of the relationship between achievement and impulse control is provided by Snyder (1968), who reports a four-year study at Massachusetts Institute of Technology.[105] In September, 1961, 721 freshmen took the Omnibus Personality Inventory with its three scales—thinking introversion, complexity, and impulse expression. At the end of four years, the students who as freshmen had a low score on the impulse-expression test had attained significantly higher final cumulative averages than did those students with high impulse-expression scores. In other words, the greater the restriction of impulse, the greater the tendency for higher grades.

Impulsivity seems to be more of a factor in the academic achievement of boys than that of girls. A survey by Garai and Scheinfeld (1968) of intellectual competence in both sexes indicates that impulsivity is generally a negative factor in the development of intellectual competence in boys, whereas it may actually exert some positive effects in girls.[106]

References to impulse control in studies of creative persons are very sparse, perhaps because it is not included in the evaluative techniques being employed. There seems to be a feeling that too much control of impulses may be inimicable to the creative process.[107] Another reason may be a failure to define the term "impulsivity" as it is used in a particular study. Impulsivity is often confused with "expression of feeling" or spontaneity; in this latter sense it may be related to creativity.

Another problem in the studies of impulsivity and creativity is confusion in the findings. Roe (1969) notes that strong control of impulses is a characteristic of creative scientists. Yet Barron, in

103 Kipnis, 1971, pp. 25–26

104 See Lavin, 1965, pp. 109–110; see M. Gilmore, 1964, p. 23

105 Snyder, 1968, pp. 59–62

106 Garai and Scheinfeld, 1968, p. 238

107 Barron, 1955, p. 484

a study of U.S. Air Force captains (1955), found that the most creative subjects did not use "suppression as a mechanism for the control of impulse" (although it appears that "suppression" may be the key term here, rather than "impulse.")[108] In his later study of personal soundness in graduate students, Barron also reportrd that impulsivity was either unrelated or negatively related to personal soundness. (In this investigation both the population and the general criteria were different from those of the previous investigation.)[109]

Two brief reports from the field of business indicate a relationship between success and control of impulsivity. Baker (1971) found that the successful stockbroker who displayed high intelligence, particularly verbal intelligence, had high scores on the self-control scales of the California Personality Inventory, whereas the scores of the unsuccessful stockbroker suggested that he might be impulsive in his social behavior.[110] Zaleznik et al. (1970) found that both managers and specialists in the conflicted groups gave evidence of impulsive behavior and a need to discharge energy.[111]

Some studies of impulsivity have dealt with its antecedents. According to Slater (1962), if parents are overly strict and punitive, the child will not build the necessary internalized controls; rather, he will continue to depend on external ones.[112] This observation is especially pertinent to a discussion of productivity, and in particular to the area of academic achievement, where there is a strong association between high academic performance and impulse control.

Some recent investigations indicate that an extended absence of the father when children are young may be associated with subsequent behavior in boys which is aggressive, impulsive, and hostile—but not "masculine" in a "competitive-aggressive" sense. There is further evidence that boys from father-absent homes are less able to delay gratification than are boys from father-present homes; they also exhibit less ability to make accurate time judgments.[113] As discussed in Chapter Three, impulsivity is only one of many adverse consequences for a child deprived of the father model.

108 Barron, 1955, p. 485

109 Barron, 1968, p. 48

110 Baker, 1971, p. 86

111 Zaleznik, Dalton, and Barnes, 1970, p. 169

112 Slater, 1962, p. 66

113 See J. Lynch, 1971, pp. 3–4

ABILITY TO ORDER

One characteristic which has appeared in our survey of all types of productive individuals is their need to control their interaction with their environments by reducing complex data to some form of order. The academic achiever, for example, shows "superior study habits," such as the ability to plan his time and to outline information in reading assignments. Lavin (1965) has observed that a "higher need for order" is associated with high academic performance.[114]

The ability to correlate and organize widely disparate, unrelated pieces of information extends to all areas of productive endeavor. The scholar's painstaking organization of ideas from the voluminous notes he has collected over the years, the scientist's formulation of a hypothesis from thousands of minute laboratory observations, the composer's organization of sound in the framework of measured time, the business executive's formulation of a plan that will meet numerous conflicting requirements—all are examples of the exacting process of handling complexity of detail.

It is among creative individuals that we find the most marked ability to deal with and to control complexity. The creative person in any field seems to have a preference for working with complex problems and is willing to expend whatever time and effort may be necessary to find a solution. He also enjoys discovering hidden relationships in apparently unrelated data and utilizing these findings in working toward some solution of a problem. There is general agreement that creative individuals have a characteristic affinity for working with complex ideas. Taylor (1963), Roe (1969), and many others have noted a preference for the challenge of complexity. MacKinnon (1962) also comments on creative architects' marked preference for the complex and, especially, the asymmetrical.[115] The creative person apparently derives real pleasure from the process of manipulating ideas and seems to have an insatiable desire for resolving them into some kind of orderly pattern.[116]

In the process of formulating a solution or seeking an under-

114 Lavin, 1965, p. 106   116 Taylor, 1963, p. 237
115 MacKinnon, 1962, p. 488

lying pattern in complex, and often confused, information and ideas, the creative person often exhibits another widely noted characteristic, his ability to tolerate ambiguity. Since anxiety reduces the tolerance of ambiguity and uncertainty, this trait is probably evidence of his low level of anxiety. As Barron reminds us, the intellectual ordering of complicated and unrelated data is a taxing process; as the complexity increases, it strains "the organism's ability to integrate phenomena." However:[117]

> Some measure of disintegration is tolerable in the interests of a final higher level of integration.

Because he is intrigued by the challenge of a problem, the creative person also seems able to remain flexible in his approach to it. This flexibility of attitude is another characteristic of creativity which has interested a number of researchers. Excessive rigidity is incompatible with the management of a difficult, perplexing, and perhaps chaotic situation. To arrive at a solution which takes into account and accepts all aspects and conflicting elements of a situation, one must possess a degree of open-mindedness. This quality is indispensable to leaders. Gardner (1948) refers to the ability of business executives to consider many courses of action prior to reaching a decision. All forms of leadership, for that matter, require the capacity to deal flexibly with conflicting points of view.

Studies of creativity reveal interesting personality differences between highly creative and less creative persons, especially with respect to their attitudes toward problem solving. Ghiselin, Rompel, and Taylor (1964) administered a Creative Process Check List to two groups of scientists. They found that the highly creative scientist feels challenged and stirred when faced with a problem and is decidedly rewarded by mastery, but that the less creative one tends to feel threatened by a problem and, in addition to occasional feelings of pleasure at mastery, feels relief from temporary insecurity when it is solved.[118]

Another characteristically "creative" trait which has engaged the attention of researchers is the ability to perceive associations between ideas which seem otherwise unrelated and remote

---

117 Barron, 1955, p. 484

118 Ghiselin, Rompel, and Taylor, 1964, p. 32

from one another. The Remote Associates Test, developed by Mednick and Mednick (1964), has been used to measure this process. In the words of its authors:[119]

> Creative thinking consists of forming new combinations of associative elements, which combinations either meet specified requirements, or are in some way useful. The more mutually remote the elements of the new combination, the more creative is the process of solution.

The precise manner in which the highly creative person handles complexity has also been explored. Garwood (1964) found that in a group of 105 young scientists the highly creative subjects scored higher than the less creative ones on composite measures of personality factors which are predisposed towards originality. Garwood concludes that these findings provide clear empirical evidence [120]

> . . . for the association of higher creativity with a greater integration of nonconscious with conscious concepts. . . . The highly creative individual obtains satisfaction from the integration of initially disordered and complex phenomena. He thus tends to admit into consciousness disordered, irrational, nonconscious material, which is ordinarily repressed, in order to achieve the satisfaction of integrating it creatively in a complex personal synthesis.

It thus appears that the unconscious plays at least some role in the creative process, and that the integration of nonconscious with conscious material may be an important step in the evolution of a final synthesis. Roe (1969) feels that this step may be particularly important in scientific discovery.[121] Because much of his vast store of knowledge and experience consists of memories which may be temporarily inaccessible to conscious recall, he may at times forego orderly, logical thinking in favor of "scanning" these memories at the preconscious and even the unconscious levels. Such scanning may reveal patterns and complex associations which were not apparent to him from the process of analysis alone.

119 Mednick and Mednick, 1964, p. 55   121 Roe, 1969, pp. 95–96
120 Garwood, 1964, p. 418

The role of the unconscious in creative thinking has interested other researchers. Mednick et al. (1964) cite the usefulness of an "incubation period" after an intensive period of work. Although there is no active thought about the problem during this period, on returning to it later, one finds that some improvement or progress seems to have taken place.[122]

All these subtle intellectual and intuitive processes apply fairly universally. However, it is only in the individual who enjoys a high degree of personal security that we are likely to find the capacity to organize complex masses of data constructively. The ability to tolerate ambiguity and confusion, to maintain a flexible outlook, to perceive relationships and patterns in a seemingly chaotic, amorphous collection of details, and from those details to evolve an effective, meaningful synthesis or solution is a significant characteristic of the most productive individuals.

PERSISTENCE

One of the characteristics which the highly productive individual brings to a situation is his willingness to persist in the solution of a problem. As Dollard and Miller (1950) have pointed out, productive and creative work requires, among other things, that an individual devote sustained attention to the task at hand. He cannot be interrupted, either by outside distractions or by the intrusion of irrelevant thoughts.[123] The highly productive individual is willing to work long hours, sometimes around the clock, and even day after day for weeks on end in order to find the solution he seeks. McClelland observes that "creative scientists are unusually hardworking to the extent of appearing almost obsessed with their work."[124]

In any profession, moreover, the vast store of knowledge necessary for success is acquired only after years of difficult and often extremely onorous application. In a study of chemists and psychologists Chambers (1964) found that, in addition to dominance and initiative, persistence and a high level of energy were typical of the most creative subjects.[125] Earlier in their lives, these men studied long hours and earned good grades; as adults they still devoted themselves tirelessly to creative research which resulted in many original products; they had strong work-oriented interests.

MacKinnon observed that the most creative architects devoted "endless attention to matters of design, planning, detailing, individualization, industrialization, technology," and other matters associate with their profession.[126] In comparison with their less creative colleagues, they seemed to have more endurance and a greater capacity for sticking to a problem over a long period of time, even a lifetime, although their flexibility permitted them to vary specific means and goals for its solution. Taylor writes that one of the motivating traits of creative persons is their intellectual persistence; he notes their characteristically high level of energy, their "vast output," and their "disciplined work habits."[127]

Although the creative person is willing to take larger calculated risks than others, he is not likely to work for the solution of a problem against hopeless odds.[128] When there is some doubt that his efforts will make a difference, he tends to turn his energies to an area which offers some hope of solution. In other words, he does not engage in a mere gamble.

There are other references to the quality of persistence in the productive person. Lavin found persistence to be associated with high academic performance, and Barron noted it both in high-soundness graduate students and in creative writers.[129] Drevdahl reported greater industriousness and more scientific activity among the most creative psychologists than in the less creative groups.[130] Oden noted that the most successful members of the Terman groups displayed perseverance, integration toward a goal, desire to excel, self-confidence, and greater satisfaction in working out a solution along vocational lines at an early age.[131] Holland reports that the scientific achievers in his study perceived themselves as scholarly and hard-working.[132] Douvan and Adelson reported their upward-aspiring group as being able to postpone immediate pleasure for the sake of long-term rewards and able to commit themselves to a long period of education.[133] Baker interprets the successful stockbroker's high scores on the

172

126 MacKinnon, 1963, pp. 272–274

127 Taylor, 1963, p. 237

128 McClelland, in Taylor, 1963, p. 238

129 Lavin, 1965, pp. 106–107; Barron, 1968, pp. 46, 242–249

130 Drevdahl, 1964, pp. 170–186

131 Oden, 1968, p. 86

132 Holland, 1964, p. 301

133 Douvan and Adelson, 1966, p. 60

responsibility and concern-for-status scales of the California Psychological Inventory as indicating that he is "efficient, persevering, and resourceful."[134]

Persistence, like other coping characteristics, is closely associated with self-esteem. In a study of the relationship between persistence in college and academic achievement, Peterson (1967) found that the students who persist in college until they graduate tend to be self-confident and relatively free of self-doubt.[135] They are verbally fluent, poised, and socially confident, and also have such assets as "better study habits" and "fewer personal and family problems" than other students.

Barker (1968) studied the relationships of persistence, self-concepts of ability, and other motivational and perceptual variables to success in college.[136] He found that the pattern differed for male and female students. In the female students persistence was predictive of college success and a higher general self-concept of ability was associated with higher college grades. In the male students there was less relationship between self-concept and persistence, although the "chronic male nonpersister" had the lowest general self-concept of all the groups. Since high self-concepts are more frequent in girls, these findings may reflect the fact that girls are usually given a more nurturing environment than boys.

The findings on less productive individuals reveal a general absence of persistence-related traits. Barron's low-soundness subjects were preoccupied and unstable. Drevdahl's lowest-ranked psychologists (noncreative nonproductive) displayed a greater degree of insecurity, anxiety, and tension than did either the creative or the noncreative productive groups. Douvan and Adelson found their downward-mobile subjects somewhat disorganized, listless, and lacking in both self-confidence and an adequate time-perspective. Oden noted that the low-productive subjects in the Terman group tended to use alcohol as an escape. Baker's unsuccessful stockbrokers were described as passive, apathetic, unambitious, and lacking both self-direction and discipline. The failing students studied by Peterson (1967) were restricted in their

134 Baker, 1971, p. 86   136 Barker, 1968 (1968A), p. 1100

135 Peterson, 1967 (1967A), p. 2076

outlook and pessimistic about their occupational futures. Other characteristics observed were laziness, passivity, defensiveness, and a tendency to disorganization under stress.

An individual's ability to persist in any task is fundamentally dependent on his attitude toward the possibility of attaining a future goal. His time perspective, in other words, is of crucial importance. Even more important, perhaps, is his attitude of hope:[137]

> Persistency depends on the time perspective of the individual. As long as there is hope that the difficulty may be overcome for that price in effort or pain which the individual is ready to pay, he goes on trying. . . .

Both time perspective and hope are consequences of the basic self-confidence which underlies all the attributes associated with effective coping.

mastery: the final decision

Regardless of the manner or the effectiveness with which an individual copes with his environment, the coping process begins with the perception of a stimulus or problem and ends with a decision-making act which in some manner concludes the situation or solves the problem. The interval between perception and the final decision may be brief or quite extended; the decision may be reached quite spontaneously, or approached deliberately. In any case, the individual will, consciously or unconsciously, go through the steps of perception and appraisal in order to arrive at a decision.

If he is a productive person, he should bring to the coping situation an adequate background of cognitive skills and previous experiences, together with a basic attitude of hope for an eventual solution. He should also be fortified with certain personality traits of independence, judgment, impulse control, facility in handling complex information, and persistence. Once he has reduced the data of the problem—no matter how complex or ambiguous it may

137 See Stotland, 1969, p. 16

be—to a simple, operational formula, he should tend to reach a decision involving the plan of action which has the best chance of solving the problem. The validity of his decision will depend on the facts that he has at his command. Just as important, however, these consequences will depend on the quality of his self-esteem and the values which he brings to the situation. The more secure he is, the more precise will be the alternatives that characterize his behavior. Decision making, in short, involves all aspects of the personality; it is the final step in the coping process.

Decision making appears to be related to the need for achievement. Van der Meer (1967) found that although the need for achievement was significantly related to the level of aspiration, there was a negative correlation between achievement need and the willingness to take risks.[138] For the group with high achievement need, there was a significant negative correlation between the risk and the level of aspiration, indicating that when one has a high level of aspiration, one does not take undue or unpredictable chances in decisions.

There are only a few references in the research literature to the decision-making powers of productive individuals, but they are of particular interest in connection with leadership. Gardner (1948) reported that decision-making ability is a characteristic of the successful business executive.[139] Baker (1971), while describing successful stockbrokers as conscientious and responsible, noted that the unsuccessful ones tend to be unduly influenced by other persons' attitudes and judgments and are also uncertain in arriving at decisions.[140] Karasick et al. (1968) found that the high school leader places a much greater importance on decisiveness and forcefulness than does the nonleader.[141]

Decisiveness has also been found characteristic of creative persons. Knapp (1956) noted that the story responses of college science majors to the Thematic Apperception Test revealed a tendency to "bring the plot to a clear and decisive conclusion."[142] MacKinnon comments that, for the highly creative architect, "it is not sufficient that problems be solved, there is the further demand that the solutions be elegant."[143] He contends that highly creative architects, who rank high in two apparently conflicting values,

138 Van der Meer, 1967, pp. 353–372
139 Gardner, 1948
140 Baker, 1971, pp. 85–86
141 Karasick, Leidy, and Smart, 1968, p. 8
142 See McClelland, 1962, p. 148
143 MacKinnon, 1962, p. 490

the esthetic and the theoretical (on the Allport-Vernon-Lindzey Study of Values test), nevertheless succeed in reconciling these two elements in their personality; they seek both truth and beauty.

Any decision is in some measure a creative act, in the sense that it entails a synthesis of some new understanding or course of action. The capacity for decision, however, depends ultimately on the personality strengths or weaknesses of the individual. A person who lacks independence tends to avoid making final decisions because he is thereby made vulnerable to possible criticism. An impulsive person may arrive at a premature decision to avoid the tension created by his inability to concentrate; he can thus deny (or avoid) the reality of a situation by saying that the matter is "closed." In contrast, the productive person must have the strength and courage to make decisions that may affect not only his own life, but perhaps the entire course of history as well.

Yet life, in the last analysis, is a fabric of the myriad small decisions which are made on a day-to-day or even an hourly basis. An individual's decision-making ability—his capacity to solve problems effectively—does not emerge as a unitary trait. Rather, it evolves through many years of practice from earliest childhood, at first with very small challenges and then with gradually increasing ones. It is only within a secure and nurturing environment that any individual is able to develop and realize the full extent of his abilities to master himself and the challenge of his surroundings.

For a full picture of the environmental factors that relate to productivity we must give some consideration to the family background within the productive individual develops. As we have seen, the qualities of self-esteem, a clear sense of identity, a highly developed value system, and the competence to cope with and master life situations are common to all productive persons, regardless of the area in which they express themselves. We can assume, therefore, that this basic personality structure also has common antecedents in the family backgrounds from which such individuals emerge.

Just as the profiles of the academic achiever, the creative person, and the leader differ somewhat in the proportion of various qualities, their home backgrounds also differ somewhat in the emphasis on various values. Moreover, there are certain factors relating both to the family structure and to the family's position within the social structure that have some bearing on the child's

the antecedents
of productivity

CHAPTER SIX

development. Nevertheless, it appears that the fundamental family relationships in the backgrounds of all productive persons share certain qualities which we might view as the source of academic achievement, creativity, and leadership.

the family structure

From the vast amount of literature on the nuclear family, defined as a household consisting of a father and mother and their offspring, three factors have emerged that seem to have some influence on the potential productivity of the family members. One is the size of the family, another is the life style and value system of the cultural or socioeconomic group within which it functions, and a third is the birth order, or ordinal position, of the child. None of these factors can be considered an absolute condition. Highly productive persons have emerged from every type of family background, and from families in every walk of life.[1] From the standpoint of statistical averages, however, the child from a small family (one with no more than three children), whose parents are at a higher educational and income level, and who is an only child or the first-born evidently has certain inherent advantages.

FAMILY SIZE

There have been numerous studies showing that large families labor under certain disadvantages with respect to the achievement motivation of their members (Rosen, 1963; Bachman, 1970; Clausen, 1966; Ackerman, 1958). The number of children in the home affects the quality and quantity of nurturance available to each; the larger the family, the smaller the individual child's share of parental attention. In a large family there is relatively greater need for interdependence, cooperation, and consensus than in the smaller family; as a result, most large families must place more emphasis on responsibility, conformity, and obedience than on individual achievement and self-expression.[2] There is less opportunity for the recognition of individual members, for

1 Stalnaker, 1961, p. 519; Moore, 1962, p. 179   2 Rosen, 1963, esp. pp. 173–177

development of individual skills, or for intensive interaction between parents and individual children. There is also more strain on economic resources.

In a large family the discipline—particularly that of the father—tends to be authoritarian, and the methods of discipline are frequently power-assertive. Consequently the children tend to be dependent on adult authority, and despite the fact that they are often made responsible for caretaking and other duties, these responsibilities are not necessarily associated with higher achievement motivation. In a large family there are increased opportunities for conflict, the formation of alignments, and scapegoating.

Behavior problems seem to occur more frequently in very large as opposed to smaller families. Clausen (1966), in reviewing some of the vast research in this area, cites studies of Hawkes, Burchinal, and Gardner (1958) showing that among children with five or more siblings there is more frequent evidence of daydreaming, inferiority feelings, and social adjustment problems than among children from smaller families. In French child guidance clinics there is an overrepresentation of children who have five or more siblings.[3] The Gluecks (1962) found that delinquency is more of a problem in larger families, even when socioeconomic level is held constant.[4]

Rosen contrasts numerous advantages generally available in the children in a smaller family group. Because there is more adult time, energy, and affection available for each child, individual physical and psychological needs can be met more easily. There is less need for rigid and authoritarian discipline structures and more use of a reasoned, democratic approach to family problems. There are more opportunities for maximum communication among the members of the small family. Because fewer persons are involved, there is less likelihood of family alignments, less need for the displacement of anxiety and hostility from one member onto another, and consequently less opportunity for the creation of scapegoats. Discipline can be based on the use of "conditional love and the manipulation of guilt feelings," rather than on force.[5]

3 See Clausen, 1966, p. 14   5 Rosen, 1963, p. 174
4 Glueck and Glueck, 1962, pp. 116ff

The small middle-class family in particular tends to emphasize achievement, standards of excellence, and upward mobility, and children are typically reinforced for school performance. Parent-child interaction and mutual enjoyment of shared activities and outings are economically more feasible for a smaller family unit. For the same reason, there are more opportunities for privacy, as well as for the recognition of individual virtuoso performances of all members.

As a group, the parents of smaller families have a higher level of formal education, a higher per-person income, and greater emotional stability than those of larger families. Usually there is less marital conflict, and hence less tension in the home. The parents are often upward-mobile and future-oriented, and the limitation of their family size is part of their life plan. The father's vocational or career pursuits, moreover, probably contribute to his ego security, so that in his family relations he tends to be more accepting, nurturant, and ego rewarding than the father of the larger family. His educational and cultural interests are customarily more extensive and he can share these interests with his children. In a smaller family, therefore, there are more opportunities for modeling and identification with the parents than in the larger family.

There is more or less general agreement on the personality traits that distinguish children from small families. Douvan and Adelson characterize the small-family child as having greater ego strength and development and a higher activity level than the member of a large family. He is more oriented to the future and has a longer time perspective; he has more poise and self-confidence and more autonomous internal control, is less inclined to yield to peer pressure, and is more concerned with educational plans and goals.[6]

Douvan and Adelson stress the fact that these personality attributes of a small-family child are generally unrelated to socioeconomic level. They found in their own study that even "within each of the two major social strata, family size maintains its effect on activity and other ego variables."[7] Clausen also cites research indicating that children from small families tend to have

6 Douvan and Adelson, 1966, pp. 273–274   7 Douvan and Adelson, 1966, p. 273

higher IQ scores than those from large families irrespective of socioeconomic group.[8]

SOCIOECONOMIC LEVEL

Although there have been a great many studies on the various effects of socioeconomic level as a factor in achievement, the continual shifts in the dividing lines and the relative status of various groups makes it difficult to generalize from any specific findings. In many communities, for example, the former working class is now the middle class, and large segments of the middle class have changed their value structure. Interpretation of some of the current research, however, requires an understanding of at least the general framework, and for this purpose the Hollingshead-Redlich description of class levels is probably still the most useful, despite the fact that it is fifteen years old.[9] Although the characteristic family patterns may no longer apply in the same group, they nevertheless exist as patterns.

According to McKinley (1964), socioeconomic distinctions carry a connotation of social status—"the position one occupies in the reward system of a society."[10] Thus, although the socioeconomic classification of a family is usually based directly on the father's occupation and educational level, indirectly it is related to his achievement mastery. Specifically, an individual —regardless of his position in the social spectrum—is rewarded according to his degree of mastery over the physical and sociological forces in the environment. A person who demonstrates such mastery is one who gives of himself and his talents and in turn receives reward for his efforts. Emphasis on work is a deeply imbedded value in our society.

Among genuinely disadvantaged families, (class V, or the lower class, on Hollingshead's scale) the manifestations of extreme social and psychological deprivation are apparent in both children and adults. Such families are characterized by lack of authority, indecisiveness, and disorganization. The parents are often absent, apathetic, or rejecting and are usually unable to respond to the challenges and demands of their family roles; hence

8 Clausen, 1966, p. 12

9 Hollingshead and Redlich, 1958, pp. 69–136

10 McKinley, 1964, p. 241

they are also poor models and are incapable of conveying "the instrumental techniques required for academic and vocational achievement." Lacking belief in their ability to guide and change their children's lives, they permit and encourage them to obtain advice and assistance from peers. Even when there is not outright rejection, there are "few limits, limited respect, and few favorable models, particularly for boys."[11] There is a high rate of psychosis and generally poor mental health. Desertion and family disruption are common.

It is difficult to make a fair appraisal of the "working-class" family. According to Hollingshead's description of 1958, about one-third of the family heads in this class (35 percent) are skilled and somewhat over half (about 52 percent) are semiskilled workers, with the balance employed in clerical and sales jobs. Members of these families live for the most part in two- or three-family homes, and the median formal education of the parents is about ten years. The children attend public school for about eleven years.[12] As a group, working-class families tend to place less value on the development of the individual child than middle- and upper-class families. There is more emphasis on immediate and short-term goals than on long-term goals. There are nearly always some material and emotional lacks, and the greater pressure on the child to earn his own living may lessen the interest in his further education.

The significance given to work, mastery, and accomplishment as factors in socioeconomic status is borne out by the importance of the father's role in the family. It is he who almost entirely determines the family's class membership. The father's role is therefore the most direct link between what is to the family either a rewarding or a depriving economic situation and the quality of interpersonal relations within the family. The gratification (or frustration) the father receives from his occupation becomes an important variable in the reward structure within the family. At all socioeconomic levels it is the father who determines the quality of the interpersonal relations within the family, not only because of his status, but also because his personal characteristics are associated with mastery of the external environment.[13]

182

11   National Institute of Child Health, 1968, pp. 30–31

12   Hollingshead and Redlich, 1958, pp. 105ff

13   McKinley, 1964, pp. 241–242; Clausen, 1966, p. 34

The father of the working-class family differs from the middle- and upper-class father in that his occupation usually provides him with relatively little recognition and ego enhancement. Because of his limited education, he works at a job which gives him little or no opportunity for self-expression, and he tends to displace his frustrations through authoritarian behavior with his family, particularly his sons. Under these circumstances his disciplinary techniques are punitive, power assertive, and tinged with aggressiveness and an almost military emphasis on discipline and obedience.

The working-class mother's relationship with her children is somewhat similar to the father's. She is generally more rigid, more coercive, and less warm than the middle- or upper-class mother, although Waters and Crandall (1967) indicate that coerciveness is decreasing.[14] Because her opportunities for informal education are severely curtailed by her role in the home, her child-rearing methods are relatively unsophisticated. Thus she is often inept at maintaining a good balance between structure and permissiveness and at helping her children develop independence. In a word, she has fewer personal resources with which to carry out her difficult job. To add to her problems, her family is likely to be larger than the middle-class family, and the drains on her physical and emotional resources are consequently much greater.

In middle- and upper-class families (which for our purposes can include Hollingshead's first three categories) there is a much higher level of education, occupational status, and material resources, and a correspondingly greater degree of emotional security. Fathers can relate more comfortably to their children and provide better models for both their sons and their daughters. Middle-class mothers are significantly more given to using direction, helping, structuring, teaching, playing interactively, lending cooperation, and observing attentively than lower-class mothers. Both parents are also much more concerned with their childrens' achievement and development.[15]

One aspect of family influence which seems to be somewhat related to socioeconomic level is the mother's employment out-

14 Waters and Crandall, 1967, p. 314   15 Walters, Connor, and Zunich, 1967, pp. 300–303

side of the home. During the past three decades there has been a steady increase in maternal employment, and as professional opportunities for women continue to expand, their outside employment can be expected to increase. At this point 40 percent of all women are gainfully employed, and 12 million of these women are working mothers.

Although considerable research has dealt with the possible influences of the mother's employment on her family, this research has certain limitations. Some investigations have relied, for example, on questionnaires administered to children, who are unlikely to be objective when asked how they feel about their mother's working. Other studies seem to be oriented to a negative approach; they have merely demonstrated that the mothers' employment does not conspicuously add to the child's adjustment problems. A more fundamental consideration is the effect of the mother's absence on the actual productivity of her children.

Complex research problems surround the question of maternal employment and its possible effect on the child's competence and social responsibility. Among the numerous variables which may influence the child are the size and the socioeconomic level of the family. Other variables, and certain aspects of the mother's role and personality, are also involved: her level of education and professional training, her motives for seeking employment, the presence or absence of actual financial need, her own self-esteem, the relative effects of part-time versus full-time employment, the age of the children, and the amount of time and energy she allots to them (whether or not employed). Further questions concern the differential effects of the mother's employment on children of one sex or the other and whether she is sufficiently competent to meet the combined demands of her dual role. Of possible additional significance are the stability of the father's employment and income and his own self-esteem. A brief report of four different studies gives some indication of the complexity of the research findings on a few of these variables.

A study by Langner and Michael (1963) indicates that the influence of a mother's employment on her children varies with the family's socioeconomic position.[16] At all socioeconomic

16 Langner and Michael, 1963, pp. 182–186, 188

levels, the children's mental health tends to be poorer in homes in which the mother works full time than when she is not employed at all. In the low and high socioeconomic groups the children enjoyed better mental health when the mother was employed part-time than when she was either not employed or worked full time; however, the mothers in the high socioeconomic group had the best mental health when they were not employed. In middle-class families the children enjoyed better mental health when the mother was not employed, but the middle-class mother herself enjoyed better mental health when she worked part time than when she was employed either full time or not at all.

Douvan and Adelson (1966) reported that in the low socioeconomic group—where the mother often works full time as a matter of necessity—low productivity in adolescents was accompanied by lower general social and extracurricular activity and dependent dating relationships; there was also a marked dependence in girls and low academic achievement in boys.[17] The mother's full-time employment seems to have more effect on the girl than on the boy; however, at this socioeconomic level parents are also less empathic with their sons. Full- or part-time employment of middle-class mothers and part-time employment of lower-class mothers seemed to have no serious detrimental effects on their daughters' development; in some cases, in fact, they offered a model of competence, activity, and conscientiousness to their daughters. Boys in middle-class families are also more frequently upward-mobile when the mother is employed part-time than when she is not employed at all.

Moore and Holtzman (1965) report no difference between adolescent boys and girls as to attitude toward school or academic competence and no more problems and tensions in families where mothers were employed than in those where the mother was not employed.[18] They did find, however, that children showed greater feelings of inadequacy in low-income homes, regardless of whether the mother was employed or not.

In a study of upper elementary school children Coopersmith (1967) found that high self-esteem was related to the length of the mother's employment, with higher self-esteem more frequent

17 Douvan and Adelson, 1966, pp. 291–309   18 Moore and Holtzman, 1965, pp. 268–270

when the mother had been employed for more than a year.[19] High self-esteem in children is related to high self-esteem in parents at all socioeconomic levels, but it is more frequent in higher-income groups. Coopersmith also found that the fathers of those children with low self-esteem often had unstable jobs or were unemployed for extended periods of time.

These studies—three of which deal with problems of mental health and one specifically with self-esteem—point not so much to the effects of the mother's employment as such as to the economic reasons for her employment, with particular reference to the level of competence of the father.

BIRTH ORDER

It appears that ordinal position, or birth order, may also be an influential factor in aiding or impeding the development of productivity (Altus, 1966; Clausen, 1966; Sampson, 1965). It was noted a century ago that a disproportionate number of outstanding people are first-born children. It is probably the first-born child's early environment which provides the greatest opportunities for his future growth and development; he generally receives more undiluted parental love, concern, and guidance (as well as subtle pressure and "achievement training") than do subsequent siblings. Moreover, he receives this intense emotional investment from his parents at the age at which he is most impressionable. Even though he may subsequently be dethroned by the arrival of another child, his position in the family remains a special one.

The first-born's self-esteem, his sense of identity, and his coping skills are probably all enhanced by his early experiences. He does not necessarily have an advantage in IQ, but he tends to develop good cognitive skills (particularly verbal skills), and both his achievement motivation and his actual achievement are often high. Through characteristic persistence and determination, he performs at a high level not only throughout school and college, but often in graduate school. He is disproportionately represented in such publications as *Who's Who* and *American Men of Science*,

 19 Coopersmith, 1967, pp. 87-95

as well as in populations of exceptionally bright persons; for example, 60 percent of the National Merit Scholarship winners in 1964 were first-born children.[20] A recent restandardization of the Strong Vocational Interest Blank reveals that an astonishingly high proportion (94 percent) of our astronauts are first-born children, and that first-born children are highly represented in the more demanding professions.[21] The situations of the only child and the first-born child are similar; the latter is, in effect, an only child during the critical early years of life, especially when there is a relatively wide age gap between him and the second-born. The only child resembles the first-born in such characteristics as cognitive skill and achievement motivation and is often grouped with the first-born in research studies, although his social position is somewhat different in that he lacks the stimulus provided by siblings.[22]

The youngest child in the family may have other assets, including somewhat better social skills than the first-born. He is likely to be more peer-oriented, empathic, and popular than his older sibling, who has been described as somewhat anxious and introverted, not a particularly good mixer, and somewhat given to overaffiliating, especially in anxiety-arousing, ambiguous social situations.[23] Part of the first child's lack of ease in social situations may result from his past experiences with parents who felt somewhat insecure in their first child-rearing attempts, as well as from the fact that initially he had no siblings with whom he could interact socially.

Family size is also a factor in the effects of ordinal position, since there are more middle children in larger families. It is the middle child who may have the greatest number of problems. As McGurk and Lewis (1972) point out, the second-born child receives less attention in early infancy than either of his siblings and consequently may fail to develop as much independence as they do in later childhood.[24] This tendency is particularly apparent when there is little age difference between the middle child and the next oldest sibling.[25] The age-spacing between births in a family is another important factor which appears to be attracting increasing attention among researchers.

20 Altus, 1966, p. 45

21 D. Campbell, 1971, pp. 639–640

22 See Lavin, 1965, p. 146

23 Schachter, 1959; Clausen, 1966, p. 22

24 McGurk and Lewis, 1972, p. 366

25 See Elliott and Elliott, 1970, pp. 369–370

The voluminous literature shows that birth order is interrelated with both family size and socioeconomic level. Moreover, it interacts in complex ways with the sex of the siblings. There are special problems in the three-child family, the two-child family, and the large family. Moreover, the personalities of the parents, their ages, and their own backgrounds are also possible factors.

the family and personality formation

It is virtually impossible to generalize concerning the implications of this complex picture for the development of the productive personality. Notwithstanding the possible influence of any or all sociological factors that affect the family structure, the intangible affective qualities within the home, and particularly those of the individual parent-child relationship, are, in the last analysis, the most potent influence on the development of a productive individual. These essential qualities can transcend the limitations of social class, material possessions, ethnic status, family size, or disadvantageous position in the order of siblings. Studies in Great Britain by Himmelweit and Sealy (1966) show, for example, that lower-class pupils who succeed in maintaining a high level of school achievement and are able to remain in school (in itself an achievement in the rigidly selective British educational system), have generally received a "much higher level of parental support" than their equally bright peers who drop out of school.[26]

Perhaps we will gain more enlightenment from exploring the retrospective researches dealing specifically with the backgrounds of productive individuals. Before beginning this exploration, however, it is important to note that certain shortcomings and risks are to some extent inherent in all retrospective *post hoc* studies of the antecedents of behavior, particularly when the antecedents being reported have occurred several years before a given investigation takes place. These risks are generally recognized and need only be summarized briefly here.

In retrospective studies researchers must content themselves with self-reports elicited for the most part by interview,

26 See Clausen, 1968, p. 165

questionnaires, or checklists which are often group-administered (if the population is large) and rely heavily on the perceptions and the memory of the respondents. As Bronfenbrenner has cautioned us, the subjective information given in such reports may be deficient in two respects. Adolescents, for example, may lack really complete or accurate knowledge about their parents, and/or their responses may willfully or unintentionally be distorted. Moreover, teachers who are asked to assist in evaluating behaviors of students may also unwittingly flavor their responses with personal bias.[27] In cases where self-reports of subjects can be supplemented by reports of at least one parent (in the Coopersmith study of self-esteem, for example), the data are probably more reliable. Other studies (that of Bing, for example) have utilized in the research design special mother-child or parent-child interaction situations in an attempt to penetrate the workings of the child's family background. These experimental situations, however, may not be exactly reproducing the early childhood experiences or parental attitudes and practices of an earlier stage in the parent-child relationship. It has been pointed out, moreover, that parental attitudes can change between one period of childhood and another. It is probably true, as stressed by Zaleznik et al. (1970), that adult memories of "important" childhood experiences are fairly accurate. It is, however, the adult's perceptions and memories of his actual feelings about a long-past event which are important, rather than the original episode itself.[28]

Coopersmith (1967) warns that we may not be able to determine whether the conditions we find are "antecedents, consequences, or correlates."[29] It is also possible that statistical correlates may reflect not the parent's influence on a child, but that of some uncontrolled factor or factors such as ordinal position or ethnic background. Moreover, the direction of causality may even be reversed; the child's past behavior may have actually influenced the parent's treatment of him.[30]

On the whole, we can agree with Yarrow, Campbell, and Burton (1968) that child-rearing research is a curious combination of loose methodology that is tightly interwoven with provocative hypotheses of development processes and relationships and that

---

27 Bronfenbrenner, 1961, p. 245

28 See Zaleznik, Dalton, and Barnes, 1970, p. 213

29 Coopersmith, 1967, p. 17

30 Bronfenbrenner, 1961, p. 246

there has been too much reliance on data "so open to measurement error, and so vulnerable in interpretation as cause-effect evidence" that it is of questionable usefulness.[31] Although certain of these limitations and weaknesses will inevitably be present in some of the child-rearing research, the findings are sufficiently valuable to our study of the productive person to warrant a brief review.

Two well-conducted retrospective studies of productive individuals and their antecedents have dealt primarily with general mental health and related characteristics, rather than with productivity itself. One of these is Barron's study of personal soundness in advanced doctoral candidates (for the most part, in the sciences) at the Institute of Personality Assessment and Research at Berkeley. Another is Westley and Epstein's investigation of the mental health of first-year students at McGill University. While neither of these studies was specifically concerned with the productivity-related areas of academic achievement, creativity, and leadership, both dealt in detail with the family backgrounds of their subjects. Both found significant strengths or weaknesses in past family life to be associated with the presence or absence of the "personal soundness" or "mental health" of the persons they were studying: the negative findings are almost as revealing as the positive. Both, moreover, are concerned with the attributes of good personality functioning.

Two other studies of great importance to our discussion deal not with productivity as such, but with one of its most essential aspects—self-esteem. The investigations of Rosenberg and Coopersmith reveal the enormous importance of the family environment in determining the quality of the child's future self-image and hence his capacity for productivity as an adult.

EMOTIONAL STABILITY

In the Barron (1968) study eighty male graduate students, most in their final year of doctorate study in one of the sciences, were evaluated on personal soundness as judged by faculty members of their respective departments and by staff members of the Institute

31 Yarrow, Campbell, and Burton, 1968,
        p. 152

of Personality Assessment and Research.[32] The population being tested was already a highly select one; it was felt that one way of being personally sound was to be a sound scientist or scholar. Personal soundness was defined as integrity, stability, and coherence of the individual personality and its functioning, as well as the soundness, balance, and degree of maturity which the individual showed in his relationship with others. It is apparent that these attributes resemble certain aspects of identity, socially responsible behavior, and coping characteristics, as discussed in previous chapters. The family backgrounds of each of the subjects were ascertained through information given on a biographical data sheet and life-data questionnaire as well as a series of four interviews with psychoanalysts and staff members.

One of the chief differences between the high and low subjects on the personal-soundness scale was the integrity, stability, and harmony of the home. Subjects in the high group reported that both of their parents had been continuously present during most of their childhood, that they had enjoyed a certain degree of economic security, and that they had lived long periods in the same house in a stable community. Parents and children alike had had excellent physical health. The homes of the lows tended to be broken by death, divorce, frequent illnesses, long father absences, and various other problems. One of the greatest percentage differences between the backgrounds of the two groups was the absence of marked family friction in the homes of the highs.

A second marked difference was the image of the father in the high group as a respected and successful man. The highs almost always spoke of their fathers as individuals whom they admired and sought to emulate and who were much respected in the community; in other words, the highs as children had had a good male model with whom to identify. A number of the lows either did not know their fathers or knew them essentially as failures.

The third most frequent differentiating variable was affection and attention from the mother. Many of the high subjects had been closely controlled at home, but the general picture was that the mother had been "loving without being seductive, and solicitous without being demanding and protective, whereas the low subjects reported mothers who were both seductive and demanding. Both high and low subjects had been influenced by the mother's personality. As boys, the highs had generally made a fairly clear break from the mother and the home circle soon after graduation from high school, but the lows tended to remain mother-dependent. In other words, the mothers of the highs had permitted their sons to gain independence and autonomy; those of the lows had dominated their sons.

A fourth factor was the presence of other siblings and the positive relationships with them in the home. The highs, as a rule, had come from larger families and had maintained more friendly relationships with their brothers and sisters than had the lows. Like the presence of a successful father, siblings in childhood served as models for later adult experience and roles.

Another valuable piece of research, Westley and Epstein's sociopsychiatric study of the mental health of first-year students at McGill University, probes the family backgrounds of emotionally healthy and unhealthy persons. The findings and its conclusions offer helpful insights with respect to productivity, although productivity as such is not mentioned. The study revealed striking differences between the families of emotionally healthy and emotionally disturbed students. The most important variable relating to the child's emotional health was found to have been the emotional rapport between his parents. When their relationship was warm and respecting, and the wife and husband both felt loved, admired, and encouraged to act in ways that they themselves admired, the children themselves were healthy and happy:[33]

> Couples who were emotionally close, meeting each other's needs and encouraging positive self-images in each other, became good parents.

It was also found that a balance of sharing and individual responsibility was most likely to lead to mature and affectionate husband-wife relationships and to emotional health in their children. Without sharing and differentiation of household and

33   Westley and Epstein, 1969, p. 158

family responsibilities, the couple's relationship tended to be remote, formal, and weak and to resemble a relationship between siblings rather than adults.[34] The full acceptance by both parents of their respective roles seemed to assure emotional health in the children.

Perhaps the most useful contribution for the purposes of this discussion was the classification of the families. Four types of families were identified as father-dominant, father-led, equalitarian, and mother-dominant. Both father-led and equalitarian types of families were essentially democratic in structure, although in the father-led family, the father had the final word.

The second family type, the father-led family, was represented by the largest proportion of emotionally healthy subjects who were described as assertive and stable, and probably good leaders. Somewhat less healthy were the offspring of the father-dominant family, who tended to be somewhat timid, withdrawn, submissive, and lacking in self-confidence, but also compulsive, self-disciplined, and industrious. Subjects from equalitarian families were described as quiet, friendly, industrious, and probably good followers and members. The poorest emotional health was found in the subjects who had come from mother-dominant homes; they were found to be not only timid and withdrawn, but also lacking in self-discipline and industry and showing serious psychopathologic symptoms. The mother-dominant families seemed to be characterized by extremely unhappy mothers and cold, impersonal family relationships.[35]

In the McGill study the father was revealed as the most important family member with respect to the solution of problems, but the key person in the development of the child's autonomy and independence seemed to be the mother. It is the mother, responsible for the day-to-day decisions of famioy life, who has the power either to encourage or to discourage decision making (an essential aspect of coping) in her children. Another important finding of the McGill study concerned the influence of parents on the formation of sex identity, as discussed in Chapter Three.

34 Westley and Epstein, 1969, pp. 160–161   35 Westley and Epstein, 1969, p. 162

SELF-ESTEEM

Rosenberg (1965) has contributed a valuable sociological study on the self-attitudes (self-esteem) of 5024 high school juniors and seniors from ten randomly selected New York State high schools; the sample represented all social classes, races, religious groups, rural and urban communities, and nationalities.[36] (Parochial and private schools were not represented.) On the same day the students from the entire group were given a ten-item Guttman scale, consisting of statements dealing with favorable or unfavorable attitudes toward the self; this was filled out anonymously in a single class period. The purpose of the scale was to rank the subjects on a single "unidimensional" continuum from very high to very low self-esteem, according to their level of agreement or disagreement with the scale items. A great deal of other information was also secured about each respondent, including his socioeconomic and cultural background, group memberships, neighborhood environment, high school activities, occupational aspirations, and values.

Analysis of the vast amount of data yielded information about self-esteem as influenced by the factors of socioeconomic level, religious affiliation, race, and nationality groups. For example, boys from middle- and upper-class homes reported closer relationships with their fathers than those from lower-class homes, and differential father-son relationships were found importantly involved in the general self-esteem advantage of upper-class over lower-class boys.[37] Upper-class children in general tended to have somewhat higher self-esteem than lower-class children, although lower self-esteem found to be especially characteristic of children whose fathers were in authoritarian occupations (such as the police or the military).

Even more important however, were the findings relating to family influences on self-esteem, including the effect of divorce and subsequent remarriage on the emotional life of the children involved.[38] It was found that divorce had greater impact on the child's self-esteem in Catholic and Jewish families than in Protestant families, that the effect was more severe when the mother was

36   Rosenberg, 1965, pp. 16ff

37   Rosenberg, 1965, pp. 35, 45

38   Rosenberg, 1965, pp. 107–110, 113ff

young at the time of separation than when she was older, and that when or if she remarried, the older children of the first marriage were more likely to suffer in self-esteem than if she did not remarry. The influences of family size and birth order were studied. The only child, especially a boy from a Jewish home, was typically higher in self-esteem than a child with siblings. The younger boy who arrived late in a family of older sisters was also likely to be high in self-esteem, as was the first girl in a family of boys.

Rosenberg concluded that parental interest in the child is the critical factor in the formation of his self-image. Whether the child belongs to the upper, middle, or lower economic group; whether he is a Protestant, a Catholic, or a Jew; whether he is male or female; or whether he comes from a large or medium-sized city or a small town, the results are essentially the same. If his parents maintain an attitude of indifference to him, this child will have a low level of self-regard.[39]

Rosenberg's data suggest, in fact, that an extreme level of parental indifference is more damaging to a child's personality development than physical punishment or even outright rejection. The parents' lack of interest in such minor matters as a child's mealtime conversation, his report card, or his friends indicates to him their basic lack of love and respect; such parents show little consideration for their child and treat him as a nonentity, with irritation, impatience, and anger. Rosenberg is not alone in maintaining that:[40]

> The feeling that one is important to a significant other is probably essential to the development of a feeling of self-worth.

Coopersmith's research centered on normal fifth- and sixth-grade boys from white middle-class neighborhoods in central Connecticut. From an original sample of 1748 students, who were given a fifty-item Self-Esteem Inventory and rated by this on a fourteen-item behavior-rating form, various types and levels of self-esteem were ascertained, and the sample narrowed to eighty-five students (and their mothers), representing five different levels of self-esteem ranging from low to high. These students were then clinically evaluated by standard intelligence, personality, and

---

39 Rosenberg, 1965, pp. 144–145   40 Rosenberg, 1965, p. 146

projective tests and by individual interviews. Their mothers completed an eighty-item questionnaire on parental attitudes and child-rearing practices and submitted to intensive individual clinical interviews. The children also responded to a questionnaire eliciting their perceptions of parental attitudes and practices; this was supplemented by their responses on the Thematic Apperception Test.

The findings, which are reported in book form, are too extensive to detail here, but some are especially noteworthy. These relate to the self-esteem of the mother, the child's perception of his parents' values, the stability of the home, the effectiveness of the father, certain personality attributes of the mother, and family decision-making practices.[41] It was found that mothers of children with high self-esteem tended to have high self-esteem themselves. Conversely, almost two-thirds of the mothers of low self-esteem children were rated below average in poise and assurance and were also found to be somewhat emotionally unstable. Low self-esteem children indicated much more often than medium or high self-esteem children that their parents valued accommodating behaviors—obedience, helpfulness, adjustment to others, kindness, good grooming, and cordial relationships with one's peers. High and medium self-esteem children felt their parents valued achievement. Reports of previous marriages were more frequent in the low self-esteem group. Low self-esteem families were also marked by much more tension and conflict between the parents than high self-esteem families.

The fathers were not interviewed, but the mothers' responses revealed that in high and medium self-esteem families the mothers were almost invariably satisfied with the father's performance in his child-rearing role, whereas about one-fourth of the low self-esteem families expressed dissatisfaction with the father's role. Fathers of the high self-esteem group were much more likely to enjoy the confidence of their sons than those in other groups, which suggests that active support from fathers is an important factor in the enhancement of a child's self-concept. The findings indicate that the mothers of high self-esteem boys

41 Coopersmith, 1967, pp. 97–100, 109–114

deal with issues directly, realistically, and effectively.[42] In other words, they are coping individuals.

A considerable difference was found between the high and low groups with regard to family decision making. In high self-esteem families major decisions were usually made by either one parent or the other (usually the father), suggesting that there was a clear designation of who is to assume leadership in matters of importance to the family. In day-to-day decisions, however, the tendency in high self-esteem families was toward sharing of the decision making between parents.[43]

All four of these studies point to the importance of a stable home life, with a father who enjoys the admiration, affection, respect, and confidence of his wife and children and a mother who is affectionate and supportive and permits a reasonable degree of independence in her children. Rosenberg emphasizes the great importance of constant parental interest in the child and all his concerns for building his self-esteem; he also found that self-esteem was independent of social class, ethnic, or religious factors. Coopersmith summarizes his study by stating that the antecedents of a child's high self-esteem can be given in terms of three indispensable parental attitudes: acceptance, clearly delineated and enforced limits, and respect and latitude for the individual within those limits. Moreover, he stresses that parents of children with high self-esteem have high self-esteem and values themselves and are concerned, attentive, and accepting in their relationship to their children.[44]

The findings of a number of studies suggest that:[45]

Above a certain minimum level of status and subsistence, occupation, education, and finances may play a lesser role than is generally assumed.

Beyond this level it appears that the individual family situation plays a more significant role in the development of self-esteem than does the broader social context.[46] In a study of tenth-grade boys Bachman (1970) reports a fairly strong correlation between family relations and self-esteem. As in the Rosenberg study,

42 Coopersmith, 1967, p. 117

43 Coopersmith, 1967, pp. 113–114

44 Coopersmith, 1967, p. 236

45 National Institute on Child Health, 1968, p. 31

46 Coopersmith, 1967, pp. 82–83

Jewish boys were above average in this respect, and there were positive, but rather weak associations between self-esteem and socioeconomic level, but the family relations measure was found to be consistently the strongest predictor of the various dimensions studied.[47]

A study by Epstein and Komorita (1971) of internal-external control in 136 lower-class black children of elementary school age suggests that even in a disadvantaged minority group, self-esteem may at least partly be established within the family.[48] It was found that although failure experiences were attributed to external causes (luck, chance, or fate), high self-esteem subjects were more "internal" than low or moderate-esteem subjects, suggesting that even in a social outgroup a child's sense of powerlessness "may be cushioned by a foundation of intrinsic self-esteem which is presumably established in the home."

Miller (1971) studied 203 eighth-grade children and their mothers in a wide range of educational, social, and ethnic backgrounds.[49] He found that even in the inner-city homes, where the mother was considered to be head of the household and assumed the role of both disciplinarian and nurturant parent, where "maternal empathy, genuineness, and positive regard" were high, the child's self-esteem was also high, and where the parent was more judgmental and less descriptive of the child's behavior, the child's self-esteem was lower.

Peck (1958) reports the results of a careful longitudinal study of thirty-four children between the ages of ten to eighteen whose families represented a fairly even cross section of social classes.[50] Annual interviews, as well as sociometric, projective, and intelligence tests and self-rating questionnaires, identified four clusters of traits in family life: consistency, democracy (versus autocracy), mutual trust and approval, and severity (versus leniency). Ego strength in children (self-esteem) was found highly correlated ($r = .74$) with a trusting family life; it was also found correlated with consistency in family life ($r = .56$). Ego strength was thus shown to be associated with a family life characterized by both stable consistency and warm, mutual trust and approval

47 Bachman, 1970, p. 135

48 Epstein and Komorita, 1971, p. 7

49 T. Miller, 1971, pp. 241–242

50 Peck, 1963, pp. 137–140

between the parents and between parents and child. Mote (1966), who explored the relationships between home environment and children's self-concepts as well as other factors, found a large number of correlations, significant at the .05 level or better, linking a supportive home atmosphere with positive child attitudes, high ability, achievement, and creativity.[51]

Studies by Rotter (1971) on interpersonal trust seem to give further validation to the influence of families, particularly fathers, on self-esteem.[52] Fathers of highly trusting sons have been found significantly higher in trust than the fathers of less trusting sons. Rotter also points out the special importance of the father as interpreting "the trustworthiness of outside agents" to the family, and especially to the son, who must also eventually make his way in the world (see Chapter Three).

In a study of forty preschool children and their mothers Schwartz (1966) found additional evidence that the antecedents of a child's high self-concept are to be found in the family.[53] She noted certain distinguishing differences between the high and low self-concept groups. In the former group there were more girls than boys, fewer only children, and more children who were members of four-person families. Children of the high group achieved a better rating on the ego variables of autonomy and regulation and control of drives. The mothers of the high group tended to be exclusively homemakers, to be slightly younger than the median age, and to be much more active in their religious observances than those of the low self-concept group. Moreover, their attitudes revealed not only their perception of the child as an individual in his own right, but also their own high self-esteem and their acceptance, warmth, and intensity of interaction with their child. There was other evidence of maternal satisfaction and adequate emotional climate. Schwartz concluded that individual differences in basic personality attributes and self-concepts are fairly well established by the age of five and that a key factor in the development of the self-concept is the nature of the parent-child interaction, with both parents and child as contributing parties.

51 Mote, 1966 (1967A), p. 3319

52 Rotter, 1971, p. 449

53 Schwartz, 1966 (1967A), pp. 2898–2899

family backgrounds of productive persons
THE ACADEMIC ACHIEVER

Academic achievement and its accompanying skills follow the same laws of social learning discussed in Chapter Four. Empathic and nurturing parents who possess a high value structure will in all probability reward and reinforce academic achievement as part of their responsibility to their children. This relationship is particularly apparent from the many investigations of the family backgrounds of low achievers. It should be borne in mind, however, that these studies vary widely both in the measuring instruments used and in the criteria for determining the degree of achievement; hence the findings can be viewed only in terms of their over-all contrast to the findings on high achievers.

Kurtz and Swenson (1951) found that low achievers generally come from homes in which there is no exchange of affection, where the children are not anxious to please the parents, and the parents have low expectations for them.[54] Barrett (1957) noted that parents of low achievers tended to manifest a neutral or uninterested attitude toward education; moreover, they were overanxious, oversolicitous, and inconsistent in their attitudes toward their children.[55] Shaw (1961), in summarizing research of the 1950s, observed that the parents of underachievers tend to have less education themselves and a more neutral or negative attitude toward education for their children than parents of high achievers, and that the parent-child relationship is more distant in general.[56] Parents of underachievers are much less inclined to push their children toward high performance in school or other areas, and they tend to make their demands at a later age than parents of achievers. Shaw also noted that broken homes, working mothers, and other family disruptions were much more frequent in the backgrounds of underachievers, and also that underachievers generally came from larger families. Sutherland (1952) found deficient and negative relationships between underachieving boys and their fathers. Underachievement was found by Roberts (1962) to be more common among youngest children in the family.[57]

54 Kurtz and Swenson, 1951, p. 478

55 Barrett, 1957, p. 194

56 Shaw, 1961, pp. 22–23

57 B. Sutherland, 1965b, p. 374; Roberts, 1962, pp. 175–183

Shaw and Dutton (1962) noted that parents of underachievers had significantly strong negative feelings toward their children; mothers in particular were fearful of their own hostile impulses, and in both parents there was a basic anxiety about sexual matters and a general suppression of their own sexuality. In both parents there was also a slight dissatisfaction with the parental role.[58] In another study Sutherland (1953) found among underachievers a tendency toward passivity, less ability to give direct expression to negative feelings, and a higher level of anxiety. She also found significantly more psychosomatic conditions (asthma and hay fever) in conjunction with unhappy home conditions.[59]

Numerous other characteristics of the low achiever's home background have been noted in other research, such as covert hostility between parents and children, parental indifference both to the child's success and to his failures, and parental punishment of failure without reward of accomplishment.[60] Certain parental attitudes or syndromes also appear to be typical in the homes of underachievers: "Don't spoil your child" (a mistaken notion that parental praise somehow weakens a child's motivation), the "double-bind" syndrome (issuance of contradictory directives to a child in various situations), the "yo-yo" syndrome (characteristic of an insecure parent's alternation of intense emotional need for the child followed by periods of neglect), the "too-much-alike" syndrome (the child's attempt to win parental approval by emulation of the parent); the "do-it-yourself" syndrome (parental refusal to provide help), and a number of other parental attitudes which serve to depress the child's self-concept and achievement motivation even in middle-class homes, where academic achievement is usually stressed.[61]

In general the low achiever's home seems to lack the basic affection and support which are indispensable to good mental health. This lack of nurturance may be further compounded by such factors as relatively low levels of education in parental models and a low value placed on formal education in general, by a poor relationship between fathers and sons, and by such special difficulties as emotional problems of parents, family disruptions, and the management of very large families. Yet the problems can

58 Shaw and Dutton, 1962, pp. 203–208   60 M. Gilmore, 1964, p. 31
59 B. Sutherland, 1965a, p. 388   61 Gilmore, 1967, pp. 46–69

also be relatively simple ones stemming from mistaken attitudes about the "proper" parent-child relationship rather than from any deep-seated problem in the parent's feeling for the child.

Pierce and Bowman (1960) present a very different picture of the home background of the high achiever.[62] They found that the parents of high achievers, as a group, had a higher level of education than those of low achievers and that fathers played a more significant role in their children's lives. Mothers of high-achieving boys were found to be less authoritarian and controlling than those of low achievers, and mothers in general reported their children as being more responsible, more independent, and more likely to be engaged in educationally related activities; they also held higher educational aspirations for them. High achievers were more often found to be first-born or only children than low achievers, and small families produced a larger percentage of high achievers than did large families. Roberts (1962) found that high achievers were more often the eldest child in the home and that their homes generally provided more opportunities for individual development in nonacademic areas than did the homes of low achievers.[63]

The influence of the parents' own values regarding formal education is indicated by Rosen's finding on achievement motivation in different ethnic groups. High achievement was more characteristic of Greeks, Jews, and white Protestants—cultures in which learning traditionally carries status—than it was of Italians, French Canadians, and Negroes.[64]

Student achievement has been found related to emotionally supportive home situations at all educational levels. Morrow and Wilson (1961) after studying two carefully matched groups of bright (IQs of 120 or above) achieving and underachieving high school boys, reported that the families of the high achievers engaged in more sharing of activities, ideas, and confidences than the families of the underachievers.[65] The parents of the high achievers were more "approving, trusting, affectionate, and encouraging (but not pressuring) with respect to achievement"; they were less restrictive and severe and their youngsters were more accepting of their standards. There was a marked difference be-

62 Pierce and Bowman, 1965, pp. 251–252   64 Rosen, 1965, p. 278

63 Roberts, 1962, pp. 175–183   65 Morrow and Wilson, 1967, pp. 252–254

tween the two groups (.01 level) with respect to the parents' simple "Golden Rule" observation of consideration and understanding. There was also a difference in the parents' interest in the child (.01 level) and in their outgoing, positive shaping of his development (.02 level). Factors such as overprotectiveness, high pressure, parental disharmony, and irregularity of home routine, which the investigators had expected to find in the homes of underachievers, were apparently not significant in this study; rather, the principal quality differentiating the two types of homes seemed to be general family morale.

It has also been found that achievement, and especially verbal ability, can be considerably enhanced in a child whose parents involve themselves continually in helping him to learn from an early age. It is often the mother who plays this role. Bing (1963) studied the effects of child-rearing practices, using a sample of sixty mothers of fifth-grade children who had similar IQs but differed in levels of verbal ability.[66] The mothers of the high-verbal group were found higher than the mothers of the low-verbal group in all categories of helping behavior: during the experimental mother-child interaction sessions, they exerted pressure for improvement and were quick to give help to their child. Moreover, the high-verbal children had received considerable verbal stimulation during infancy and early childhood. They had been allowed to take part in adult conversations and had received less punishment for poor speech and school work than the low-verbal children. Their parents had given them more storybooks; they had also been more restrictive and less permissive than the low-verbal mothers. Bing concludes from these findings:[67]

> The essential condition for the development of verbality is probably the close relationship with an adult, and verbal ability is fostered by a high degree of interaction between mother and child.

One interesting observation in this study was that the fathers' reading time was strongly associated with high verbal ability for girls, but not for boys. It is possible that fathers reinforce and praise girls for their reading, whereas they tend to praise

66 Bing, 1967, pp. 205–222   67 Bing, 1967, p. 220

and reward physical or athletic activities in the boys, or possibly skill in mathematics and science, instead of the quality of their reading. The characteristic peer-group involvement of boys at this age may also influence the amount of reading they do, since they are usually more encouraged by their mothers to be physically active, especially outdoors, than are girls.

Other studies demonstrate that active involvement of helping and affectionate mothers can enhance childhood verbal skills. Mothers of children with high reading-readiness scores appear to be more verbal and affectionately demonstrative in interacting with their children than the mothers of children in low reading ability.[68] Trotta (1967) found significant differences, in both practices and personalities, between mothers of slow and fast readers.[69] The former were much more likely to help their sons merely by supplying the answer, whereas the mothers of achievers more often went into an explanation of the material being read, thereby enhancing the child's comprehension. The underachievers' mothers also showed lack of confidence in their children, an inability to tolerate errors, and a domineering attitude; the achievers' mothers were more child-centered and concerned with developing the independence of their child.

There is other evidence that the mother may play a vital role in enhancing the development of achievement skills. A six-year longitudinal study by Feld (1967) demonstrated that mothers who stress achievement in their sons in early childhood later have adolescent sons who are low in test anxiety.[70] This study suggests that early maternal stress on accomplishment produces subsequent independence, whereas insistence merely on independence is more likely to produce dependent adolescents. Chance (1961) also found that independence training, if started too early, could interfere with adequate progress in reading and arithmetic.[71] Conceivably, a certain amount of early maternal overprotection and attendant pressure may act as a stimulant for higher achievement in later years.

Maternal helping behavior and stress on accomplishment is not synonymous with maternal control. One difference between achievers and underachievers is in their perceptions of their

68 See Bandura and Huston, 1967, p. 269   70 Feld, 1967, pp. 408–414
69 Trotta, 1967 (1967B), p. 1215   71 Chance, 1965, p. 45

mother's degree of control: underachievers view their mothers as more controlling than do high achievers. Davids and Hainsworth (1967), studying two groups of highly intelligent boys, found that low achievers see their mothers as more controlling than the mothers see themselves to be, and that the reverse is true of the high achievers.[72] The writers point to the implications of these findings for an understanding of the impulsivity and poor self-discipline of the low achiever. Although control itself is not defined, it is possible to infer that the mothers of the high achievers may have been controlling but also nurturant in handling their sons, while in the underachievement group there may have been control but little or no nurturance.

Another investigation of maternal control in combination with maternal nurturance indicates that the mother's influence on academic achievement may persist even to the college years. Heilbrun and Waters (1968) studied 102 college students to determine the relationship between underachievement and perceptions of maternal child-rearing practices.[73] It had previously been found that in adolescents perceived maternal control mediates reinforcement sensitivity, while perceived maternal nurturance influences anticipated reinforcement outcome. In college there are fewer extrinsic reinforcers than in earlier years. It was found that college students classified as "high control" (reinforcement-oriented) with backgrounds of low nurturance (producing anticipated negative reinforcement) were marked underachievers. Conversely, those who were both high-control and high-nurturance subjects (anticipating positive reinforcement) were found to be achievers. In other words, a college student who perceives his mother primarily as a controlling and nonnurturing individual is likely to be conditioned to anticipate negative reinforcement and to be less motivated toward genuine achievement than is a student with a background of maternal control combined with nurturance.

There is almost universal agreement that the father is also a vital influence not only on the sex identity of the child, but also on his achievement. A number of studies have dealt with the relationship between the father's absence from the family and the

72 Davids and Hainsworth, 1967, pp. 29–37   73 Heilbrun and Waters, 1968, p. 913

son's intellectual functioning (Biller, 1970; Biller and Borstelmann, 1967; Bronfenbrenner, 1967). In a study of forty-four white third-grade boys Blanchard and Biller (1971) demonstrated clearly how the presence or absence of fathers can influence the academic achievement of their sons.[74] The boys were divided into four groups: early father-absent (father absent before age five, usually due to divorce or separation), late father-absent (after age five), low father-absent (father available less than six hours per week), and high father-present (father available more than two hours per day). It was found that the academic performance of the high father-present group was markedly superior to that of the other three groups. The early father-absent boys were generally underachievers; the late father-absent and the low father-present boys usually functioned somewhat below grade level. In every comparison, the high father-present group performed consistently above grade level. The authors conclude that fathers who are regularly available to their sons can serve as models to them of perseverance and achievement motivation. A previous study by Biller (1968) also indicates that in families where the father can be present a reasonable part of the time, it is probably the quality of the father-son relationship rather than the quantity of the father-son interaction that is most influential in the boy's development.[75]

Perhaps the most dramatic of all the studies of the influence of the home on achievement is the famous Terman Study of the Gifted, with its numerous follow-up studies extending over a period of forty years.[76] A group of individuals, who in 1921 to 1922 all had IQ scores placing them in the top 1 percent of the population, diverged in actual achievement performance into markedly different levels of success. In 1960, at which time the original subjects were approximately fifty years of age, they were divided into two groups of the 100 most and the 100 least successful. The A group included fifty-nine members of the professions (members of university faculties, lawyers, physical or biological scientists, doctors, and an assortment of other professional roles), thirty top-level business, industrial, or financial executives, six high-ranking State Department officials, and four others in important administrative positions. The C group contained only five

74 Blanchard and Biller, 1971, pp. 302–305   76 Oden, 1968, esp. pp. 55–58

75 See Blanchard and Biller, 1971, p. 305

relatively unsuccessful professionals and thirteen others in positions of limited responsibility in business and semiprofessional occupations; the great majority of the Cs (62 percent) were in clerical, sales, and small-business occupations and the skilled trades and crafts, and the remainder were in semiskilled occupations. The median annual earned income (at 1959 levels) of those in the A group who were employed full-time was $23,900; for the Cs it was $7,178.

As noted in Chapter Two, the two groups (though equal in intelligence and cognitive skills near the beginning of their lives) were reliably different in self-esteem. In addition, there were marked differences in the home backgrounds of the two groups. The parents of the A group were better educated than those of the Cs (although the differences were significant only for the fathers); there was also an educational advantage favoring the grandparents of the As. Consequently, the A parents had a higher occupational status than did the C parents. The home libraries of the A families were more extensive; the fathers of the A group showed broader range of interests and had received more recognition and honors in the business and professional world than the C fathers. They also assumed more community responsibilities and were members of more organizations than the C fathers. Most important, the pressure for academic achievement was greater on the part of the parents of the A group, and their children were encouraged to "forge ahead in school, to earn better grades, and to go to college." Independence and initiative were encouraged; there was an expectation of a high level of accomplishment.[77] In other words, the level of family education, the stability of the home, the parental encouragement, and the pressure for achievement had all been decisive factors in differentiating the groups.

Parent preferences have been found to have a marked influence on the child's academic achievement and educational choices. Nichols and Holland (1963) reported a study of over 1000 National Merit Scholars which was designed to predict their academic and extracurricular accomplishments in science, art, and other fields during their first year of college.[78] Home backgrounds were studied, along with other factors. The parents'

77 Oden, 1968, pp. 72–74, 77–83, 92   78 Nichols and Holland, 1963, p. 25

educational level appeared to be related to achievement. It was also found that when parents preferred the conventional, realistic, and perhaps the more social occupations, these preferences were negatively correlated with artistic achievement in their children. When parents emphasized traits of social desirability and conformity (such as being happy, well-adjusted, dependable, curious, studious, and self-controlled), these traits were in general negatively correlated with achievement. There was a positive relation, however, to achievement in the parents' desire for the children to be independent, aggressive, self-reliant, ambitious, and able to defend themselves. It was also reported that the fathers' attitudes and values were more highly related to achievement criteria in the students than were those of the mother.

It is almost self-evident that the broken home has great impact on the emotional well-being of its members, and consequently will affect not only their achievement but productivity in all areas. This conclusion was strongly evident in the Barron and McGill University studies discussed earlier. The following two studies illustrate further the effect of the broken home on achievement.

Engemoen (1966) studied the influence of the broken home on the test performances of first-grade children.[79] Children from both broken and united homes were compared with respect to intelligence, social readiness, achievement at the end of the first grade, socioeconomic status, and adjustment. While the differences on these criteria were for the most part not statistically significant, it was found that the children from united homes had a higher level of reading achievement, were chosen more often (in sociometric ratings) in both work and play situations, and were rated as showing less signs of withdrawal or maladjustment than the children from the broken homes. It was suggested that a recent parental separation might affect a child's school achievement more than a long-standing marital rift.

A study of college dropouts illustrates the problem at the upper end of the educational scale. Nicholi (1972) reported at a meeting of the American Psychiatric Association that of the 1454 undergraduates who withdrew from Harvard during a five-year

79 Engemoen, 1966 (1967A), p. 2726

period, 43.3 percent left for psychiatric reasons.[80] When compared with the general undergraduate population, the dropout sample had "significantly" higher percentages of both divorced and deceased parents. It was also found that students who dropped out and failed to return to college had a significantly higher percentage of divorced parents than the general dropout population.

As might be expected, a high percentage of psychiatric dropouts described their homes in terms of overt conflict. Also, although students with public school backgrounds tended to drop out more frequently than private school students, there was a higher proportion of the more serious psychiatric illnesses in the students with private school backgrounds.

Similarly dismal is the home background of the high school dropout. The principal characteristics in the home life of the dropout seems to be poor communication among family members, general parental unhappiness, and social isolation. Mussen et al. (1969) stress that not all dropouts come from deprived homes, although one study in which dropouts were matched in age, sex, school background, socioeconomic status, and minority-group membership did show significant differences in family and peer influences as well as in individual personality traits.[81]

It is apparent from the research studies of dropouts that socioeconomic level is not the primary influence on academic achievement. Rather, achievement motivation is related to certain personality characteristics generated in the family matrix, irrespective of the family's position in the social matrix. Johnson (1966) studied two groups of adolescents from contrasting socioeconomic groups who had achieved high scores on the School and College Ability Test (SCAT).[82] He found no significant differences between the two groups on "scholarship points" in English, algebra, citizenship, or physical education nor on their National Merit Scholarship Qualifying Test (NMSQT) scores in English and other areas. There were also no significant differences in scores on the Allport-Vernon-Lindzey Study of Values Test (measuring theoretical, esthetic, political, economic, or religious values) nor in their work habits, traits of self-control and

80 Nicholi, 1972, pp. 2–3

81 See Mussen, Conger, and Kagan, 1969, pp. 732–733

82 Johnson, 1966 (1967A), pp. 3226–3227

responsibility, or plans to attend college. In short, these two groups of gifted students, representing both high and low socioeconomic environments, were more alike than they were different.

Frierson (1964) also studied characteristics of gifted children from both upper and lower socioeconomic backgrounds who were in upper elementary grades of a highly urban area —Cleveland, Ohio.[83] Those with an IQ of 125 or above, classified as gifted regardless of family status, were in special enrichment classes and were compared with average pupils. The personality profiles of the upper- and lower-status gifted groups were found to be closer to each other than the profiles of the lower-status gifted and average groups.

A third study by Cloninger (1972) was conducted on the academic achievement of 600 entering freshmen at the College of Basic Studies, at Boston University.[84] Sixty percent of this class were male students whose mean Scholastic Aptitude Test scores were 523 on the verbal scale and 519 on the math scale. Cloninger describes the membership of this college as representing both privileged and underprivileged classes, with about one-third of the students coming from private schools. He found no significant differences in academic performance associated with any key demographic factors such as family income, the education and occupation of the father, the mother's education, the standing of the high school attended, and previous work experience.

In addition to the numerous investigations of family influences on achievement, there is also some research dealing specifically with the effect of home environment on IQ. Of particular interest are such studies as that of Radin (1972), which demonstrates the importance of the father in the intellectual development of his son.[85] Radin studied two groups of white fathers, twenty-one in lower-class homes and twenty-one in middle-class homes, and observed the relationship between paternal child-rearing practices, sex-role preferences, and the intellectual functioning of their four-year-old sons. She found that the boys' IQs were positively and significantly correlated with paternal nurturance, and negatively and significantly correlated with paternal

83 Frierson, 1964 (1967A), p. 495

84 Cloninger, 1972, esp. p. 35

85 Radin, 1972, pp. 353–361

restrictiveness. Together, these two factors accounted for more than one-third of the variance in IQ.

This study also showed that both these factors were related to class differences. Middle-class fathers interacted more with their sons and were more nurturant than lower-class fathers. The differentiating factors between the two groups appeared to be the father's responsiveness to the child's needs, his empathy with him, and the degree to which he consulted with him. In other words, "fathering" was clearly related to class-level differences in the child's cognitive functioning. These findings agree with the results of a number of previous studies showing that the mother's child-rearing practices also differ with class membership.

There is ample evidence that child-rearing attitudes and practices are influenced to a certain extent by class membership. However, it is also apparent that class membership is not in itself the determining factor in scholastic achievement, since the individual parent-child relationship has more direct bearing on the child's performance. The same conditions may obtain in the case of general cognitive functioning.

An earlier study by Hurley (1965) found an actual relationship between parental rejection and children's intelligence-test scores.[86] He found that parental acceptance-rejection differences seemed to account for more than 30 percent of the variance in the IQ scores of eight-year-old girls. Hurley also points to strands of evidence from additional studies which show that "punitive, coercive, and repressive interpersonal experiences have a brutalizing and intellectually impoverishing influence upon humans." He concludes that many parental rejection practices which have been accepted on the contemporary American scene as fairly normal are actually likely to damage the child's intellectual development considerably. Hurley is not clear regarding the extent to which social and educational differences are associated with the relationship between parental acceptance or rejection and the child's IQ, although he indicates the phenomenon may be more marked among families in which the parents are less well educated.

Other attempts have been made to relate "mental ability" to

86 Hurley, 1967, pp. 113

factors of parental acceptance, educational success, and socioeconomic level. According to Covington (1966), children who are educationally successful tend to perceive their parents as being more accepting than those who are educationally unsuccessful, irrespective of their socioeconomic status.[87] In this study subjects were divided into four groups: high mental ability, high socioeconomic level; high mental ability, low socioeconomic level; low mental ability, high socioeconomic level; and low mental ability and low socioeconomic level. Covington found that children who were high in both variables tended to perceive their parents as more accepting and were somewhat more educationally successful than those who were low in both variables. He also found, however, that children of high mental ability and low socioeconomic levels tended to perceive their parents as more accepting than do those of low mental ability and high socioeconomic levels.

It has been known for over twenty years, from various longitudinal studies, that a child's IQ does not necessarily remain constant (Bayley, 1949; Bradway, 1944). Research studies conducted at the Fels Institute, reported by Kagan et al. (1958), add further evidence of this fact.[88] Researchers studied 140 children between the ages of six and ten, obtaining continuous Binet IQ data on each. They found that in some of the children (the "ascenders") the IQ increased, and in others (the "descenders") it decreased over the four-year period. The TAT and Rorschach test were used to identify certain personality differences in both types of children. The ascenders showed significantly more "achievement imagery" and "themes of curiosity about nature" and fewer "themes of passivity" than did the descenders. Kagan et al. conclude that:[89]

> High need achievement, competitive striving, and curiosity about nature are correlated with gains in IQ score because they may facilitate the acquisition of skills that are measured by the intelligence test.

They also suggest that such characteristics in a child (achievement need and striving to compete) would probably motivate him

87 Covington, 1966 (1967A), p. 2871

88 Kagan, Sontag, Baker, and Nelson, 1966, pp. 393–398

89 Kagan, Sontag, Baker, and Nelson, 1966, p. 398

to improve his intellectual abilities only if his social environment provided him with rewards of praise and recognition. In other words, the achievement-oriented children probably came from homes where parents often praised and reinforced intellectual activity.

Certain home conditions have been identified in the backgrounds of productive persons which might be called prerequisites for the development of such individuals. These conditions include a stable and harmonious relationship between parents who themselves have a basic sense of self-esteem, a supportive and nurturing parent-child relationship, and a basic structure of firm, but reasonable discipline within which the children may operate with a degree of confidence and security.

It may be assumed that all these prerequisite conditions are usually present in the background of the high achiever. In addition, various other conditions have been noted which appear to reinforce the possibility of high achievement in the various family members. In most cases, but not always, there is a fairly high level of parental education and occupation; often both parents have completed college or further training. There is also usually a marked parental interest in education. Goertzel and Goertzel (1962), who studied family backgrounds of 400 eminent men and women, found "a love of learning and achievement" to be a characteristic of 90 percent of the homes.[90] With this interest in and love for education there are accompanying parental expectations for educational achievement in the children. In addition, opportunities are often provided for the development of special nonacademic skills (music and dancing lessons, athletics, and various hobbies).

The father plays a vital role, especially in enhancing the intellectual functioning of a young son. The mother is likely to be actively involved, especially with the younger child, in a helping, supportive role which may enhance later development of his verbal skills. This maternal helping behavior is likely to be accompanied by a certain amount of benevolent and affectionate control and possibly even a degree of overprotection and subtle pressure, which, however, probably give the child a sense of direction and

90   Goertzel and Goertzel, 1962, p. 28

support. There is also evidence that "independence training" in young children may result in reduced independence (and possibly also achievement skills) at a later age.

Birth order and family size play some role in favoring the achievement motivation of certain members, particularly the first-born child and children of small families. There are also cultural differences in parental attitudes toward education, as well as social-class differences in child-rearing practices, which influence achievement motivation. These factors are secondary, however, to the quality of the individual parent-child relationship.

THE CREATIVE PERSON

Of all the studies dealing with family backgrounds of creative personalities, those of MacKinnon and Roe are perhaps the most illuminating. In his study of the childhoods of highly creative architects, MacKinnon (1962) identified a number of characteristics which seem to shed light on the unique traits of the mature creative person.[91]

The parents of the child who has become an outstandingly creative architect appear to have had a deep and abiding respect for him, combined with a confidence that he would be able to act appropriately; thus from very early in life he was given an unusual amount of freedom—freedom to explore his surroundings and practice in making independent decisions which probably served him well in maturity.

Strong emotional ties between child and parents seemed to be generally absent. MacKinnon emphasizes, however, that this lack of intense emotional involvement may have worked to the child's advantage, since there was less opportunity for the development of either overdependency or rejection. There was a high incidence of mothers who led active and independent lives apart from their husbands and children.

Because of the relative degree of emotional distance between parents and child, there were what MacKinnon terms "ambiguities" in the child's identification with the parents. He tended

214   91   MacKinnon, 1962, pp. 491–493

to identify either with both or with neither of them. However, he was by no means deprived of adequate models: relatives and friends—many of them important and prominent in the community—were available and exerted a strong influence. Moreover, the father, who was usually engaged in an exceptionally demanding career, served as an excellent example of effectiveness and resourcefulness.

Two-thirds of the families emphasized the development of a strong personal code of ethics rather than mere adherence to formal religion. The values most often stressed were integrity (forthrightness, honesty, and respect for other people) and quality (including pride, care in and enjoyment of work, and development of talent). Other values encouraged were intellectual and cultural endeavor, success and ambition, and being respectable and "doing the right thing."[92]

Within these families there also existed clear ethical and behavior standards, which the child was expected both to follow and adopt. Consistent and predictable discipline, explicitly known and seldom infringed rules, and infrequent punishment were characteristic. This type of discipline closely resembles that of the high self-esteem family identified by Coopersmith.

The parents were not overconcerned about the development of the child's specific skills and abilities. Although one or both of them were often artistic, they did not pressure the child in the development of similar skills; they certainly encouraged his interest in art at an early age, but he was not in any way coerced into the choice or adoption of a particular career.

The fact that the families were reported to have moved about quite often may have affected the child in two ways: first, by enriching his cultural and personal experiences in a great variety of ways and second, by isolating him somewhat from the immediate neighborhood in which the family happened to be living. The child, almost without exception, showed an interest and skill in drawing and painting at an early age.

Roe's findings concerning the childhood environment of the creative physical scientist produce a picture which is like the

92 MacKinnon, 1962, p. 492

background of the architect in a number of ways.[93] Roe has stressed that in the background of virtually every important scientist there is someone whom he respected and who placed a high value on intellectual pursuits. In many cases the parents themselves were well educated and members of some profession; they generally gave sympathetic support to the child's early interest in scientific hobbies. According to one physicist:[94]

> *Father never helped me make anything. On the other hand if I asked him how to do something he always knew and he had tools around. . . . He never gave me any formal instruction but I learned a lot.*

If, as was true in a few cases, the parents or members of the immediate family were not interested in science or matters of intellectual importance, a budding scientist had a close association with someone—a friend or, particularly, a teacher—who took a keen interest in his affairs and gave him much encouragement. The science teacher was possibly a kind of father-figure to such a boy; he typically went out of his way to provide him with equipment for experimental purposes, guided him in projects, and in general served as friend and mentor.

The family environment was supportive and stable. There was a minimum of unnecessary restrictions to discourage exploration of the environment and usually a minimum of punitiveness in the administration of discipline. The father did not "boss" the family; comments such as the one above suggest that father-son relationships were friendly and positive.

McCurdy (1956), who has also investigated the background of scientists with particular reference to superior science students, feels that three conditions are particularly encouraging to the development of the scientific achiever. The family has usually had sufficient economic security to offer the child an adequate laboratory or workshop facilities, in many cases in his home, the child has had adequate time to develop his scientific skills in out-of-school hours, and there has been a parental attitude which permitted the child's self-development.[95] Certainly

216   93 Roe, 1960, pp. 66–77   95 See Roe, 1960, pp. 71–72

94 Roe, 1960, p. 71

the young scientific achiever was encouraged to explore independently, as is illustrated by the following remark:[96]

> *Having to make my own way (intellectually) meant a lot. I don't like guidance. I don't like spoon-feeding. I don't like pampering. It's much better to be thrown on your own.*

Implicit in both these descriptions of childhood environments there are certain common elements. The child was respected as a person. He was given a considerable amount of freedom to explore and experiment on his own. There appears to have been an absence of strong emotional ties with either parent, which did not, however, preclude a generally positive, friendly relationship, particularly with the father. A basic emotional security seemed to pervade the family structure; otherwise the healthy involvement in and enthusiasm for creative hobbies and projects would not have been possible. There appear to have been in both types of backgrounds other adults who served as models in addition to the parents—teachers and admired persons. There was an absence of any kind of coercion on the part of the parents for the child to be "trained" for a specific profession or vocation. There was, however, a rich intellectual and cultural milieu to provide plenty of informal educational development for the child. Discipline was at a minimum and was administered fairly and only when necessary.

There appears to be little in other writings on the family background of creative persons that conflicts with the above picture. Drevdahl (1964) found evidence that highly creative psychologists had had significantly more educational stimulation as children than their colleagues, that there were "fewer signs of neuroticism" in their backgrounds, that they had exhibited creativity early in life, that matters of "social adjustment" were of relatively little importance to them, and that they were more attached to their homes and families than those who were less creative. One puzzling finding was a "significantly stronger attachment and positive feeling toward the mother" than was evident in the other groups.[97]

96 Roe, 1960, pp. 70–71   97 Drevdahl, 1964, pp. 173–175

Datta and Parloff (1967) studied 742 young scientists and found that, while both creative and less creative groups described their parents as moderately affectionate, nonrejecting, and encouraging of their independence, the parents of the most creative students appeared to assume integrity and responsibility in their children and did not feel the need for authoritarian methods of control.[98] Holland (1963) concluded that parents of creative children appear to be more permissive and more nurturant of their ideas and impulses than parents of less creative students; he adds that creative students are likely to come into conflict with the demands of their teachers for conforming, nonexploratory behavior, whereas the more authoritarian parent may have a child who is a typical achiever.[99] Weisberg and Springer (1961) reported a correlation of .5 between the integrity of the father-child relationship and the level of creative test performance.[100] Singer (1961) found that members of the high-fantasy (creative) group had significantly more contact with their parents than the less creative group and usually chose one parent (the father).[101] Studies of Watson (1957), Ellinger (1964), Nichols (1964), Getzels and Jackson (1961), and others are in essential agreement as to the importance of a flexible, somewhat permissive parental attitude toward discipline in enhancing the spontaneity and curiosity of the young creative child.[102] According to Dewing (1970), three highly important variables in child rearing which influence creativity are nonauthoritarian discipline, diverse and relatively intellectual interests, and a parent-child relationship which is not characterized by overdependence. Dewing reminds us that creativity has always suffered (or even been nonexistent) in authoritarian, repressive societies.[103]

There is some evidence that highly creative children have some personality characteristic of both sexes. Sensitivity has been considered a feminine trait. A study by Biller, Singer, and Fullerton (1969) of sex-role development and creative potential in kindergarten boys indicated that boys with mixed sex-role preferences were significantly higher on the creative measure than boys with consistent sex-role patterns.[104] There was no meaningful relationship between the various creativity subtests and IQ, but the

98 Datta and Parloff, 1967, p. 149
99 Holland, 1963, p. 523
100 See Arasteh, 1969, p. 170
101 See Arasteh, 1969, p. 170
102 See Arasteh, 1969, pp. 168–184
103 Dewing, 1970, pp. 399–404
104 Biller, Singer, and Fullerton, 1969, pp. 291–295

factor of socioeconomic status correlated .36 (.05 level of significance), indicating that the range of intellectual experience and stimulation available to a child in an upper-middle-class home may facilitate the development of creative potential. It was also considered possible that in the upper-middle-class home the child may identify with both mother and father in the early years, and since strict lines of sex identification are considered less important, he encounters a wider range of experience.

Perhaps the principal contrast with the parental background of the high achiever is the factor of independence. As Getzels and Jackson indicate, there appears to be somewhat more vigilance, especially on the part of the mother, in the high-achiever's home than in the home of the creative person.[105] It is exceedingly difficult to generalize fairly on this matter: the distinction between vigilance and warm interest and concern, on the one hand, and between permissiveness and neglect, on the other, is a fine one. Excessive rigidity and control on the part of parents would be detrimental not only to creativity in children, but also to the building of good achievement skills, and certainly to achievement motivation. Moreover, high parental expectations of the child are found in the homes of achievers, and although they may be subtly expressed, they are undoubtedly present in any home which values intellectual accomplishment in any field, whether or not it is labeled "creative" in orientation.

LEADERSHIP

Essentially the same family environment appears in the background of productive leaders which is found in the childhood of achievers and creative persons. Again, fundamental stability of the home and parental relationship is usually a prerequisite, and the importance of the father's role is underscored in nearly all the research in this area. The mother's role in the background of the person who subsequently becomes a successful leader is seen as a supportive, rather than a dominant one.

In the research on business leaders, for example, Gardner (1948) found that one important factor in success was that the

---

105   Getzels and Jackson, 1962, pp. 69–71

mother's role in her son's development had been primarily supportive.[106] The advancing executive needed to make a clear break in his emotional ties with his mother, and a positive identification with his father was seen as indispensable to a man if he were to fit successfully into the hierarchy of authority of a business organization. A man who was still emotionally at odds with his father was regarded as a poor prospect for promotion to more responsibility.

The Harvard Business School studies are essentially in agreement with the Gardner study. Zaleznik et al. (1970) found the top-ranked leaders (the oriented managers), to have the highest score on both mother and father affection of the four groups studied.[107] The mother had been an active disciplinarian, a role which she shared with the father, but usually the father had had the final say. The oriented managers viewed their parents as having been relatively demanding but highly affectionate. They could identify with both parents to a greater extent than the other groups, apparently because both parents could be loved and admired. Their home had been characterized by a kind of trust. Injury to self-esteem was never a question, and identification was on the basis of loyalty to the parents. The family relationships reported by the remaining groups were characterized by various lesser degrees of affection and closeness; and in the home background of the lowest group, the conflicted specialists, there was relatively little affection from either parent and a tendency for the mother to be dominant in the home.

An earlier Harvard Business School study by Moment and Zaleznik (1963) revealed a similar pattern in the high versus low leadership types.[108] The top-ranked "stars" were close to their family in early relationships. Strong father identification and early experiences of independence had made it possible for these men to develop a deep sense of responsibility; they were strongly internalized and had a "rich fantasy life." Many of them were first-born children. The lowest-ranked group (the underchosen) had come from backgrounds marked by marital instability and apparent unhappiness; they were lowest among the four groups in their perceived closeness to their families during childhood.

106 Gardner, 1948

107 Zaleznik, Dalton, and Barnes, 1970, pp. 218, 221–225, 233, 236–237

108 Moment and Zaleznik, 1963, pp. 138–145

Investigations of leadership in other areas reveal similar trends. Cox (1970), in studying men and women who had been college leaders ten years earlier, found a correlation of .602 (significant beyond the .01 level) between their mental health as adults and the emotional climate of their childhood homes.[109] Allen (1955) investigated family backgrounds of 316 Methodist ministers and found statistically significant differences between the more and the less successful men in terms of certain family and childhood factors.[110] The more successful ministers had been accepted by their fathers as equals; moreover, their fathers had usually belonged in the professional and managerial ranks. They had had more extensive education and were more happily married than the fathers of the less successful ministers. The successful minister, as a rule, was an only child, and his father also tended to be an only child. Again we can see the factors of father-son identification, adequate education, emotional security in the home, and an abundance of parental support contributing to adult success and productivity.

There have been interesting reports from leadership studies among adolescents. Two Purdue University-sponsored surveys have dealt with this topic. One investigation, by Karasick et al. (1968), indicates that leadership in high school students is to some extent related to the mothers' educational level.[111] More than one-third of those in the low leadership group reported that their mothers had not completed high school, and only 12 percent had mothers who were college graduates; in the high group only 26 percent of the mothers had not completed high school, and 22 percent had finished college. Another finding was that school grades were strongly related to leadership.

A second study, by Erlick (1968), dealt with the "style of life" of students and their families.[112] Style of life was defined as a composite of active involvement and participation in extracurricular and community activities on the part of both students and their parents, as well as factors related to academic achievement. Students with an "extensive or elaborated" style of life reported that at least one, and often both, of their parents was actively involved in community and service-oriented activities and that

109 Cox, 1970, p. 88
110 Allen, 1955, pp. 188–189
111 Karasick, Leidy, and Smart, 1968, pp. 3–4
112 Erlick, 1968, pp. 21–22

they themselves were participating actively in school extracurricular activities; they were also receiving better than average grades in school, and there was other evidence of security and good functioning in their homes. Subjects with "limited or restricted" styles of life reported conditions which were nearly the opposite of those cited by the leadership group.

A study of social mobility (which is somewhat related to leadership) was carried out by Douvan and Adelson (1966) with adolescents in Michigan: sharp contrasts in the family backgrounds of the upward- and downward-mobile children were observed.[113] The upward-mobile boys portrayed their parents as less harsh than the downward-mobile parents: they were less dependent on their parents and more often shared leisure activities with them. Very few of them had been physically punished, although psychological methods of punishment had been used. The family life of the downward-mobile boys was characterized by harsh punishment, high dependency, and low autonomy. Physical punishment was more frequently used, and there was marked ambivalence in the attitudes of the children toward their parents.

An excellent study of familial antecedents of the traits of leadership and responsibility was carried out under the direction of Bronfenbrenner (1961). From a sample of 400 tenth-grade students in a medium-sized upstate New York city, eight groups carefully matched for sex and social class were administered a 100-item Parent-Activity Inventory eliciting information in twenty different dimensions of parent-child relationships; teachers' ratings were also utilized. The findings showed that:[114]

> Parental rejection and neglect impede the development of responsibility and leadership in both boys and girls. The emergence of effective behavior is a function of an optimal balance of affection and control which is different for the two sexes and entails different risks in the process of socialization.

Bronfenbrenner adds that inadequate levels of parental support and authority in American middle-class culture tend, on one hand, to interfere with the development of leadership and responsibility in boys and, on the other hand, to oversocialize girls

222   113 Douvan and Adelson, 1966, pp. 63, 66

114 Bronfenbrenner, 1961, p. 268

through an "overdose of parental affection and control." The role of the father is important in both cases. Moreover, both responsibility and leadership are damaged when the parent of the same sex is not involved in the child-rearing process. If the adolescent is to be viewed as a leader by his peers, the background of an affectionate relationship with his parents is critical. Hence parental child-rearing practices and the sex of the child are both factors.

the family as a source

The family background of all three types of productive persons is, it seems, essentially the same. Although there are exceptions, the prerequisites for the development of productivity appear to be a basically stable and conflict-free home environment, a strong father who is respected and admired by all members of the family, and an emotionally secure and supportive mother. Over and above these fundamentals there are other factors which appear to enhance both the desire and the opportunity for productive development. In the case of the academic achiever these include an interest in the child's education, and perhaps a specific model in terms of parents who are themselves fairly well educated, as well as active involvement and concern, particularly on the part of the mother, for the development of academic skills.

In the home environment of the creative person there seems to be less conscious pressure to meet parental standards; rather, there is the unspoken assumption that the child will live up to them. As a result, he is granted a rather marked degree of independence and autonomy, and the parent-child relationship is characterized more by a deep respect for the child as an individual than by constant and intimate association. The home itself usually provides a richly varied intellectual and cultural climate, in which the child has an opportunity to explore a variety of identifications without the pressure of rigid conformity to traditional sex-role behavior patterns.

The background of the leader perhaps contains less overt emphasis on conscious development of skills than on the factors of empathy and sensitivity to the feelings of others. The warmth of the relationship between the child and the father and the child and the mother is especially marked and is probably an essential factor in developing the supreme emotional security needed to deal with stresses and tensions that are a concomitant of any leadership position.

Here, then, is the family background of a productive person. Regardless of the area in which he chooses to make his primary contribution, he will have acquired early in life the emotional bases of success and the positive self-attitudes that enable him to develop the skills and competence to cope with and master his environment.

The productive person is unique, both in himself and in the contribution he makes to society. However, the quality of productivity is not unique, nor is it limited to some special few. Individuals are productive in many different ways and to many different degrees. For this reason an understanding of the personality characteristics of the contributing, productive individual, and of the manner in which they develop, has important implications for the enhancement of productivity in all persons, and especially in those persons who will at some point in the future take their places in society as adults.

enhancement
of productivity

CHAPTER SEVEN

225

characteristics of the productive personality

The extensive research literature in the fields of academic achievement, creativity, and leadership provides us with three slightly different personality profiles of the individuals who attain notable success in each of these areas. The academic achiever has considerable cognitive skill which is exemplified in verbal and mathematical competence, efficient and orderly work habits, an ability to control his impulses, intellectual curiosity, independence, and persistence. The picture of the creative person is similar in a number of respects. If he is creative in the theoretical or scientific area, his academic background must be extensive, and also intensive within his own specialty; hence he must also be an academic achiever.

If he is artistically creative, he is oriented more to the intuitive, perceptive, imaginative approach than to the intellectual, analytical approach of the scientist. Whereas the physical scientist is typically highly masculine in his attitudes, the artistically creative person is often less fixed in his sex-role identity and is perhaps somewhat more gregarious. There are also creative persons in such fields as architecture and mathematics whose characteristics appear to lie midway between these two types. All creative persons possess to some degree the intellectual qualities of divergent thinking.

The personality characteristics of the leader also resemble those of the other types (particularly the academic achiever), but the balance is slightly different. The leader shows a marked ease in social relationships, and his empathy, judgment, sense of fairness and responsibility, and skill in communication arouse the respect and trust of others. These qualities are also typical of the achiever and the creative person, but the leader expresses them more directly in his interpersonal relationships.

In spite of these differences, all three types of highly productive persons bear more resemblance to each other than to the less productive persons in their respective areas. The most conspicuous characteristic which differentiates the highly productive individual from others is self-esteem. High self-esteem is associated with high productivity, whether it is exemplified in academic achievement, creativity, or leadership; low self-esteem is characteristic of the low achiever, the noncreative person, and the follower. In research not specifically concerned with the areas of achievement, creativity, and leadership, such as studies on general mental health, a similar relationship is found between mental health, as defined by the particular researcher, and self-esteem.

Although intelligence has long been equated with ability, IQ score has been found to be a generally inadequate predictor even of academic achievement. It does not measure factors of impulsivity and memory, which are involved in scholastic performance. Altogether IQ accounts statistically for only 35 to 40 percent of the variance in academic performance, and above a certain level which is probably a requirement for general performance, there appears to be no relationship at all between IQ and creativity. It is therefore evident that personality characteristics and other variables must exert considerable influence on all forms of productivity. The significance of motivation, which is ultimately related to the degree of anticipated reward, and the problem of male underachievement so conspicuous in our schools serve indirectly to underscore the importance of self-esteem as a personality asset.

Another quality common to productive individuals is a clear sense of identity. The productive person knows who he is and where he is going; he is confident in his unique role and feels comfortable with himself and what he is doing. Although the concept of identity is less easily defined than self-esteem, it seems the most appropriate description of this aspect of the mature, contributing, and productive person. It embodies not only his self-esteem and self-respect, but also his clear and realistic perception of himself and his capabilities. He is confident of, happy with, and effective in his uniqueness as an individual.

One special aspect of identity is the individual's "sex identity." This is an omnibus term which actually describes the presence or absence of specific behavior traits associated with mature acceptance of one's own gender. Clear, positive gender identity is typical of the productive individual. His relationships with the opposite sex—one indication of his security in his gender role—are generally stable and rewarding; in contrast the low-productive person (according to the marriage and divorce statistics cited by Cox, Oden, Barron, and others) has more difficulty establishing permanent and satisfactory heterosexual relationships. The love of vigorous and active sports, usually identified with the masculine role, has also been found to differentiate the highly productive from the less productive male.

Social responsibility, another characteristic of the productive individual, is expressed through a wide range of behavior. It appears, however, one hallmark of productive persons as a group is a mature social awareness and concern in the broad sense of the term. Their contributions are motivated, directly or indirectly, by an empathic, altruistic, and sympathetic feeling not only for specific individuals, but for humanity in general. Thus, whether these qualities are expressed in the spontaneous sensitivity, friendliness, and interpersonal skills that characterize the leader or in the deep concern for social and humanitarian issues that characterizes the physical scientist's keen sense of professional standards, the productive person, almost by definition, has a highly developed internal value system which commits him to a fundamental integrity in his own behavior and an inherent respect and esteem for others.

The basis of an internalized system of values is the degree to which the individual's own behavior contributes to his self-esteem—that is, the degree to which he feels that he is the person he should be. Hence the productive individual is relatively free of crippling feelings of guilt. Because his basic orientation is an empathic concern for others he feels more troubled by an inability to resolve the larger social problems of inequality, suffering, and injustice—by the discrepancy between what is and what ought to be—than by a burden of unresolved guilt and anxiety over his own behavior.

The productive individual is also one who grapples with the problems of life rather than retreating from them. Thus he brings to any situation a fundamental attitude of hope which is based on an inner assurance that, whatever the nature of the task, he will be rewarded by a sense of accomplishment and the approval of those who in his own mind represent the group or standards with which he identifies. Hope enables an individual to extend himself into the future, to establish remote, not easily attainable, but ultimately highly rewarding goals. This attitude stems from his own previous experiences of having often been recognized and rewarded for his efforts by the persons on whom he is dependent for support.

Because the productive person is secure in himself and in his trust in his environment, he can perceive a confronting stimulus or problem clearly, accurately, and realistically. Far from being disconcerted by a difficult situation, he welcomes the challenge of ambiguity, uncertainty, and complexity. Moreover, his freedom to observe the environment not only contributes to his intellectual curiosity, but also enhances his capacity to appraise alternative courses of action. Thus, he also brings to any situation well-developed cognitive skills which enable him to cope with the situation effectively. Among these cognitive assets are a good memory, uninhibited by affective conflicts, and well-developed verbal and mathematical skills, including the ability to utilize their respective symbols in the acquisition of information and the formulation of a solution or decision.

The degree to which any person is productive is the degree to which he can master the life situations which confront him. The process of coping therefore entails not only accurate perception and appraisal of the problem, but the capacity to arrive at a decision regarding his own course of action; effective coping must lead to a result. Hence the productive individual is also characterized by independence (confidence in his own judgment), control both of his own impulses and of the situation through his ability to order its complexities, and by the persistence and single-mindedness which enable him to pursue a problem to its conclusion. Finally, he has the strength and courage to reach a decision, with full cognizance of its consequences for himself as well as for others.

development of the productive personality

The productive individual does not "spring full-blown from his mother's forehead." Rather, the qualities which distinguish him from others are shaped by a long developmental process which can be traced, in theory, as far back as birth.

The productive person's sense of identity—his conscious recognition of himself as a distinct and valuable individual——evolves only after many years of developmental identification, during which a child unconsciously models himself after the behavior and ideals of his parents, and subsequently of other persons in his social milieu who are important to him. Theoretically the earliest forms of identification are already operative in infancy. The first acts of swallowing nourishment and experiencing satisfaction of hunger produce not only physical gratification, but a sense of psychological well-being in which lie the beginnings of self-esteem or psychological security. Something akin to self-esteem is thus experienced almost from birth; it must therefore be viewed as a prerequisite both of the identification process and of the establishment of a mature sense of identity.

In the primary identifications of infancy during which the baby becomes aware of his closeness to another human being (at first his mother), a basic ingredient in the relationship is the quality of generative empathy, which is enhanced by the mother's expressions of smiling, vocalization, and loving gesture. As the infant's perception of his external environment expands beyond his basic physiological needs, identification with his father becomes an increasingly important factor in his development. All identifications are based on the child's continuing need for psychological safety (self-esteem); accordingly, he selects and adopts the characteristics of those models who contribute most to this need. In subsequent years other identifications with siblings and individuals outside the family such as peers, teachers, older adults, and more casual acquaintances are operative in a child's growth. It is on the quality of these relationships and influences that the child's optimum personal development depends; this quality is determined, however, by his initial perception of himself in relation to the principals within the family matrix—his parents.

A fundamental aspect of identity is the child's self-identification of his own gender. An awareness of sex differences may occur as early as two years, but the crucial period in which the child establishes actual identification of his own sex is probably somewhere between the ages of four and six. There is substantial evidence that clear and unambiguous sex identity is fostered by a warm and empathic relationship with both parents, in which the father and the mother play separate but equally important roles. The father's influence seems to be more critical in this area than in any other aspect of development, for children of both sexes; in fact, there is some evidence that it may be more significant in some respects than the role of the mother. The absence or loss of a father does not affect a daughter's sex typing as such, but it is reflected in an impaired ability to relate to adult males. In sons the mother's attitude toward a weak, irresponsible, or absent father has been shown to be a causative factor in confused sex identity, manifested either in exaggerated masculinity and sexual aggression or in homosexual behavior.

The developmental process by which a child becomes a socially responsible adult is known as socialization; its ultimate goal is to enable the individual to govern his own behavior according to the principles of personal conduct and concern for others which reflect society's judgment of morality. Socialization is the continuation of the early identification processes; it originates in an empathic relationship with another person. According to social learning theory, a child's social behavior is acquired in three ways. He learns by observing the behavior of those around him and by identifying with the behavior of those who are significant to him; as his cognitive skills of vocabulary, memory, and time perception mature, he develops the powers of anticipation and foresight; finally he learns through his own experiences with the outcome of actions to relate behavior to its consequences and to apply value judgments to his own behavior in terms of its consequences for others.

Successful socialization of any child depends on the empathy, nurturance, and warmth in the parents' child-rearing practices and attitudes, on an optimum level of communication between and among family members, on successful and adequate development of the child's own cognitive skills, and on the parents' ability to handle discipline problems in a way that produces the desired behavior in the child, rather than guilt over his failure to behave in the desired way. Socialization also depends on the effectiveness of the models—determined first by their expressive qualities of empathy and nurturance and by their competence in an area significant to the child's immediate needs.

The process of socialization is a lengthy one, and for this reason it is accomplished effectively only in an environment that is consistent and nurturing during the child's formative years.

Families differ in their philosophies and their child-rearing practices, and to some extent these differences are related to the cultural orientation of various ethnic groups, as well as to socioeconomic pressures. On the whole, however, the basic conditions for social development are a warm and empathic parent-child relationship characterized by authoritative parental limits and the reinforcement of approved behavior by praise and affection. Since discipline lies in the child's desire to avoid the loss of love, it can be effective only when there is love to be lost.

Socialization may be impeded by such factors as a child's special learning difficulties or sensory-motor handicaps; it is certainly hindered by inconsistencies and conflicts in values among a child's socializing agents—his parents, teachers, and peers —especially when his principal socializing agents, his parents, fail to provide him with the basis for formulating a value system of his own to guide his judgments.

There are certain dimensions of family structure which have some bearing on the affective environment that is available to the developing child. Members of small families with an adequate income to provide both psychological and economic security probably enjoy more opportunities for individual recognition, encouragement, and personal development than do those of large families subject to constant economic pressure and frustration.

232

Similarly, opportunities are probably more accessible to the only or first-born child than to middle and later-born siblings. Yet children have often emerged from the midst of large families in modest and even impoverished circumstances to reach high levels of accomplishment as adults, testifying to the presence somewhere in their backgrounds of a high degree of affective security. In other words, these demographic factors may exert indirect influence in the sense that they influence the parent's basic orientation. These factors have less direct influence, however, than the individual parent-child relationship in developing the self-confidence, coping skills, and other personality strengths that are the basis of productivity.

Retrospective studies of the family backgrounds of productive persons reveal that these backgrounds are essentially similar. The home and parental relationship are generally stable and harmonious, there is a strong father who assumes responsibility for family leadership, and the mother is affectionate and supportive, but not dominating. Self-esteem and competence are generally high in the parents as well as in the children.

Apart from these common characteristics, the home backgrounds of academic achievers, creative individuals, and leaders differ slightly in their emphasis on values and vocational goals. The parents of the academic achiever tend to stress the values of formal education, to develop specific skills in their children, and to devote constant care and attention to the early development, in both boys and girls, of high verbal ability. The father's involvement is significant in the intellectual development of his son. Independence is usually not stressed in the earliest years.

In the home that fosters creativity there appears to be a distinct stress on independence which has probably tended to promote in the child freedom of exploration and opportunities for various creative endeavors. There is an abundance of respect for the child as an individual and an assumed expectation of a strong personal code of ethics. Although overt parental pressure for achievement is usually absent, the provision of a rich variety of informal educational opportunities indicates a subtle but pervasive interest in intellectual accomplishment, which is probably strengthened by the high level of education and professional training often found in both father and mother in such homes.

In the background of leaders there appears to have been considerable emphasis on a warm and affectionate parent-child relationship and a respect and concern for others, rather than on specific skills and competencies. The father-son bonds are exceptionally strong, and the homes are marked by a high sense of values and a sense of social responsibility, concern, and individual obligation to be involved in social action.

One aspect of the productive person—his physical health—has received relatively little comment in the research literature except from a few investigators; it has not, therefore, been dealt with in previous chapters. Barron (1968) did find a striking difference in the health of his high-soundness and low-soundness groups. The various follow-ups of the Terman study also found that reports of good or very good physical health characterized a larger percentage of the A (successful) than the C (unsuccessful) subjects, and that the differences between the two groups became more marked as they grew older.[1] This same study also found that the A subjects reported themselves as having greater physical energy than did the Cs. Reports from the investigations of Zaleznick et al., McClelland, and Barron, describing the active involvement of outstanding individuals in competitive sports and strenuous physical pursuits, suggest that the physical condition of these individuals was one of healthful vigor.

There are also references to the presence or absence of psychosomatic complaints in certain groups of individuals which are of significance to this discussion because they are closely associated with self-esteem. Rosenberg noted that "secondary physiological manifestations of anxiety," such as insomnia, hand trembling, nervousness, nail biting, and shortness of breath, were reported much less frequently by high self-esteem subjects than by those with low self-esteem.[2] Coopersmith similarly found more frequent reports of emotional problems and psychosomatic complaints among his low self-esteem subjects than among those of high self-esteem.[3] Rosenberg maintains that persons with low self-esteem may be more prone to psychosomatic complaints and

234   1   Oden, 1968, pp. 63, 70, 81, 91   3   Coopersmith, 1967, pp. 132ff
        2   Rosenberg, 1965, pp. 22ff

symptoms because low self-esteem is itself associated with various anxiety-producing personality traits. These include a somewhat unstable self-image, a tendency to present a false front to others, vulnerability to criticism, and habitual feelings of isolation and loneliness, all of which could logically be expected to increase anxiety.[4]

It appears that good physical health is a concomitant of productivity, at least in the general case. It also appears that low self-esteem hampers productivity not only in the psychological sense, but also because the accompanying state of anxiety may give rise to numerous minor, but far from negligible, physical symptoms.

social and professional implications

From this survey of a large number of research findings, a substantial amount of information has emerged which has direct bearing on the basic personality structure of those individuals who are effective in contributing to the society in which they live, regardless of the particular area or capacity in which they do so. In addition, a fairly clear picture emerges of the specific child-rearing attitudes and practices which are characteristic of the family backgrounds of productive persons. From a synthesis of all this information, certain fundamental conclusions can be drawn:

1 High self-esteem is clearly a consistent characteristic of a productive person in any field of endeavor. Moreover, it appears to underlie, and to be prerequisite to, the development of all the other attributes of a productive individual: his sense of identity; his social competence, concern, and maturity; and his numerous coping skills and characteristics.

2 High self-esteem develops in a family environment characterized by empathy, concern, and reinforcement. It appears to be the result of a continuous nurturance during the child's formative years in a loving and supportive, but

4 Rosenberg, 1965, pp. 166–167

also structured and consistent, social environment characterized by firmly upheld standards, values, and parental expectations. There is evidence that this environment is operative almost from infancy, and that it is the child's parents (or those who relate to him as parents) who are primarily responsible for his emotional development, as well as his physical and intellectual development, through the processes of identification and socialization.

3   In the light of present evidence, there is every reason to believe that the characteristics which underlie productivity can be acquired by any child in any environment, given the basic conditions for the development of self-esteem.

Self-esteem is not a new term in psychology; it has appeared in the writings of Freud, Erikson, Fenichel, Sullivan, and others. It is only recently, however, that close examination of its microstructure has suggested self-esteem as a suitably definitive concept by which to explain variances in the level of productive behavior. Although the nature of self-esteem requires further exploration, it appears from the findings thus far that self-esteem should properly be conceptualized as a basic, continuous psychological need of all persons. This concept applies not only to the normal processes of growth and development in the well-functioning child, but also to the modification of low-productive and nonproductive behavior in the poorly functioning child, adolescent, or adult. It should provide the basis for a new theoretical model of personality functioning which will not only serve to explain growth and development of successful persons more adequately than have past models, but will also provide a firmer basis for the treatment and remediation of the problems of malfunctioning persons. Putting the matter differently, if the presence of a given factor fosters growth, its absence will result in lack of growth. In short, in any discussion of a theory of personality development, especially with respect to children and adolescents, we should consider both developmental and therapeutic approaches as based on the same premise.

CURRENT APPROACHES TO THERAPY

Reports on the effectiveness of current therapy programs have, on the whole, been discouraging. Part of the difficulty is that significant research on the factors associated with improvement is difficult to design and implement. Limited budgets have handicapped most programs, and as a rule treatment facilities have had to give first priority to immediate therapy needs, usually on only a short-term basis. Some of the limitations on effectiveness, however, are inherent in the approach to treatment itself.

The lack of a clearly defined and unified theoretical model of personality development has led to a tendency to treat isolated symptoms, rather than any underlying cause. The result has been a multiplicity of approaches to therapy, each based on some fragmented model of the ill or dysfunctioning personality. Most of them lay claim to some degree of therapeutic success within a limited framework, but on closer examination there is little indication of results. As Meltzoff and Kornreich (1970) note, there is "no current evidence that one traditional method is more successful than another in modifying psychopathology, alleviating symptoms, or improving general adjustment."[5] In fact, there are instances in which psychotherapy may even have had negative effects. Bergin (1971) observes that although therapeutic results during the past four decades have been "modestly positive":[6]

> The averaged group data on which this conclusion is based obscure the existence of a multiplicity of processes occurring in therapy, the existences of a multiplicity of processes occurring in therapy, some of which are now known to be either unproductive or actually harmful.

The lack of structure of traditional methods has also added to a complexity of theory and technique which further compounds the problem. Eysenck and Beech (1971) have been highly critical of the complex cognitive approaches in which many psychologists are now involved and contend that if science is to be self-correcting, some oversimplification is a necessary

---

5 Meltzoff and Kornreich, 1970, p. 200   6 Bergin, 1971, p. 263

beginning:[7]

> If we begin by considering all the complexities involved in real-life
> events, we will never arrive at a scientific theory; if we are willing
> to over-simplify, we are at least enabled to make a beginning, and
> thus to correct our errors.

Much of the confusion over the various theoretical approaches to psychotherapy is owing to the lack of any means of
evaluating the results. Over the years treatment programs have
been concerned primarily with the process, rather than with the
outcome, and there has been little follow-up on the results. This is
especially the case with parent education and therapy, school
counseling programs, family clinics, and behavior-modification
programs. The lack of a definite approach or direction in therapy
makes adequate follow-up difficult, since there is no basis for
isolation of a single variable, random selection of subjects, and
careful matching of experimental and control groups.

The success of treatment methods in child-guidance clinics
has seldom been thoroughly investigated. In a ten-year follow-up
investigation of 579 children who had undergone treatment at
the Institute of Juvenile Research in Illinois, Levitt et al. (1959)
found that this group differed significantly from a control group
of 427 subjects on only two of twenty-six variables, and even these
differences were not sufficient to be more than chance.[8] When the
study was narrowed down to those children who had made at
least ten, and an average to twenty-six, clinic visits, there was still
no significant evidence that treatment had led to any improvement. These findings cannot be generalized to all child-guidance
situations, of course, but they do point to the need for investigation in this field with adequate control groups.

In addition to the lack of adequate follow-up on the results
of treatment programs, there is rarely any objective measure of
success. In most cases the only measure available is the evaluation
of either the therapist or the patient. Under these circumstances
there is no way to make a conclusive judgment, since what each
participant perceives as success will depend on his own goals and

7 Eysenck and Beech, 1971, p. 603   8 See Meltzoff and Kornreich, 1970,
                                                                        p. 158

aspirations, which may differ vastly for the therapist and the patient.[9]

One serious limitation of most therapeutic methods is that they are designed primarily in terms of the value system of the therapist, rather than the patient. They presuppose certain cognitive skills, a certain degree of motivation, and in some cases the ability to cope with detailed procedures and record keeping. As a result, the therapeutic techniques intended to correct deviant behavior actually fail to reach those persons who are most in need of attention.[10] Even among those who seek and are accepted for treatment in mental-health facilities, the dropout rate is 30 to 60 percent. About two-thirds of the treated group seem to benefit to some extent; however, this estimate may be high, since in most instances the criteria for improvement are set by the patient's own therapist and there are very few follow-up studies. Actual treatment for deviant behavior is apparently no more frequent for children than for adults. Levitt (1971) estimates that only about one-third of the children referred to child-guidance clinics are given any kind of formal treatment.[11]

CHILD-DEVELOPMENT PROGRAMS

Programs and projects to aid parents in providing a better home and family milieu for their children have been conducted for many years.[12] The social work profession dates back to the early 1900s, and various family counseling services have been in operation for as long as fifty years. Such counseling is generally based on the social and emotional factors involved in family relationships, largely in terms of psychoanalytic theory. More recently these programs have expanded to include behavior-modification techniques, which are based on the use of various reward systems to motivate social development. Other programs include lectures, discussion groups, and printed materials to educate parents on the physical, social, and economic aspects of family life as they affect the child, as well as specific parent training designed to improve the child's development of cognitive skills.

---

9 Meltzoff and Kornreich, 1970, p. 172   11 Levitt, 1971, p. 491

10 Bandura, 1969, pp. 52–53   12 S. White, 1972, chaps. 10 and 13

It is difficult to determine the extent to which these various programs have been of benefit to the child. In most cases, as with psychotherapy, the approach is either fragmented or global and the goals are ambiguous; experimental studies lack any theoretical model and are seldom designed for random selection of subjects, control groups, or adequate follow-up procedures. The few available studies on parent-education projects reveal no significant changes in either the parent or the child, although parents report that they have more information about child behavior than they had before.[13] Most of the programs, moreover, have involved only mothers, and all of them are based on a general middle-class orientation. Hence they do not reach the members of economically or socially deprived subcultures or the disorganized or multiproblem family.

From the limited number of studies designed with control groups and follow-up procedures, it appears that the programs which focus on a clearly delineated problem are more effective than those with a broad-spectrum approach. Parent training oriented to the development of cognitive skills, language and reading skills, and academic achievement has produced measurable increases in the child's level of performance, although the gains tend to be lasting only when there is continued nurturance as a result of a change in the mother's attitude. Evidently the benefits of parent training extend to siblings as well; improved performance in the target child is often accompanied by corresponding improvements in the performance of other children in the family.[14]

behavior-modification programs Behavior-modification practices are based on the application of standard laboratory methodology to behavioral development through a planned program of reinforcement. Although this approach has introduced some structure to the research on parent-child relations, specific reinforcement methods have not been universally successful and are open to challenge.[15] One of the more serious drawbacks of this approach is that its application by the parent is inherently contradictory: parents are placed in the position of trying to eliminate

13   S. White, 1972, pp. 93–103
14   Gilmore, 1971b, p. 84
15   Meltzoff and Kornreich, 1970, p. 476

behavior which they may at the same time be reinforcing. They may, for example, be inadvertently providing the model for the very same aggressive or negative behavior for which they now hold the child responsible. They may be unconsciously accepting or supportive of behavior which they profess to disapprove, or they may be creating a nonempathic environment to which the child can respond in no other way. Without a basic change in the parents themselves, any changes in the child as a result of behavior-modification techniques are likely to be minimal or short-lived.

Another limitation of behavior-modification programs is the difficulty in implementing them. Efforts to train parents in such reinforcement devices as a point system have not met with notable success. In discussing the experiments with both token rewards and social reinforcement (expressions of affection), Patterson comments on the problem of administering either system on an adequate research basis.[16] In some cases parents have been coerced into participating; in others they are very little involved with their children. Some fail to follow up the token reward with social reinforcement; others forget, or are too busy with other tasks. Moreover, because of the multitude of clerical and other tasks which such systems entail, they are vulnerable to inaccuracies, lapses of memory, and eventual loss of interest on the part of the participants. These problems are further compounded by the fact that, on one hand, token rewards provide little inducement to middle-class children, whose physical and material needs are already fulfilled, and on the other hand, a program of rituals and record keeping is generally unsuitable at other socioeconomic levels.

These same handicaps apply to an even greater extent to the use of behavior-modification techniques by teachers in the regular classroom situation. However, there have been a number of experimental studies on classroom procedure with delinquent and predelinquent children in which the teachers involved were trained in the various reinforcement techniques.[17] The reports of the experimental programs themselves have been encouraging in some cases, but unfortunately there is insufficient follow-up in-

16 Patterson, 1971a, pp. 751ff   17 See Patterson, 1971a, p. 771

formation to evaluate their actual success. The reported improvements in behavior are not supported by any data on the child's behavior after he is returned to the regular classroom, nor is there any information on the teacher's application of newly learned principles and techniques in other teaching situations after the experimental period.

Behavior-modification techniques also fail to meet the requirement of simplicity from the standpoint of theory, since they deal primarily with isolated symptoms rather than underlying causes. Experimental studies have usually focused on various behavioral problems, which are more accessible to change than learning problems, and the emphasis appears to be on the behavioral process, rather than on the child's productivity. In a recent review of current research, O'Callaghan notes that out of twelve projects, ten are concerned with the parents' acquisition of information and its effect on their behavior—not the child's. Moreover, three of the studies involve direct payment to parents for their participation, and only one includes a control group.[18]

As Patterson (1971) points out, there are some "eminently testable statements about the antecedents of deviant behavior and an alternative set of assessment procedures" which should be explored in future behavior-intervention research.[19] For example, although self-esteem has not been investigated as a possible variable in behavior modification, it has been difficult to differentiate a token-reward program from one utilizing social reinforcement (an esteeming environment), and Bandura reports that a combination of tokens and social reinforcement seems to build self-esteem in severely deprived children.[20]

In an experimental program with delinquent boys, it was found that a token system alone did not teach the most important social skills; however, Phillips et al. (1973) report considerable success with a "parent-teacher," a specially trained parent surrogate who communicated with enthusiasm, made liberal use of praise, encouraged the boys to be reinforcing in their interaction with each other, and included them in program decisions.[21] In a study of a Boston University program for parents of low-achieving junior high students, Pigott (1970) found that when the parents

18   O'Callaghan, 1973, pp. 3–24

19   Patterson, 1971a, p. 763

20   Patterson, 1971a, pp. 752, 759;
     Bandura, 1969, p. 227

21   Phillips, Phillips, Fixen, and Wolf, 1973,
     pp. 75–59

employed tokens alone, the student's scholastic improvement was only temporary; however, when the tokens were preceded by verbal and other empathic reinforcement to increase his self-confidence, he generally continued to perform at this higher level as long as the empathic milieu was sustained.[22] Repeated experiments in the Boston University programs have also demonstrated improvement in the grades of low achievers when parents employed only verbal techniques to increase self-esteem.[23]

These findings clearly point to self-esteem as an important factor in behavior modification. In fact, if a token system or similar device is not effective without empathic interaction and an observable change in behavior can be accomplished by fostering self-esteem without the use of tokens, then in all probability the dependent variable is actually an esteeming environment. A study of reinforcement techniques conducted at the University of Oregon indicates that a smile, a nod, or an "attending"—all necessary factors in the development of self-esteem—may become the focus of future behavior-intervention programs.[24]

self-esteem counseling Another approach to child development has been to help parents specifically to establish a nurturing, empathic parent/child relationship which will increase the child's level of productivity by increasing his self-esteem. Parents are counseled in the behavioral expressions by which such a relationship is established and maintained—their smiles, their words of approval, affection, and encouragement, and their warm demonstrations of physical affection. Problems of deviant behavior, psychosomatic reactions to anxiety, and poor academic performance are almost invariably accompanied by low self-esteem, and in such cases programs of systematic parent training and education conducted by specially trained parent counselors are meeting with substantial success. The counselors attempt to demonstrate to participating parents the importance of developing and maintaining self-esteem in their children, as well as specific means by which self-esteem can be enhanced, maintained, or restored.

In one study of the effects of such parent counseling, Perkins (1970) worked with three groups of bright underachieving boys

22 K. Pigott, personal communication

23 Gilmore, 1971c, pp. 40–49

24 Patterson, 1971a, p. 752

and their mothers.[25] In one group counseling was given to the mothers alone, in a second it was given to the boys alone, and in a third the mothers and boys were counseled together; there was also a control (noncounseled) group. The counseling emphasized to the mothers the importance of maintaining a genuinely warm and empathic relationship with their sons. Comparison with the control group showed that in all three of the counseled groups the boys had increased their grade-point averages. More significantly, not only was the improvement just as great in the group in which the mothers alone were counseled, but it also was maintained at a significant level five months after the experimental period. Perkins concludes that counseling mothers in groups in the establishment of empathic relationships seems to be more effective in improving the child's scholastic achievement and self-confidence than counseling only the child.

Another fruitful exploration of parent counseling has been under way since 1965 at the Boston University School of Education, where a series of programs have been conducted by graduate students trained to counsel parents, either individually or in small groups, in the use of specific techniques which help them to be more empathic, nurturant, and expressive with their children.[26] These programs were initially directed to the parents of children doing C-level scholastic work. Since then they have been expanded to include a wider range of academic and behavioral problems. Parents are invited to participate in a program of weekly half-hour counseling sessions for a period of about fifteen weeks. Fathers are required to be present for a majority of the meetings. Instead of focusing on the child's various "objectionable" traits, the counselors deal with three positive goals for his development: establishment by the parents of an empathic relationship with their child, specific methods of improving and maintaining the child's self-esteem, and improving the child's academic achievement.

Over the years approximately 450 families, with children at all levels of public school, have participated in these programs. Each project has been designed for a control group of students matched for academic record, IQ level, and percentile rank on

25 Perkins, 1969 (1970A), p. 2809   26 Gilmore, 1971d, pp. 65–68

reading and arithmetic achievement tests, and whenever possible, the subjects have been selected at random. A comparison of the records of the experimental and control groups at the end of the school year has shown significant academic improvement in about 70 percent of all the students who have been involved in the programs.[27]

In addition to the evaluation of grade-point averages, a special behavior rating scale is administered to parents and teachers in October and again in June to elicit their perceptions of the child's progress in social behavior. The ratings show that there has been improvement in the areas in about 80 percent of the cases; they also show reductions in the frequency of psychosomatic disorders, such as overweight, asthmatic conditions, and enuresis, and in many cases there are reports of improved academic achievement in other children in the family. Although follow-up studies have not been possible on all programs, in some programs the child has continued to improve during the following year and even for some years afterward.[28] Results have also been encouraging with parent counseling in crisis situations.[29] Most of the programs thus far have involved children in the public schools, but some pilot studies with small groups of private school, college, and low-income parents have produced promising results.

THE SELF-ESTEEM CONSTRUCT

There is widespread feeling that a new theoretical approach to personality functioning is needed if psychotherapy is to meet its responsibility for helping the poorly functioning person to become more productive. Levitt comments that in treating behavioral problems in children "rigid orthodoxies find scant empirical support" and innovative approaches are the order of the day.[30] The emphasis has turned from theories concerned with the inner psychic and emotional life of the individual to consideration of ways in which the developing individual is influenced by his interaction with the external environment. As Garfield (1971)

27 Gilmore, 1971d, pp. 65–68

28 M. Zundell, personal communication

29 Gordon, 1971, pp. 69–73

30 Levitt, 1971, p. 491

notes, it is no longer possible to rely solely on counseling or therapy to modify or remake a person:[31]

> *More attention will have to be paid to social or environmental variables as contrasted with essentially intrapsychic ones. . . .*

For any personality theory to be definitive and workable, however, the theoretical model must meet certain fundamental requirements. In order to cover the entire spectrum of human behavior, it must be associated with some primary physiological need. It must be predictable, simple, and based on implementation by those who are most directly involved in the individual's growth and development. The results must be observable and measurable and capable of unbiased verification. Finally, the model must be one that is universally applicable. Let us examine the self-esteem construct in terms of these requirements.

It is not sufficient to formulate a theory of personality based on an abstract concept such as the "life instinct," as in psychoanalytic theory, or the "self," as in behavior modification. A theoretical model of personality development should be constructed on some aspect of personality that is related to basic human requirements.

The beginning of all physical and psychological growth depends on basic physiological processes, and in any living organism one of the primary requirements for these processes is nourishment. Self-esteem, as described by Fenichel and others, is in essence the psychological reaction associated with the awareness of having received nourishment from some external source. Both its origin and its development are dependent on constant nurturance and the direct fulfillment of physical and psychological needs.

Another requirement for a theoretical model of personality is that the results of its application must be predictable. The validity of any concept in human behavior can be predicated only on its ability to predict behavior when other influencing variables are held constant. This requirement is clearly fulfilled by the direct evidence that an empathic and supportive environment engenders high self-esteem, and hence greater personal effectiveness

31 Garfield, 1971, p. 293

and productivity, whereas the lack of such an environment impairs, and may even prevent such development. Moreover, if a child's empathy and nurturance are interrupted, his productivity is observed to decrease, and when the nurturing environment is restored, his growth and development resume. Repeated experiments have demonstrated that if parents, after a period of neglect or critical response, recreate an empathic and nurturing relationship with their child, his productivity is restored. The child who has known little empathy and has developed longstanding defenses against his needs, may require some time to develop a basic trust in his surroundings. The need for constant nurturance is apparent even in children with high self-esteem, since the deprivation of affection in a customarily empathic relationship increases the likelihood of guilt feelings.

A theoretical model must be simple in principle; that is, it must be predicated on some underlying causal factor, rather than on the variety of behavioral expressions which are merely symptomatic of the problem. A full diagnosis of the low academic achiever, for example, commonly reveals such accompanying conditions as anxiety-related ailments, social problems with peers, hyperkinesis, impulsivity, and reading and language difficulties—most of which can actually be traced to the individual's loss or deficiency of self-esteem.

The history of education is marked by the repeated failure of misdirected efforts to improve academic achievement by dealing with individual symptoms. Remedial reading programs, exercises in "visual acuity," changes in the curriculum, the use of various behavior-modification systems, and constant reminders to the child that he needs more "motivation" have all failed to reach the root of the problem. The basic factor in motivation is self-esteem, and not one of us is motivated to achieve or create anything unless we feel that those close to us basically care about our success.

The simpler the theory, all other things being equal, the simpler should be the methods of applying it. A smile, a kind word, a warm gesture of physical affection—it is such basic interaction which creates self-esteem in children. Parents need not be thrown into conflict over rules of discipline or the "correct" or recommended thing to do or say in a given situation; they need not be burdened with involved artificial systems of awarding tokens, implementing complex schedules, and keeping voluminous records. Since the differentiating factor in the child's productivity is self-esteem, why not simply focus on those measures which will serve to meet this need by promoting greater empathy and nurturance in his social environment? All that is needed is a simple, genuine parental concern for the child and a positive, nurturing relationship—which is, after all, the functional basis of the family structure.

Another aspect of this approach to personality development is that it focuses on an activity that carries with it the greatest reinforcement in the child's peer and adult world—academic achievement. Rosenberg has found that no single thing contributes to the child's self-esteem as much as a good report card. A good report card at the same time improves the parents' self-esteem, since it reflects on their competence as parents. Since high self-esteem in parents leads, in turn, to increased self-esteem in their children, the net effect tends to be a spiraling one. This is primarily because in our society evidence of learning is associated with both social and occupational status—that is, with mastery of the environment. Academic achievement is, therefore, more than demonstration of cognitive skills. It is a value, which in its development requires the acquisition of some of the characteristics we prize and reward in others, such as honesty, intellectual integrity, consideration for others, creativity, and social responsibility. As a result, in focusing on academic achievement parents are providing an environment which increases the child's opportunities for productive development in general.

It is important that the nurturing environment be provided by those who are directly involved in meeting the child's basic needs—his parents. The term "parent" has been used throughout in the general sense of biological parent, but it refers to any person or persons assuming the primary responsibility for the early and continuing physical and emotional needs of the child. Ideally, empathy, an essential ingredient of this relationship, is established quite early with the biological mother. Empathy, however, lies in the relationship rather than in the biological functions that may have preceded it, and such a relationship can develop with any concerned and caring adult functioning in a parental role. There are circumstances in which, for any of a variety of reasons, an infant may have lacked the crucial early contacts with any parent, and yet the growing organism is amazingly viable. Productive persons can and do emerge from any empathic adult-child relationship.

The results of any theoretical model of personality must be observable and measurable. Otherwise, the theory itself is not subject to verification and remains only a hypothesis. If a parent, teacher, or counselor is giving a child any form of treatment or assistance, any change in the child's functioning must be attributable to the treatment, and the change must be sufficient to be measurable, either by the teacher's evaluation of his academic work, by ratings of teachers or observers, or by some other quantifiable means. The self-esteem construct lends itself to such quantified evaluations: the change in the parental environment should produce a corresponding change in the child's academic work.

For the results to be considered conclusive, the measurement must also be unbiased. Hence any change in the child's behavior must be verified by someone who is not involved in the parent-counselor-child relationship. Evaluation by one or more of the child's teachers, as evidenced by their assignment of grades, is often the best source of verification. The Boston University studies of self-esteem counseling have utilized teachers' as well as parents' ratings of progress in academic achievement and social responsibility. In some projects teachers have not been informed that a counseling situation was involved.

The final requirement of a useful theoretical model is that it apply, in both principle and practice, to all individuals. The self-esteem construct is not limited to the value system of a specific cultural or socioeconomic group; nor is it limited by such factors as age, educational level, or degree of personality malfunctioning. Hence it is applicable to personality growth and development, as well as to treatment and remedial situations.

Although the use of the self-esteem construct in the treatment of psychosis has not yet been researched, therapy based on building the patient's self-esteem may be more successful than attempts to treat various symptoms of malfunctioning. Low self-esteem, with its accompanying anxiety, is often expressed in various behavioral and physical conditions symptomatic of a single cause. Bandura notes that most psychological functions are to some extent interdependent, and that desirable changes in one area of behavior may therefore produce beneficial modifications in other areas which are not directly involved in the treatment program.[32] For example, in a program involving children with perceptual disorders (dyslexia), Baker (1970) found that counseling mothers on their relationship with their children not only improved academic achievement, but reduced both enuresis and asthma attacks.[33] In the parent counseling program at Boston University, it has been found that focusing upon the single concept of self-esteem improves academic achievement, physical health, and general behavior not only of the target child, but also of the siblings.[34] The stressing of an empathic relationship with the runaway or alienated adolescent also appears to offer a positive approach to the rehabilitation. The evidence thus far suggests that the self-esteem construct may well prove useful as a therapeutic framework as well as a developmental one.

nurturance of the productive personality

The theoretical and empirical data assembled here do not represent new discoveries. They do suggest that the causative factors in the development of those personality characteristics fundamental to all productive functioning lie in certain environmental antecedents. It is primarily the empathy, nurturance, and esteem in the family milieu which result in the development of the productive personality—and the lack of these conditions which often produces a poorly functioning individual.

An essential process in the development of productivity in any individual is the enhancement of his self-esteem. This process may be initiated at any age, but the most significant role is played by the persons who constitute the individual's earliest

32 Bandura, 1969, p. 90   34 Gilmore, 1971b, p. 84

33 Gilmore, 1971a, p. 80

social environment—his mother and father. Many parents with growing children will find it necessary to redefine and clarify their goals and objectives for their family and children if they are to be successful in enriching, stabilizing, and strengthening the family environment in such a way as to increase their children's self-esteem. In such cases they may need professional help.

Most research points to a harmonious family relationship in the background of the productive person. Yet disagreements need not be traumatic or disturbing. Some studies have revealed that such factors as parental disharmony, high pressure to achieve, and parental overprotectiveness are not in themselves factors in lack of achievement; but rather, that the antecedents of success are to be found in family relations characterized by understanding, approval, trust, and observance of the Golden Rule. A happy, productive home is not characterized by complete absence of controversy and conflict over ideas and interests, but by the method used in the solution of problems. In a home based upon empathic relationships, conflicts can be resolved by the use of respectful and considerate communication, patience, and understanding.

The above findings suggest that the quality of family relationships which meet the child's self-esteem needs is within the reach of practically all parents. We are just beginning to discover the factors which change and improve self-esteem, not only within the family, but also in business and professional situations. Programs in parent counseling, well designed with measured outcomes, indicate that parents of children of all ages and all socioeconomic levels earnestly want more professional help with their children. There is evidence that deeply concerned parents are capable of changing their fundamental relationships with their children with the help of skilled counseling; there is also evidence that the resulting changes, which are reflected in their children's continued academic and social productivity, are relatively permanent.

These findings pose a twofold challenge for all those in the helping professions—particularly for psychologists, educators, and pediatricians. Their first responsibility, perhaps, is to instruct all parents and prospective parents in the basic principles of interaction with their children. A second responsibility is to help parents of school-age children to provide more empathy and nurturance in their homes.

The public school, which can reach more families than any other single organization in our society, bears a special responsibility in this respect. Academic achievement is so highly valued and rewarded in our culture that the report card, according to Rosenberg, exerts a unique degree of influence on a child's self-concept.[35] As a result high self-esteem is strongly associated with academic performance, and an individual who views himself, for whatever reason, as deficient in this area tends to lose self-confidence. For example, under stress of perceived failure, the able seventh-grade students studied by Gibby and Gibby (1967) not only performed less effectively, but also evidenced a lowered self-concept and decreased intellectual productivity. In another experiment Diller (1954) found that the self-concept of college students was enhanced by success.

Carlton and Moore (1966, 1968), who allowed culturally disadvantaged children to select and dramatize stories, found not only that the subjects improved in self-concept and reading ability, but that the self-concept changes were relatively permanent. Lamy (1965) found that a child's first-grade reading achievement could be predicted by his perception of himself when he was still in kindergarten.[36]

One attempt by both counselors and teachers to improve the self-esteem of students has not been successful. Higgins (1971) at the University of Pittsburgh tried to increase self-esteem in thirty students who had received the lowest scores on Coopersmith's Self-esteem Inventory.[37] These students were randomly assigned to three different groups. In one group, which received counseling, two contacts were also made with the students' parents; a second group received only group counseling; a third control group received no treatment. In addition, some teachers participated in an in-service training program which would help them to improve conditions for self-esteem in the classroom. At the end of a nine-week period the subjects were retested on the Self-esteem Inventory, and the results showed no significant change in either

35 Rosenberg, 1965, p. 140

36 See Purkey, pp. 23, 25–26

37 Higgins, 1971 (1972A), p. 4351

of the two counseled groups which could be attributed to the counseling or to the benefits of the teacher-training program. The project directors concluded that within the time and space limitations imposed by the school situation, they could not demonstrate that working with teachers, parents, and counselors could increase self-esteem in students. The project, however, appears to have many theoretical and design weaknesses; for example, "two contacts" with parents cannot be said to constitute adequate par-

The results of classroom experiments in improving social behavior, academic achievement, and self-esteem have been mixed. The findings on behavior-modification techniques are inconclusive. Teachers' and counselors' attempts to increase self-esteem seem to have produced uncertain results. Nevertheless, the level of self-concept is clearly a factor in academic achievement, and there is little doubt that an empathic, concerned teacher can facilitate a child's acquisition of learning skills through various types of reinforcement, such as oral and written recognition and other rewards.

The relationship between the parents and the school, however, must be a reciprocal one. Since the development of a child's self-esteem precedes his entrance into school by a number of years, in all probability the self-esteem characteristics that he acquires within his family and brings with him to the classroom are the chief determinants of his performance. Hence a more effective means of enhancing a child's general productivity as well as his academic performance lies in reaching the parents of children who show signs of either learning or behavior problems at the elementary school level.

In this respect the needs of low-income families are a special concern. Parents of this group may need substantial help in learning to establish more empathic relations with their children, since the social and economic pressures of their own lives hinder them in reaching out empathically or using words of feeling and affect. Current methods of parent counseling and family therapy are based on a minimum verbal-cognitive level which is geared essentially to the middle class. It is difficult to counsel parents of the low-income group, since they doubt the possibility of being competent to bring about a positive outcome in their children's academic achievement. Moreover, their community and peer groups may envy, but not reward, the high-achieving student.

One of the major hurdles in working with the deprived family, of course, is posed by the basic orientation of the teacher or counselor, which often prevents him from communicating with real empathy with the parents. However, efforts are currently being made to counsel these parents by experimenting with different approaches. Instead of emphasizing academic and achievement skills, the counselor may stress the importance of improving communication within the family or he may focus on some other situation which is viewed as an immediate problem. Home visits may be necessary, in order to provide parents with at least the security of their own surroundings. Moreover, mothers may be unable to leave younger children alone, and fathers are often unable or unwilling to participate in any other setting. As a rule, parents in this group are more task- than verbal-oriented and may find it difficult to sit, talk, and listen; they may, however, be comfortable conversing with the counselor while they are working at some familiar—and often necessary—task. A graduate student at Boston University has successfully trained parents (whom she had already counseled on the self-esteem approach with their own children) to counsel other families in their neighborhood. Significant improvement in the children's scholastic achievement has resulted from the work of these paraprofessionals. It is through approaches such as these, which have been tried with some degree of success, that there is some hope of reaching and helping those families who are likely to be the ones most in need of help.

One solution to many of society's problems lies in strengthening the value system and general functioning of the family unit itself. Self-esteem accounts for productivity only in the sense that it enables the individual to function within a social structure which gives direction to the expression of his self-esteem. Empathy and nurturance will foster self-esteem, but self-esteem alone will be of little avail in a family without a commitment to a sound set of human values.[38]

38 Ackerman, 1958, p. 101

The highly productive person with his accompanying sense of social responsibility, good physical and mental health, and effective coping skills develops within the family which values social concern and the acquisition of learning. Academic training and the development of other skills which directly or indirectly contribute to one's effectiveness are attainable goals which are included in the value system of such a family.

Thus, to avoid perpetuating from one generation to another the weak value structure which defeats productive expression, perhaps one of the fundamental responsibilities of the public school is to help parents to fulfill their important social roles. Unfortunately, there is no facility that educates people in parenthood, so that parents themselves feel that they have amateur status. If professional assistance at the school can help them to increase their child's self-esteem, their own self-confidence will increase as they observe the improvement in the academic and social functioning of their offspring. This gives them hope; and since advanced educational opportunities can then be viewed as a possible reality, the values and aspirations of the entire family can be raised. With enhancement of the productivity of each family unit, there is a corresponding benefit to all of society.

Ackerman, N. W., 1958: *The psychodynamics of family life*, New York: Basic Books.

Ackerman, N. W., 1971: The growing edge of family therapy. *Family Process*, 10, 143–156.

Albert, R. S., 1969: Genius: Present-day status of the concept and its implications for the study of creativity and giftedness. *American Psychologist*, 24, 743–753.

Allen, P. J., 1955: Childhood backgrounds of success in a profession. *American Sociological Review*, 20, 186–190.

Allinsmith, W., and T. C. Greening, 1955: Guilt over anger as predicted from parental discipline: A study of superego development (Program of the Sixty-third Annual Convention of the American Psychological Association). *American Psychologist*, 10, 320.

Altus, W. D., 1966: Birth order and its sequelae. *Science*, 151(3706), 44–49.

Arasteh, J. D., 1969: Creativity and related processes in the young child. In S. Chess and A. Thomas (eds.), *Annual progress in child*

bibliography

psychiatry and child development, 1969, New York: Brunner/Mazel, pp. 152–184.

Arieti, S., 1970: The role of cognition in the development of inner reality. In J. Hellmuth (ed.), *Cognitive studies,* New York: Brunner/Mazel, vol. I, pp. 91–110.

Aronfreed, J., 1968: *Conduct and conscience,* New York: Academic.

Bachman, J. G., 1970: *Youth in transition,* Ann Arbor, Mich.: Institute for Social Research, vol. II.

Baker, W. G., III, 1971: The successful investor. *Psychology Today,* 5(6), 59–86.

Bandura, A., 1969: *Principles of behavior modification,* New York: Holt.

Bandura, A., and A. D. Huston, 1967: Identification as a process of incidental learning. In G. R. Medinnus (ed.), *Readings in the psychology of parent-child relations,* New York: Wiley, pp. 259–272.

Bandura, A., and R. H. Walters, 1959: *Adolescent aggression,* New York: Ronald.

Banta, J., 1970: Tests for the evaluation of early childhood education: The Cincinnati Autonomy Test Battery (CATB). In J. Hellmuth (ed.), *Cognitive studies,* New York: Brunner/Mazel, vol. I, pp. 424–490.

Barker, L. W., 1968: An analysis of achievement, motivational, and perceptual variables between students classified on the basis of success and persistence in college. Doctoral dissertation, West Virginia University. *Dissertation Abstracts,* 1968A, 29 (4), 1100.

Barrett, H. O., 1957: An intensive study of 32 gifted children. *Personnel and Guidance Journal,* 36, 192–194.

Barron, F., 1955: The disposition toward originality. *Journal of Abnormal and Social Psychology,* 51, 478–485.

Barron, F., 1964: The relationship of ego diffusion to creative perception. In C. W. Taylor (ed.), *Widening horizons in creativity,* New York: Wiley, pp. 80–86.

Barron, F., 1968: *Creativity and personal freedom,* Princeton, N.J.: Van Nostrand.

Baumrind, D., 1971a: Current patterns of parental authority. *Developmental Psychology Monograph,* 4(1), part 2.

Baumrind, D., 1971b: Harmonious parents and their preschool children. *Developmental Psychology,* 4, 99–102.

Becker, W. C., 1964: Consequences of different kinds of parental discipline. In M. L. Hoffman and L. W. Hoffman (eds.), *Review of child development research,* New York: Russell Sage Foundation, vol. I, pp. 169–208.

Bell, N. W., and E. F. Vogel (eds.), 1960: *A modern introduction to the family*, New York: Free Press.

Bell, R. Q., 1971: Stimulus control of parent or caretaker behavior by offspring. *Developmental Psychology*, 4, 63–72.

Bergin, A. E., 1971: The evaluation of therapeutic outcomes. In A. E. Bergin and S. L. Garfield (eds.), *Handbook of psychotherapy and behavior change: An empirical analysis*, New York: Wiley, pp. 217–270.

Bieber, I., et al., 1962: *Homosexuality*, New York: Basic Books.

Biller, H. B., 1969: Father dominance and sex-role development in kindergarten-age boys. *Developmental Psychology*, 1, 87–94.

Biller, H. B., 1970: Father absence and the personality development of the male child. *Developmental Psychology*, 2, 181–201.

Biller, H. B., and R. M. Bahm, 1971: Father absence, perceived maternal behavior, and masculinity of self-concept among junior high school boys. *Developmental Psychology*, 4, 178–181.

Biller, H. B., and W. Barry, 1971: Sex-role patterns, paternal similarity, and personality adjustment in college males. *Developmental Psychology*, 4, 107.

Biller, H. B., D. L. Singer, and M. Fullerton, 1969: Sex-role development and creative potential in kindergarten-age boys. *Developmental Psychology*, 1, 291–296.

Bing, E., 1967: Effect of childrearing practices on development of differential cognitive abilities. In G. R. Medinnus (ed.), *Readings in the psychology of parent-child relations*, New York: Wiley, pp. 205–222.

Blair, G. E., 1967: The relationship of selected ego functions and the academic achievement of Negro students. Doctoral dissertation, Florida State University. *Dissertation Abstracts*, 1968A, 28(8), 3013.

Blanchard, R. W., and H. B. Biller, 1971: Father availability and academic performance among third-grade boys. *Developmental Psychology*, 4, 301–305.

Bonime, W., 1969: Masturbatory fantasies and personality functioning. In J. H. Masserman (ed.), *Dynamics of deviant sexuality*, New York: Grune & Stratton, pp. 32–50.

Borke, H., 1971: Interpersonal perception of young children: Egocentrism or empathy? *Developmental Psychology*, 5, 263–269.

Brenner, M., 1971: Caring, love, and selective memory. *Proceedings 79th annual convention, American Psychological Association*, pp. 275–276.

Brewster Smith, M., 1968: Competence and socialization. In J. A. Clausen (ed.), *Socialization and society*, Boston: Little, Brown, pp. 271–320.

Brewster Smith, M., 1969: *Social psychology and human values*, Chicago: Aldine.

Bronfenbrenner, U., 1961: Some familial antecedents of responsibility and leadership in adolescents. In L. Petrullo and B. M. Bass (eds.), *Leadership and interpersonal behavior*, New York: Holt, pp. 239–271.

Bronfenbrenner, U., 1969: The split-level American family. In D. Rogers (ed.), *Readings in child psychology*, Belmont, Calif.: Brooks/Cole, pp. 208–218.

Campbell, D. P., 1971: Admissions policies: Side effects and their implications. *American Psychologist*, 26, 636–647.

Campbell, P. B., 1965: Self concept and academic achievement in middle grade public school children. Doctoral dissertation, Wayne State University. *Dissertation Abstracts*, 1966A, 27(6), 1535–1536.

Caplin, M. D., 1966: The relationship between self-concept and academic achievement and between level of aspiration and academic achievement. Doctoral dissertation, Columbia University. *Dissertation Abstracts*, 1966A, 27, 979–980.

Carlsmith, L., 1964: Effect of early father absence on scholastic aptitude. *Harvard Educational Review*, 34(1), 3–21.

Chambers, J. A., 1964: Relating personality and biographical factors to scientific creativity. *Psychological Monographs*, 78(7), no. 584.

Chance, J. E., 1965: Independence training and first graders' achievement. In M. Kornrich (ed.), *Underachievement*, Springfield, Ill.: Thomas, pp. 39–48.

Chess, S., and A. Thomas (eds.), 1969: *Annual progress in child psychiatry and child development, 1969*, New York: Brunner/Mazel.

Chiang, H., and A. Maslow (eds.), 1969: *The healthy personality: Readings*, New York: Van Nostrand–Reinhold.

Chowdhry, K., and T. M. Newcomb, 1952: The relative abilities of leaders and non-leaders to estimate opinions of their own groups. *Journal of Abnormal and Social Psychology*, 47, 51–57.

Clausen, J. A., 1966: Family structure, socialization, and personality. In Hoffman and Hoffman (eds.), *Review of child development research*, New York: Russell Sage Foundation, vol. II, pp. 1–53.

Clausen, J. A., 1968: Perspectives on childhood socialization. In J. A. Clausen (ed.), *Socialization and society*, Boston: Little, Brown, pp. 132–181.

Cloninger, J. M., 1972: A study of noncognitive predictors of academic achievement in a two year general education program. Doctoral dissertation, Boston University School of Education.

Cohen, R. J., 1970: The effects of environmental conditions upon sex typing characteristics. Doctoral dissertation, Boston University School of Education.

Coopersmith, S., 1967: *The antecedents of self-esteem*, San Francisco: Freeman.

Covington, H. D., 1966: A comparative study of children's perceptions of parental acceptance and their educational success. Doctoral dissertation, Ohio State University. *Dissertation Abstracts*, 1967A, 27(9), 2871.

Cox, R. D., 1970: *Youth into maturity: A study of men and women in the first ten years after college*, New York: Mental Health Materials Center.

Datta, L. E., and M. B. Parloff, 1967: On the relevance of autonomy: Parent-child relationshops and early scientific creativity. *Proceedings 75th annual convention, American Psychological Association*, pp. 149–150.

Davids, A., 1966: Psychological characteristics of high school male and female potential scientists in comparison with academic achievers. *Psychology in the Schools*, 3, 79–87.

Davids, A., 1968: Cognitive styles in potential scientists and in underachieving high school students. *Journal of Special Education*, 2, 197–201.

Davids, A., and P. K. Hainsworth, 1967: Maternal attitudes about family life and child rearing as avowed by mothers and perceived by their underachieving and high-achieving sons. *Journal of Consulting Psychology*, 31, 29–37.

Dell, H. L. D., 1967: The evaluation of teaching procedures designed to increase empathy. Doctoral dissertation, Ball State University. *Dissertation Abstracts*, 1968A, 29(5), 1447–1448.

Dewing, K., 1970: Family influences on creativity: A review and discussion. *Journal of Special Education*, 4, 399–404.

Dittes, J. E., 1959: Effect of changes in self-esteem upon impulsiveness and deliberation in making judgments. *Journal of Abnormal and Social Psychology*, 58, 348–356.

Domino, G., 1971: Cinematographic creativity and personality. *Proceedings 79th annual convention, American Psychological Association*, pp. 413–414.

Douvan, E., and J. Adelson, 1966: *The adolescent experience*, New York: Wiley.

Douvan, E., and M. Gold, 1966: Modal patterns in American adolescence. In Hoffman and Hoffman (eds.), *Review of child development research*, New York: Russell Sage Foundation, vol. II, pp. 469–528.

Drevdahl, J. E., 1964: Some developmental and environmental factors in creativity. In C. W. Taylor (ed.), *Widening horizons in creativity*, New York: Wiley, pp. 170–186.

Edgerly, R. F., 1971: Parental counseling in Norwell junior high school. *Journal of Education*, 154(1), 54–59.

Elliott, J. L., and D. H. Elliott, 1970: The effects of birth order and age gap on aspiration level. *Proceedings 78th annual convention, American Psychological Association*, pp. 369–370.

Elman, J., A. Press, and P. Rosenkrantz, 1970: Sex roles and self-concepts: Real and ideal. *Proceedings 78th annual convention, American Psychological Association*, pp. 455–456.

Engemoen, B. L., 1966: The influence of membership in a broken home on test performance of first grade children. Doctoral dissertation, North Texas State University. *Dissertation Abstracts*, 1967A, 27(9), p. 2726.

Epstein, R., and S. S. Komorita, 1971: Self-esteem, success-failure, and locus of control in Negro children. *Developmental Psychology*, 4(1), 2–8.

Erikson, E. H., 1950a: *Childhood and society*, New York: Norton.

Erikson, E. H., 1950b: Growth and crises of the "healthy personality." In M. J. E. Senn (ed.), *Symposium on the healthy personality*, Caldwell, N.J.: Progress Associates, pp. 91–146.

Erikson, E. H., 1960: The problem of ego identity. In M. Stein, A. J. Vidich, and D. M. White (eds.), *Identity and anxiety*, New York: Free Press, pp. 37–87.

Erikson, E. H., 1968: *Identity: Youth and crisis*, New York: Norton.

Erlick, A. C., 1968: Counseling needs of high school students: Report of poll no. 85. *Purdue Opinion Panel (Purdue University)*, 28(2).

Eysenck, H. J., and R. Beech, 1971: Counterconditioning and related methods in behavior therapy. In A. E. Bergin and S. L. Garfield (eds.), *Handbook of psychotherapy and behavior change: An empirical analysis*, New York: Wiley, pp. 543–611.

Feld, S. C., 1967: Longitudinal study of the origins of achievement strivings. *Journal of Personality and Social Psychology*, 7, 408–414.

Fenichel, O., 1945: *The psychoanalytic theory of neurosis*, New York: Norton.

Fitzgerald, A. C., 1970: Influence of the father on child development. Unpublished paper, Boston University School of Education.

Florestano, T. E., 1970: The relationship of college leadership and post-college leadership as measured by the Leadership Opinion Questionnaire and a leadership inventory. Doctoral dissertation, University of Maryland. *Dissertation Abstracts International*, 1971A, 32(1), 173.

Foote, N. N., and L. S. Cottrell, 1955: *Identity and interpersonal competence*, Chicago: University of Chicago Press.

Foster, F. P., 1968: The human relationships of creative individuals. *Journal of Creative Behavior*, 2, 111–118.

Freud, A., 1946: *The ego and the mechanisms of defence*, New York: International Universities Press.

Freud, A., and D. Burlingham, 1944: *Infants without families: The case for and against residential nurseries*, New York: International Universities Press.

Frierson, E. C., 1964: A study of selected characteristics of gifted children from upper and lower socioeconomic backgrounds. Doctoral dissertation, Kent State University. *Dissertation Abstracts*, 1967A, 28(2), 495.

Fromm, E., 1955: *The sane society*, New York: Rinehart.

Fromm, E., 1956: *The art of loving*, New York: Harper.

Gamewell, J., 1967: An investigation of the use of two instruments for assessing intellective and nonintellective aspects of intelligence as predictors of post degree success of psychology graduate students. Doctoral dissertation, Colorado State College. *Dissertation Abstracts*, 1968A, 28(8), 3022–3023.

Garai, J. E., and A. Scheinfeld, 1968: Sex differences in mental and behavior traits. *Genetic Psychology Monographs*, 77 (part 2), 169–299.

Gardner, B. B., 1948: *What makes successful and unsuccessful executives?* New York: Society for the Advancement of Management.

Garfield, S. L., 1971: Research on client variables in psychotherapy. In A. E. Bergin and S. L. Garfield (eds.), *Handbook of psychotherapy and behavior change: An empirical analysis*, New York: Wiley, pp. 271–298.

Garwood, D. S., 1964: Personality factors related to creativity in young scientists. *Journal of Abnormal and Social Psychology*, 68, 413–419.

Gebhard, P. H., J. H. Gagnon, W. B. Pomeroy, and C. V. Christenson, 1965: *Sex offenders: An analysis of types*, New York: Harper–Hoeber.

Gergen, K. J., 1971: *The concept of self*, New York: Holt.

263

Gershman, H., 1968: The evolution of gender identity. *American Journal of Psychoanalysis*, 28, 80–90.

Getzels, J. W., and P. W. Jackson, 1962: *Creativity and intelligence*, New York: Wiley.

Ghiselin, B., R. Rompel, and C. W. Taylor, 1964: A creative process check list: Its development and validation. In C. W. Taylor (ed.), *Widening horizons in creativity*. New York: Wiley, pp. 19–33.

Gilmore, J. V., 1951: A new venture in the testing of motivation. *College Board Review*, 1, 221–226.

Gilmore, J. V., 1953: Noncognitive factors in the academic achievement of M.I.T. undergraduates. Unpublished paper, Boston University School of Education.

Gilmore, J. V., 1967: Parental counseling and academic achievement. *Journal of Education*, 149(3), 46–69.

Gilmore, J. V., 1968: The factor of attention in underachievement. *Journal of Education*, 150(3), 41–66.

Gilmore, J. V., 1971a: The effectiveness of parent counseling with other modalities in the treatment of children with learning disabilities (review of a doctoral dissertation by B. E. Baker, Boston University, 1970). *Journal of Education*, 154(1), 74–82.

Gilmore, J. V., 1971b: Group of individual parent counseling? A study at Upham Elementary School, Wellesley, Massachusetts. *Journal of Education*, 154(1), 83–85.

Gilmore, J. V., 1971c: Parent counseling: Theory and application. *Journal of Education*, 154(1), 40–49.

Gilmore, J. V., 1971d: A summary of graduate students' research projects on parent counseling. *Journal of Education*, 154(1), 65–68.

Gilmore, M. C., 1964: An investigation of the non-intellectual and environmental factors in academic achievement. Unpublished paper, Radcliffe College.

Glueck, S., and E. Glueck, 1962: *Family environment and delinquency*, Boston: Houghton Mifflin.

Goertzel, V., and M. G. Goertzel, 1962: *Cradles of eminence*, Boston: Little, Brown.

Goff, C. E., 1969: A study of the relationship between noncognitive factors and general intelligence to academic achievement at the junior high school level. Doctoral dissertation, Boston University School of Education.

Gordon, S. A., 1971: Parent counseling and crisis intervention. *Journal of Education*, 154(1), 69–73.

264

Gould, J., and W. L. Kolb (eds.), 1964: *A dictionary of the social sciences*, New York: Free Press.

Green, M. M., 1963: Overachieving and underachieving gifted high school girls. In L. D. Crow and A. Crow (eds.), *Educating the academically able*, New York: McKay, pp. 203–205.

Haan, N., 1963: Proposed model of ego functioning: Coping and defense mechanisms in relationship to IQ change. *Psychological Monographs*, 77(8), no. 571.

Hall, C. S., and G. Lindzey (eds.), 1957: *Theories of personality*, New York: Wiley.

Harper, L. V., 1971: The young as a source of stimuli controlling caretaker behavior. *Developmental Psychology*, 4, 73–88.

Harrington, C., 1970: *Errors in sex-role behavior*, New York: Columbia University Teachers College Press.

Harris, H., 1970: Development of moral attitudes in white and negro boys. *Developmental Psychology*, 2, 376–383.

Hartley, R. E., 1969: A developmental view of female sex role definition and identification. In D. Rogers (ed.), *Readings in child psychology*. Belmont, Calif.: Brooks/Cole, pp. 230–240.

Hartup, W. W., 1970: Peer interaction and social organization. In P. H. Mussen (ed.), *Carmichael's manual of child psychology*, 3d ed., New York: Wiley, vol. II, pp. 361–456.

Hartup, W. W., and E. A. Zook, 1960: Sex-role preferences in three- and four-year-old children. *Journal of Consulting Psychology*, 24, 420–426.

Harvey, O. J., 1965: Cognitive aspects of affective arousal. In S. S. Tomkins and C. E. Izard (eds.), *Affect, cognition and personality*, New York: Springer, pp. 242–262.

Heilbrun, A. B., Jr., and D. B. Waters, 1968: Underachievement as related to perceived maternal child rearing and academic conditions of reinforcement. *Child Development*, 39, 913–921.

Helson, R., 1967: Sex differences in creative style. *Journal of Personality*, 35, 214–233.

Herzog, E., and C. E. Sudia, 1970: *Boys in fatherless families*, U.S. Office of Child Development, Children's Bureau, Publ. 0-385-852.

Hetherington, E. M., 1972: Effects of father absence on personality development in adolescent daughters. *Developmental Psychology*, 7, 313–326.

Higgins, J. C., 1971: A pupil personnel services program to develop self-esteem. Doctoral dissertation, University of Pittsburgh. *Dissertation Abstracts*, 1972A, 32(8), 4351.

265

Hinsie, L. E., and R. J. Campbell, 1970: *Psychiatric dictionary*, 4th ed., New York: Oxford University Press.

Hoffman, M. L., 1969: Childrearing practices and moral development: Generalizations from empirical research. In D. Rogers (ed.), *Readings in child psychology*, Belmont, Calif.: Brooks/Cole, pp. 174–184.

Hoffman, M. L., 1970: Moral development. In P. H. Mussen (ed.), *Carmichael's manual of child psychology*, 3d ed., New York: Wiley, vol. II, pp. 261–359.

Hoffman, M. L., and L. W. Hoffman (eds.), 1964: *Review of child development research*, New York: Russell Sage Foundation, vol. I.

Hoffman, L. W., and M. L. Hoffman (eds.), 1966: *Review of child development research*, New York: Russell Sage Foundation, vol. II.

Holland, J. L., 1963: Creative and academic performance among talented adolescents. In R. E. Grinder (ed.), *Studies in adolescence*. New York: Macmillan, pp. 511–524.

Holland, J. L., 1964: The assessment and prediction of the creative performance of high-aptitude youth. In C. W. Taylor (ed.), *Widening horizons in creativity*, New York: Wiley, pp. 298–315.

Hollander, E. P., 1961: Emergent leadership and social influence. In L. Petrullo and B. M. Bass (eds.), *Leadership and interpersonal behavior*, New York: Holt, pp. 30–47.

Hollingshead, A. B., and F. C. Redlich, 1958: *Social class and mental illness*, New York: Wiley.

Hughes, H. K., 1969: The enhancement of creativity. *Journal of Creative Behavior*, 3(2), 73–83.

Hurley, J. R., 1967: Parental acceptance-rejection and children's intelligence. In G. R. Medinnus (ed.), *Readings in the psychology of parent-child relations*, New York: Wiley, pp. 106–116.

Impellizzeri, I. H., 1961: Nature and scope of the problem. In L. M. Miller (ed.), *Guidance for the underachiever with superior ability*, U.S. Office of Education Bull. OE-25021, pp. 1–14.

Jacobson, E., 1964: *The self and the object world*, New York: International Universities Press.

Jahoda, M., 1958: *Current concepts of positive mental health*, New York: Basic Books.

Johnson, R. M., 1966: A comparison of gifted adolescents from high and low socioeconomic backgrounds on school achievement and personality traits. Doctoral dissertation, University of Denver. *Dissertation Abstracts*, 1967A, 27, 3226–3227.

Jones, J. G., 1966: Relationships among identity development and intellectual and nonintellectual factors. Doctoral dissertation, University of Wisconsin. *Dissertation Abstracts*, 1967A, 28(3), 941.

Joseph, E. D., 1966: Memory and conflict. *Psychoanalytic Quarterly*, 35, 1–17.

Kagan, J., 1965: Reflection-impulsivity and reading ability in primary grade children. *Child Development*, 36, 609–628.

Kagan, J., 1966: Reflection-impulsivity: The generality and dynamics of conceptual tempo. *Journal of Abnormal Psychology*, 71, 17–24.

Kagan, J., 1968: On cultural deprivation. In D. C. Glass (ed.), *Environmental influences*, New York: Rockefeller University Press and Russell Sage Foundation, pp. 211–250.

Kagan, J., and H. A. Moss, 1962: *Birth to maturity: A study of psychological development*, New York: Wiley.

Kagan, J., L. W. Sontag, C. T. Baker, and V. L. Nelson, 1966: Personality and IQ change. In J. F. Rosenblith and W. Allinsmith (eds.), *The causes of behavior II: Readings in child development and educational psychology*, 2d ed., Boston: Allyn and Bacon, pp. 393–398.

Karasick, B., T. R. Leidy, and B. Smart (eds.), 1968: Characteristics differentiating high school leaders from nonleaders: Report of poll no. 83. *Purdue Opinion Panel (Purdue University)*, 27(2).

Kennedy, W. A., 1960: A multidimensional study of mathematically gifted adolescents. *Child Development*, 31, 655–666.

Kipnis, D., 1971: *Character structure and impulsiveness*, New York: Academic.

Kohlberg, L., 1964: Development of moral character and moral ideology. In M. L. Hoffman and L. W. Hoffman (eds.), *Review of child development research*, New York: Russell Sage Foundation, vol. I, pp. 383–431.

Krebs, D. L., 1970: Altruism: An examination of the concept and a review of the literature. *Psychological Bulletin*, 1970, 73, 258–302.

Kurtz, J. J., and E. J. Swenson, 1951: Factors related to overachievement and underachievement in school. *School Review*, 59, 472–480.

Kurtzman, K. A., 1967: A study of school attitudes, peer acceptance, and personality of creative adolescents. *Exceptional Children*, 34, 157–163.

Langner, T. S., and S. T. Michael, 1963: *Life stress and mental health*, New York: Free Press.

Lavin, D. E., 1965: *The prediction of academic performance*, New York: Russell Sage Foundation.

Lazarus, R. S., 1966: *Psychological stress and the coping process*, New York: McGraw-Hill.

Leites, N., 1971: *The new ego: Pitfalls in current thinking about patients in psychoanalysis*, New York: Science House.

Lekarczyk, D. T., and K. T. Hill, 1969: Self-esteem, test anxiety, stress, and verbal learning. *Developmental Psychology*, 1, 147–154.

Lenrow, P. B., 1965: Studies of sympathy. In S. S. Tomkins and C. E. Izard (eds.), *Affect, cognition and personality*, New York: Springer, pp. 264–294.

Lett, W. R., 1968: Some postulated correlates of creativity and need achievement. Doctoral dissertation, University of California, Berkeley. *Dissertation Abstracts*, 1968A, 29(4), 1106.

Levitt, E. E., 1971: Research on psychotherapy with children. In A. E. Bergin and S. L. Garfield (eds.), *Handbook of psychotherapy and behavior change: An empirical analysis*, New York: Wiley, pp. 474–494.

Lewis, H. B., 1971: *Shame and guilt in neurosis*, New York: International Universities Press.

Lynch, J. P., 1971: Possible relationships between father absence and impulsivity. Unpublished paper, Boston University School of Education.

Lynch, M. A., 1960: Use of the Gilmore sentence completion test as a predictive instrument in relation to academic achievement in certain high school students. Master's thesis, Boston University School of Education.

Lynd, H. M., 1958: *On shame and the search for identity*, New York: Harcourt, Brace.

Maccoby, E. E., 1968: The development of moral values and behavior in childhood. In J. A. Clausen (ed.), *Socialization and society*, Boston: Little, Brown, pp. 227–269.

MacKinnon, D. W., 1962: The nature and nurture of creative talent. *American Psychologist*, 17, 484–495.

MacKinnon, D. W., 1963: Creativity and images of the self. In R. W. White (ed.), *The study of lives*, New York: Atherton, pp. 251–278.

MacKinnon, D. W., 1968: Selecting students with creative potential. In P. Heist (ed.), *The creative college student: An unmet challenge*, San Francisco: Jossey-Bass, pp. 101–116.

MacLeod, R. B., 1962: Retrospect and prospect. In H. E. Gruber, G. Terrell, and M. Wertheimer (eds.), *Contemporary approaches to creative thinking*, New York: Atherton, pp. 175–212.

268

Maslow, A. H., 1954: *Motivation and personality*, New York: Harper.

May, R. R., 1971: A method for studying the development of gender identity. *Developmental Psychology*, 5, 484–487.

McClelland, D. C., 1962: On the psychodynamics of creative physical scientists. In H. E. Gruber, G. Terrell, and M. Wertheimer (eds.), *Contemporary approaches to creative thinking*, New York: Atherton, pp. 141–174.

McGurk, H., and M. Lewis, 1972: Birth order: A phenomenon in search of an explanation. *Developmental Psychology*, 7, 366.

McKinley, D. G., 1964: *Social class and family life*, New York: Free Press.

Mednick, S. A., and M. T. Mednick, 1964: An associative interpretation of the creative process. In C. W. Taylor (ed.), *Widening horizons in creativity*, New York: Wiley, pp. 54–68.

Mednick, M. T., S. A. Mednick, and E. V. Mednick, 1964: Incubation of creative performance and specific associative priming. *Journal of Abnormal and Social Psychology*, 69, 84–88.

Meeks, A. R., 1961: What can be done at the elementary level? In L. M. Miller (ed.), *Guidance for the underachiever with superior ability*, U.S. Office of Education Bull. OE-25021, pp. 31–42.

Meltzoff, J., and M. Kornreich, 1970: *Research in psychotherapy*, New York: Atherton.

Mendel, G., 1965: Children's preferences for differing degrees of novelty. *Child Development*, 36, 453–465.

Mendelsohn, G. A., and B. B. Griswold, 1964: Differential use of incidental stimuli in problem solving as a function of creativity. *Journal of Abnormal and Social Psychology*, 68, 431–436.

Miller, L. M., (ed.), 1961: *Guidance for the underachiever with superior ability*. U.S. Office of Education Bull. OE-25021.

Miller, T. W., 1971: Communicative dimensions of mother-child interaction as they affect the self-esteem of the child. *Proceedings 79th annual convention, American Psychological Association*, pp. 241–242.

Mischel, W., 1970: Sex-typing and socialization. In P. H. Mussen (ed.), *Carmichael's manual of child psychology*, 3d ed., New York: Wiley, vol. II, pp. 3–72.

Moment, D., and A. Zaleznik, 1963: *Role development and interpersonal competence*. Boston: Harvard School of Business Administration.

Moore, B. M., and W. H. Holtzman, 1965: *Tomorrow's parents: A study of youth and their families*, Austin, Tex.: University of Texas Press.

Moore, S., 1962: Science interest peak at age 12. *Science News Letter*, 82(11), 178–179.

Morrow, W. R., and R. C. Wilson, 1967: Family relations of bright high-achieving and underachieving high school boys. In G. R. Medinnus (ed.), *Readings in the psychology of parent-child relations*, New York: Wiley, pp. 247–255.

Mote, F. B., 1966: The relationship between child self concepts in school and parental attitudes and behaviors in child rearing. Doctoral dissertation, Stanford University. *Dissertation Abstracts*, 1967A, 27(10), 3319.

Murphy, L. B., and collaborators, 1962: *The widening world of childhood: Paths toward mastery*, New York: Basic Books.

Murphy, L. B., 1970: The problem of defense and the concept of coping. In E. J. Anthony and C. Koupernik (eds.), *The child in his family*, New York: Wiley-Interscience, pp. 65–86.

Murstein, B. I., 1970: Self and ideal self discrepancy and the choice of marital partner. *Proceedings 78th annual convention, American Psychological Association*, pp. 459–460.

Mussen, P. H., 1961: Some antecedents and consequents of masculine sex-typing in adolescent boys. *Psychological Monographs*, 75, no. 506.

Mussen, P. H., J. J. Conger, and J. Kagan, 1969: *Child development and personality*, 3d ed., New York: Harper.

Mussen, P., and E. Rutherford, 1966: Parent-child relations and parental personality in relation to young children's sex-role preferences. In J. F. Rosenblith and W. Allinsmith (eds.), *The causes of behavior II: Readings in child development and educational psychology*, 2d ed., Boston: Allyn and Bacon, pp. 167–178.

Mussen, P., E. Rutherford, S. Harris, and C. B. Keasey, 1970: Honesty and altruism among preadolescents. *Developmental Psychology*, 3, 169–194

Nash, J., 1965: The father in contemporary culture and current psychological literature. *Child Development*, 36, 261–297.

National Institute of Child Health and Human Development, 1968: *Perspectives on human deprivation: Biological, psychological, and sociological*, U.S. Department of Health, Education, and Welfare Publ. 0-328-458.

Nicholi, A. M., 1972: Reflections from Harvard on 1 million dropouts. *Frontiers of Psychiatry*, 2, 1–3.

Nichols, R. C., and J. L. Holland, 1963: Prediction of the first year college performance of high aptitude students. *Psychological Monographs*, 77(7), no. 570.

O'Callaghan, J. B., 1973: An investigation of selected current parent training programs with implications for future efforts. Unpublished paper, Harvard University School of Education.

Oden, M. H., 1968: The fulfillment of promise: 40-year follow-up of the Terman gifted group. *Genetic Psychology Monographs*, 77(1), 5–93.

Parsons, T., and R. F. Bales, 1955: *Family, socialization and interaction process*, New York: Free Press.

Patterson, G. R., 1971a: Behavioral intervention procedures in the classroom and in the home. In A. E. Bergin and S. L. Garfield (eds.), *Handbook of psychotherapy and behavior change: An empirical analysis*, New York: Wiley, pp. 751–775.

Patterson, G. R., 1971b: Parents as dispensers of aversive stimuli. In E. McGinnies and C. B. Ferster (eds.), *The reinforcement of social behavior*, Boston: Houghton Mifflin, pp. 167–174.

Peck, R. F., 1963: Family patterns correlated with adolescent personality structure. In R. E. Grinder (ed.), *Studies in adolescence*, New York: Macmillan, pp. 133–140.

Perkins, J. A., 1969: Group counseling with bright underachievers and their mothers. Doctoral dissertation, University of Connecticut. *Dissertation Abstracts*, 1970A, 30(7), 2809.

Pervin, L. A., L. E. Reik, and W. Dalrymple (eds.), 1966: *The college dropout and the utilization of talent*. Princeton, N.J.: Princeton University Press.

Peterson, R. S., 1967: A longitudinal study of nonintellectual characteristics of college dropouts. Doctoral dissertation, University of Oregon. *Dissertation Abstracts*, 1967A, 28(6), 2076.

Petrullo, L., and B. M. Bass (eds.), 1961: *Leadership and interpersonal behavior*, New York: Holt.

Phillips, E. L., E. A. Phillips, D. L. Fixen, and M. M. Wolf, 1973: Achievement place: Behavior shaping works for delinquents. *Psychology Today*, 7(1), 74–79.

Pierce, J. V., and P. H. Bowman, 1965: Motivation patterns of superior high school students. In M. Kornrich (ed.), *Underachievement*, Springfield, Ill.: Thomas, pp. 214–252.

Pruyser, P. W., 1963: Phenomenology and dynamics of hoping. *Journal for the Scientific Study of Religion*, 3, 86–96.

Purkey, W. W., 1970: *Self concept and school achievement*, Englewood Cliffs, N.J.: Prentice-Hall.

Quimby, V., 1967: Differences in the self-ideal relationship of an achiever group and an underachiever group. *California Journal of Educational Research*, 18(1), 23–31.

271

Radin, N., 1972: Father-child interaction and the intellectual function of four-year-old boys. *Developmental Psychology*, 6, 353–361.

Rawlings, E. I., 1970: Reactive guilt and anticipatory guilt in altruistic behavior. In J. Macaulay and L. Berkowitz (eds.), *Altruism and helping behavior*, New York: Academic, pp. 163–177.

Reiss, S. M., 1966: Dimensions of self-concept and achievement in bright eleventh-grade male students. Doctoral dissertation, University of Nebraska. *Dissertation Abstracts*, 1966A, 27(6), 1667–1668.

Roberts, H. E., 1962: Factors affecting the academic underachievement of bright high-school students. *Journal of Educational Research*, 56, 175–183.

Roche Report, 1971: Rorschach study reflects sex-role changes in our society: Special report. *Frontiers of Psychiatry*, 1(11), 5, 8.

Roe, A., 1960: Crucial life experiences in the development of scientists. In E. P. Torrance (ed.), *Talent and education*, Minneapolis: University of Minnesota Press, pp. 66–77.

Roe, A., 1969: The psychology of the scientist. In H. Chiang and A. H. Maslow (eds.), *The healthy personality: Readings*, New York: Van Nostrand–Reinhold, pp. 91–100.

Rogers, D., (ed.), 1969: *Issues in child psychology*. Belmont, Calif.: Brooks/Cole.

Rosen, B. C., 1963: Family structure and achievement motivation. In R. E. Grinder (ed.), *Studies in adolescence*, New York: MacMillan, pp. 169–186.

Rosen, B. C., 1965: Race, ethnicity, and the achievement syndrome. In M. Kornrich (ed.), *Underachievement*, Springfield, Ill.: Thomas, pp. 253–278.

Rosenberg, M., 1965: *Society and the adolescent self-image*. Princeton, N.J.: Princeton University Press.

Roth, R. M., and H. A. Meyersburg, 1965: The non-achievement syndrome. In M. Kornrich (ed.), *Underachievement*, Springfield, Ill.: Thomas, pp. 279–288.

Rotter, J. B., 1966: Generalized expectancies for internal versus external control of reinforcement. *Psychological Monographs*, 80(1), no. 609.

Rotter, J. B., 1971: Generalized expectancies for interpersonal trust. *American Psychologist*, 26, 443–452.

Rutherford, E., and P. Mussen, 1968: Generosity in nursery school boys. *Child Development*, 39, 755–765.

Sampson, E. E., 1965: The study of ordinal position: Antecedents and outcomes. In B. A. Maher (ed.), *Progress in experimental personality research*, New York: Academic, vol. II, pp. 175–228.

Schachter, S., 1959: *The psychology of affiliation*, Stanford, Calif.: Stanford University Press.

Schaefer, C. E., 1967: Biographical inventory correlates of scientific and artistic creativity in adolescents. Doctoral dissertation, Fordham University. *Dissertation Abstracts*, 1967B, 28(3), 1173–1174.

Schafer, R., 1959: Generative empathy in the treatment situation. *Psychoanalytic Quarterly*, 28, 342–373.

Schafer, R., 1968: *Aspects of internalization*, New York: International Universities Press.

Schwartz, S. C., 1966: Parent-child interaction as it relates to the ego functioning and self-concept of the pre-school child. Doctoral dissertation, Columbia University. *Dissertation Abstracts*, 1967A, 27(9), 2898–2899.

Sears, R. R., E. E. Maccoby, and H. Levin, 1957: *Patterns of child rearing*, Evanston, Ill.: Row, Peterson.

Shatkin, S. D., 1966: Underachievement: A review of the literature. Unpublished paper, Brown University.

Shaw, M. C., 1961: Definition and identification of academic underachievers. In L. M. Miller (ed.), *Guidance for the underachiever with superior ability*, U.S. Office of Education Bull. OE-25021, pp. 15–30.

Shaw, M. C., and B. E. Dutton, 1962: The use of the Parent Attitude Research Inventory with the parents of bright academic underachievers. *Journal of Educational Psychology*, 53, 203–208.

Silverman, I., 1964: Self-esteem and differential responsiveness to success and failure. *Journal of Abnormal and Social Psychology*, 69, 115–119.

Simon, W., and J. Gagnon, 1969: Psychosexual development. *Transaction*, 6(5), 9–17.

Sisk, D. A., 1966: The relationship between self concept and creative thinking of elementary school children: An experimental investigation. Doctoral dissertation, University of California, Los Angeles. *Dissertation Abstracts*, 1967A, 27(8), 2455.

Slater, P. E., 1962: Parental behavior and the personality of the child. *Journal of Genetic Psychology*, 101, 53–68.

Smith, C. P., 1969: *Achievement-related motives in children*, New York: Russell Sage Foundation.

Snyder, B. R., 1968: The education of creative science students. In P. Heist (ed.), *The creative college student: An unmet challenge*, San Francisco: Jossey-Bass, pp. 56–70.

Sorrentino, R. M., 1971: An extension of theory of achievement motivation to the study of emergent leadership. Doctoral dissertation,

273

State University of New York, Buffalo. *Dissertation Abstracts International*, 1971A, 32(3), 1625.

Stalnaker, J. M., 1961: Recognizing and encouraging talent. *American Psychologist*, 16, 513–522.

Staub, E., 1971: A child in distress: The influence of nurturance and modeling on children's attempts to help. *Developmental Psychology*, 5, 124–132.

Stein, E. V., 1971: Faith, hope and suicide. *Journal of Religion and Health*, 10, 214–225.

Stein, M. I., 1963: *Personality measures in admissions: Antecedent and personality factors as predictors of college success*. New York: College Entrance Examination Board.

Stotland, E., 1969: *The psychology of hope*, San Francisco: Jossey-Bass.

Sutherland, B. K., 1965a: Case studies in educational failure during adolescence. In M. Kornrich (ed.), *Underachievement*, Springfield, Ill.: Thomas, pp. 376–389.

Sutherland, B. K., 1965b: The sentence-completion technique in a study of scholastic underachievement. In M. Kornrich (ed.), *Underachievement*, Springfield, Ill.: Thomas, pp. 364–375.

Sutherland, R. L., W. H. Holtzman, E. A. Koile, and B. K. Smith (eds.), 1962: *Personality factors on the college campus*. Austin, Tex.: Hogg Foundation for Mental Health.

Sutton-Smith, B., and B. G. Rosenberg, 1961: Impulsivity and sex preference. *Journal of Genetic Psychology*, 98, 187–192.

Taylor, C. W., 1963: The creative individual: A new portrait in giftedness. In L. D. Crow and A. Crow (eds.), *Educating the academically able*, New York: McKay, pp. 233–240.

Torrance, E. P., 1959: Research notes from here and there: Current research on the nature of creative talent. *Journal of Counseling Psychology*, 6, 309–316.

Trent, J. W., 1968: A dialogue on creativity. In P. Heist (ed.), *The creative college student: An unmet challenge*, San Francisco, Jossey-Bass, pp. 3–17.

Trezise, R. L., 1966: A descriptive study of the life styles of a group of creative adolescents. Doctoral dissertation, Michigan State University. *Dissertation Abstracts*, 1967A, 27(9), 2754–2756.

Tribou, V., 1958: The use of the Gilmore sentence completion test in the prediction of academic achievement in a junior college. Master's thesis, Boston University School of Education.

Trotta, J. O., 1967: A comparison of the achievement motivation of mothers of retarded readers and mothers of achieving readers. Doctoral dissertation, Temple University. *Dissertation Abstracts*, 1967B, 28(3), 1215.

Tweedie, M. J., 1965: A study of the relationship between memory process, environmental stimuli, and the delay of gratification. Doctoral dissertation, University of Michigan. *Dissertation Abstracts*, 1966B, 27(2), 618–619.

Van der Meer, H. C., 1967: Decision-making: Need for achievement and probability preference under chance and skill orientation. *Acta Psychologica*, Amsterdam, 26(4), 353–372.

Vroegh, K., 1971a: Masculinity and femininity in the elementary and junior high school years. *Developmental Psychology*, 4, 254–261.

Vroegh, K., 1971b: The relationship of birth order and sex of siblings to gender role identity. *Developmental Psychology*, 4, 407–411.

Wade, S., 1968: Differences between intelligence and creativity: Some speculation on the role of environment. *Journal of Creative Behavior*, 2(2), 97–101.

Walters, J., R. Connor, and M. Zunich, 1967: Interaction of mothers and children from lower-class families. In G. R. Medinnus (ed.), *Readings in the psychology of parent-child relations*, New York: Wiley, pp. 297–303.

Ward, W. C., 1969: Creativity and environmental cues in nursery school children. *Developmental Psychology*, 1, 543–547.

Ward, W. D., 1969: Process of sex-role development. *Developmental Psychology*, 1, 163–168.

Waters, E., and V. J. Crandall, 1967: Social class and observed maternal behavior from 1940 to 1960. In G. R. Medinnus (ed.), *Readings in the psychology of parent-child relations*, New York: Wiley, pp. 304–315.

Webster's third new international dictionary of the English language, 1971: Springfield, Mass.: G. & C. Merriam Co.

Webster's new world dictionary of the American language: College edition, 1962: New York: World.

Weisbroth, S. P., 1970: Moral judgment, sex, and parental identification in adults. *Developmental Psychology*, 2, 396–402.

Westley, W. A., and N. B. Epstein, 1969: *The silent majority*, San Francisco: Jossey-Bass.

White, K., 1968: Anxiety, extraversion-introversion, and divergent thinking ability. *Journal of Creative Behavior*, 2, 119–127.

White, R. W., 1966: Competence and the psychosexual stages of development. In J. F. Rosenblith and W. Allinsmith (eds.), *The causes of behavior II: Readings in child development and educational psychology*, 2d ed., Boston: Allyn and Bacon, pp. 300–308.

275

White, R. W., 1969: Adult growth and emotional maturity. In H. M. Chiang and A. H. Maslow (eds.), *The healthy personality: Readings*, New York: Van Nostrand–Reinhold, pp. 22–29.

White, S., 1972: Federal programs for young children: Review and recommendations. Unpublished research survey. Cambridge, Mass.: Huron Institute.

Whiting, J. W. M., and I. L. Child, 1953: *Child training and personality: A cross-cultural study*. New Haven, Conn.: Yale University Press.

Wyden, P., and B. Wyden, 1968: *Growing up straight*, New York: Stein and Day.

Yarrow, M. R., J. D. Campbell, and R. V. Burton, 1968: *Child rearing: An inquiry into research and methods*, San Francisco: Jossey-Bass.

Zaleznik, A., G. W. Dalton, and L. B. Barnes, 1970: *Orientation and conflict in career*. Boston: Harvard School of Business Administration.

Ackerman, N. W., 178, 253
Albert, R. S., 2, 3, 4
Allen, P. J., 221
Allinsmith, W., and T. C. Greening, 111
Altus, W. D., 186, 187
Arasteh, J. D., 28, 30, 33, 218
Arieti, S., 49, 50
Aronfreed, J., 52, 55, 60, 61, 62, 90–91, 101–102, 103, 104, 105–106, 109, 111, 115, 117, 118, 121, 125, 126, 127, 132, 133, 139
Aronfreed, J., and V. Paskal, 104
Bachman, J. G., 21–22, 164, 178, 197–198
Baker, B., 250
Baker, W. G., III, 40, 167, 173, 175
Bandura, A., 52, 53, 54, 55, 56, 63, 66, 100, 115, 118, 171, 239, 242, 250

Bandura, A., and A. D. Huston, 204
Bandura, A., and R. H. Walters, 86–87
Banta, J., 165
Barker, L. W., 22, 173
Barrett, H. O., 200
Barron, F., 2, 23, 26, 28, 29, 32, 48, 50, 72, 73, 75, 79, 92, 94, 143, 155, 157, 166–167, 169, 172, 173, 190–191, 234
Baumrind, D., 129–131
Bayley, N., 212
Becker, W. C., 111, 121–122, 129, 131
Bell, R. Q., 62
Bergin, A. E., 237
Bieber, I., 87
Biller, H. B., 79, 80, 84, 205–206
Biller, H. B., and R. M. Bahm, 81
Biller, H. B., and W. Barry, 79

name index

Biller, H. B. and L. J. Borstelman, 205–206
Biller, H. B., D. L. Singer, and M. Fullerton, 218
Binet, A., 1–2, 4, 17
Bing, E., 189, 203
Blair, G. E., 22
Blanchard, R. W., and H. B. Biller, 206
Block, J., and B. C. Martin, 175
Block, J., and E. Turula, 84
Bonime, W., 87
Borke, H., 101
Bradway, K., 212
Brenner, M., 153
Brewster Smith, M., 37–38, 139, 144, 145
Bronfenbrenner, U., 78–79, 81, 189, 205–206, 222
Burkhart, R. C., 96
Campbell, D. P., 187
Campbell, P. B., 22
Caplin, M. D., 22
Carlsmith, L., 82
Carlton, L., and R. H. Moore, 252
Chambers, J. A., 95, 157, 171
Chance, J. E., 204
Chowdhry, K., and T. M. Newcomb, 34
Clausen, J. A., 178, 179, 180, 181, 182, 186, 187, 188
Cline, V., J. M. Richards, and C. Abe, 27
Cloninger, J. M., 3, 210
Cohen, R. J., 80–81
Coopersmith, S., 2, 16, 17, 22, 40, 47, 50, 81, 131, 132, 144, 157, 160, 185–186, 189, 190, 197, 215, 234
Covington, H. D., 212
Cox, R. D., 37, 72–73, 74, 221
Cox, D. B., and R. A. Bauer, 160
Crutchfield, R. S., R. Albrecht, and D. G. Woodworth, 64

Datta, L. E., and M. D. Parloff, 218
Davids, A., 21–22, 164, 166
Davids, A., and P. K. Hainsworth, 205
Davis, J. A., 3
Dell, H. L. D., 102
Dewing, K., 218
Diller, L., 252
Dittes, J. E., 163
Domino, G., 32
Dollard, J., and N. E. Miller, 171
Douvan, E., and J. Adelson, 38, 46, 98, 133, 158, 172, 173, 180, 185, 222
Douvan, E., and M. Gold, 17
Drevdahl, J. E., 2, 32, 73–74, 75, 95, 96, 97, 157, 159, 172, 173, 217
Drews, E. M., 96
Durr, W. K., and R. R. Schmatz, 93
Eissler, K. R., 44
Ellinger, B. D., 218
Elman, J., A. Press, and P. Rosenkrantz, 70
Elliott, J. L., and D. H. Elliott, 187
Engel, M., 16–17
Engemoen, B. L., 208
Epstein, R., and S. S. Komorita, 198
Erikson, E. H., 2, 44–45, 48–50, 57, 61, 64, 65, 75
Erlick, A. C., 221
Eysenck, H. J., and R. Beech, 237–238
Feld, S. C., 204
Fenichel, C., 50, 57, 58, 77, 137–138, 236
Fisher, S., and S. E. Cleveland, 96
Fishman, J. A., 3
Fitzgerald, A. C., 83
Florestano, T. E., 36
Foote, N. N., and L. S. Cottrell, 115

278

Foster, F. P., 96
Frenkel-Brunswick, E., 96
Freud, A., 115, 136, 137
Freud, A., and D. Burlingham, 136, 137
Freud, S., 54, 56, 60, 76–77, 111, 236
Frierson, E. C., 210
Fromm, E., 48, 79
Gamewell, J., 143, 150
Garai, J. E., and A. Scheinfeld, 166
Gardner, B. B., 37, 47, 169, 175, 219–220
Garfield, S. L., 245–246
Garwood, D. S., 32, 170
Gebhard, P. H., J. Gagnon, W. B. Pomeroy, and C. V. Christenson, 87
Gergen, K. J., 36, 50, 160
Gergen, K. J., and R. A. Bauer, 160
Gershman, H., 67, 75–76
Getzels, J. W., and P. W. Jackson, 26, 218, 219
Ghiselin, B. R., 26
Ghiselin, B. R., R. Rompel, and C. W. Taylor, 169
Gibby, R. G., Sr., and Gibby, R. G., Jr., 22, 252
Gilmore, J. V., 18, 60, 143, 146, 201, 240, 243, 244, 245, 250
Gilmore, M. C., 21, 94, 158
Gladwin, T., 144
Glueck, S., and Glueck, E., 179
Goertzel, V., Goertzel, M. G., 213
Goff, C. E., 146
Gordon, S. A., 245
Green, L. A., 96
Green, M. M., 158
Greenacre, P., 44, 45
Guilford, J. P., 25, 26
Haan, N., 74, 94, 151, 161
Haarer, D. L., 22, 151

Hall, C. S., and Lindzey, 7
Harding, K. L., 22
Harper, L. V., 62, 64
Harrington, C., 76
Hartley, R. E., 127
Hartup, W. W., 35
Hartup, W. W., and E. A. Zook, 76
Harvey, O. J., and J. A. Clapp, 146, 147–148, 149
Hawkes, G. R., L. Burchinal, and B. Gardner, 178
Hebb, D. O., 146
Heilbrun, A. B., Jr., and D. B. Waters, 205
Heinecke, C. M., 111
Helson, R., 32
Herzog, E., and C. B. Sudia, 80
Hetherington, E. M., 76, 81, 84
Higgins, J. C., 252
Himmelweit, H. T., and A. P. Sealy, 188
Hinsie, L. E., and R. J. Campbell, 47, 52, 108, 114, 136
Hoffman, M. L., 85, 102, 103, 115, 116, 117, 119, 122, 123, 129, 131
Hoffman, M. L., and H. D. Saltzstein, 122
Holland, J. L., 21, 29, 32, 36, 95, 172, 218
Holland, J. L., and W. B. Webb, 35
Hollingshead, A. B., and F. C. Redlich, 181, 182
Holzman, P. S., and R. W. Gardner, 160
Horney, K., 2
Hughes, H. K., 29
Hurley, J. R., 211
Hurwitz, I., 164
Impellizzeri, I. H., 20
Jacobson, E., 45, 47, 50, 70, 77–78, 110

279

Jahoda, M., 3, 45, 140
James, W., 112, 143, 146–147
Jennings, H. H., 34
Johnson, R. M., 83, 209
Jones, J. G., 21–22
Joseph, E. D., 152
Jung, C., 7
Kagan, J., 63, 64, 165
Kagan, J., and H. A. Moss, 53, 71
Kagan, J., L. W. Sontag, C. T.
   Baker, and V. L. Nelson, 142,
   212
Karasick, B., T. R. Leidy, and B.
   Smart, 35, 36, 98, 158, 162, 175,
   221
Keefer, K. E., 23
Kennedy, W. A., 94
Kinsey, A. C., 87
Kipnis, D., 161, 162, 166
Knapp, R. H., 112, 175
Kohlberg, L., 14, 75, 77, 78, 132
Krebs, D. L., 105
Kurtz, J. J., and E. J. Swenson, 200
Kurtzman, K. A., 33
Lamy, M. W., 252
Langner, T. S., and S. T. Michael
   87, 164, 184
Lavin, D., 18, 19, 20, 93, 142, 158,
   166, 168, 172, 187
Lazarus, R. S., 139, 159, 160, 164,
   165
Leites, N., 44, 45
Lekarczyk, D. T., and K. T. Hill,
   151
Lenrow, P. B., 106
Lett, W. R., 32
Levine, G. R., and J. T. Simmons,
   122
Levitt, E. E., 238, 239, 245
Lewin, K., 174
Lewis, H. B., 47, 64, 113, 159,
   160, 163–164
Lichtenstein, H., 44, 45
Lynch, J. P., 167

Lynch, M. A., 20, 146
Lynd, H. M., 45, 51, 55, 57, 98
Maccoby, E. E., 53, 66, 115, 154
MacFarlane, J., and N. Honzik,
   131
MacKinnon, D. W., 2, 8, 26–28,
   30, 32, 47, 49, 96, 97, 142, 143,
   150, 159, 168, 142, 175,
   214–215
MacLeod, R. B., 48
Mahler, M. S., 44
Marcel, G., 147
Maslow, A. H., 2, 5, 7, 15, 32, 46,
   73, 97–98, 112, 142, 155
May, R. R., 76
McClelland, D. G., 29, 46–47, 72,
   73, 95, 96, 112, 171, 172
McGurk, H., and M. Lewis, 187
McKinley, D. G., 181, 182
Mednick, S. A., and M. T.
   Mednick, 170
Mednick, M. T., S. A. Mednick,
   and E. V. Mednick, 171
Meeks, A. R., 20
Meltzoff, J., and M. Kornreich,
   237, 239, 240
Mendel, G., 143
Mendelsohn, G. A., and B. B.
   Griswold, 153
Messick, S., and F. Damarin,
   63–64
Midlarsky, E., and J. H. Bryan,
   104
Miller, T. W., 198
Mischel, W., 85
Moment, D., and A. Zaleznik,
   38–39, 98, 220
Moore, B. M., and W. H.
   Holtzman, 185
Moore, S., 178
Morrow, W. R., and R. C. Wilson,
   202
Morse, R. J., 22, 151
Moss, H. A., 62, 64

280

Mote, F. B., 199
Mowrer, O. H., 145
Murphy, L. B., 50, 58–59, 115, 136–137, 138, 141
Murray, H., 44
Mussen, P. H., 79
Mussen, P. H., J. J. Conger, and J. Kagan, 52, 79, 85, 123, 126, 132, 164, 209
Mussen, P. H., and E. Rutherford, 78, 83, 84
Mussen, P. H., E. Rutherford, S. Harris, and C. B. Keasy, 5, 77, 78, 85
Nash, J., 79
National Institute of Child Health, 14, 17, 80, 84, 182, 197
Nicholi, A. M., 208–209
Nichols, R. C., 218
Nichols, R. C., and J. L. Holland, 207
O'Callaghan, J. B., 242
Oden, M. H., 2, 4, 25, 72, 73, 75, 98, 172, 173, 206–207, 234
Parsons, T., and R. F. Bales, 114
Patterson, G. R., 122, 241, 242, 243
Peck, R. F., 198
Perkins, J. A., 243–244
Pervin, L. A., L. E. Reik, and W. Dalrymple, 94
Peterson, R. S., 173, 174
Petrullo, L., 33
Phillips, E. L., E. A. Phillips, D. L. Fixen, and M. M. Wolf, 242
Pierce, J. V., and P. H. Bowman, 202
Piers, E. V., and D. B. Harris, 16–17
Pigott, K., 242–243
Pruyser, P. W., 146, 147
Purkey, W. W., 22, 23
Quimby, V., 21–22
Radin, N., 210

Rawlings, E. I., 105
Reid, J. B., F. J. King, and P. Wickwire, 32
Reiss, S. M., 21–22
Roberts, H. E., 200, 202
Robson, K. S., and Moss, 62
Roe, A., 2, 29, 73, 143, 150, 153, 156, 157, 170, 215–216, 217
Rogers, C. R., 31
Rogers, D., 78, 79, 83
Rosen, B. C., 178, 179, 202
Rosenberg, M., 2, 16, 41, 132, 190, 193–195, 234, 235, 252
Rosenhan, D., and G. M. White, 103
Roth, R. M., and H. A. Meyersburg, 158–159
Rotter, J. B., 139–140, 199
Rutherford, E., and P. H. Mussen, 123
Sampson, E. E., 186
Sanford, N., 74
Schachter, S., 187
Schaefer, C. E., 30
Schafer, R., 21, 44, 50, 53, 56, 57, 58, 59, 60, 61, 77, 78, 90, 116
Schwartz, S. C., 199
Sears, R. R., E. E. Maccoby, and H. Levin, 122, 131
Shatkin, S. D., 21, 93
Shaw, M. C., 200
Shaw, M. C., and B. E. Dutton, 201
Silverman, I., 22, 148
Simon, W., and J. Gagnon, 67, 75
Singer, D. L., 218
Sisk, D. A., 32
Slater, P. E., 167
Smith, C. P., 158
Snyder, B. R., 166
Sorrentino, R. M., 36
Spitz, R., 59
Stalnaker, J. M., 21, 93, 158, 178
Staub, E., 107

281

Stein, M. I., 74
Stotland, E., 145, 147, 148, 149, 174
Sullivan, H. S., 3, 50, 236
Sutherland, B. K., 200, 201
Sutherland, R. L., W. H. Holtzman, E. A. Koile, and B. K. Smith, 23
Sutton-Smith, B., and B. G. Rosenberg, 165
Taylor, C. W., 25, 26, 142, 157, 168, 172
Terman, L., 2, 4, 25, 72, 73, 75, 98, 172, 173, 206–207, 234
Torrance, E. P., 26, 30
Trent, J. W., 25
Trezise, R. L., 25
Tribou, V., 20
Trotta, J. O., 204
Tweedie, M. J., 153, 165
Van der Meer, H. C., 175
Vener, A. M., and C. A. Snyder, 76
Vroegh, K., 68–69
Wade, S., 27, 31
Walters, J., R. Connor, and M. Zunich, 183

Ward, W. C., 142
Ward, W. D., 76
Waters, E., and V. J. Crandall, 183
Watson, G., 96, 218
Webb, W. B.
Webster, H., 74
Weisberg, P. S., and K. J. Springer, 32–33, 218
Weisbroth, S. P.
Westley, W. A., and N. B. Epstein, 24, 47, 74, 85, 94, 98, 190, 192
White, K., 31
White, R. W., 6, 44
White, S., 239, 240
Whiting, J. W. M., and I. L. Child, 111
Whiting, J. W. M., and B. Whiting, 107
Wyden, P., and B. Wyden, 87
Yarrow, M. R., J. D. Campbell, R. V. Burton, 122, 189–190
Zaleznik, A., G. W. Dalton, and L. B. Barnes, 39–40, 72, 149, 167, 189, 220
Zimbardo, P. G., and R. Formica, 159

academic achievement, early
    studies, 3
and impulse control, 163–167
and intelligence, 17–19
measures of, 19
noncognitive factors, 19–21
and self-esteem, 21–25
sex differences in, 20
academic achiever, characteristics
    of, 17–25
    see also productive personality
achievement motivation   see
    aspiration level; motivation;
    family environment
affiliation, in dependent persons,
    94, 159–160
in first-born child, 187
in leaders, 36, 38–39
aggression, and guilt, 109
control of, 78, 116, 167
and power-association disciplines,
    86–87, 122–123, 129
sexual expression of, 86–87, 113
    see also sex identification;
    socialization

aggressiveness   see sex identity
alienation, and downward .
    mobility, 38,
in dropouts, 94, 209
and guilt, 110, 113
and impulsivity, 161–162
and perception, 142
altruism, 100–105
acquisition of, 101–104
age of appearance, 101
and empathy, 101–102
and guilt, 105, 108
in productive persons, 90,
    92–93, 134
sex differences, 105
as a social value, 101, 103, 105
and sympathy, 105–106
and trust, 140
    see also social responsibility
anaclitic identification, 57
anticipation   see hope
anxiety, and creativity, 31–32
dependency, 159–160
impulsivity, 163–164
memory, 152

subject index 283

and perception, 142, 160
psychosomatic disorders,
  234–235
appraisal   see coping; judgment
architects   see creative person
artistic creativity   see creative
  process
aspiration level, 38–41
as measure of self-esteem, 39
  see also hope
associative thinking   see
  ordering ability
attention, and memory, 153
and perception, 143
and persistence, 171
authority   see socialization
autonomy   see independence
average   see productivity
behavior modification, experimental programs, 241–143
parent-child programs, 240–241
  see also family size; socioeconomic level
business executives   see leader
child development   see
  identification; socialization
child-rearing practices   see family
  environment
closure   see impulsivity
cognitive skills, coping ability,
  149–153, 154
effect of father absence, 81–83,
  205–206
and impulse control, 164
and internalization of values,
  92, 132
and judgment, 65
and parental child-rearing
  practices, 203–204, 210–213
and self-image, 21
sex differences in, 82
and social effectiveness, 93–94
in social learning, 117–118, 154
  see also coping skills

communication   see empathy;
  interpersonal competence
competence   see coping
complexity   see ordering ability
confused sex identity   see sex
  identification
conscience (superego), 107–108
functions of, 90, 108
and identity, 50
and impulse control, 164
  see also socialization
superego identification, 56, 66,
  78–79
control   see impulse control
coping, basis of, 136–141
early stages, 58–59, 136–138
and mastery, 136, 174–177
perception of self as effectual,
  135–139
personal values, 139
self-esteem, 14, 137, 139
steps in, 141, 144
trust, 140
coping characteristics, 155–176
decisiveness, 175
impulse control, 161–167
independence, 155–161
ordering ability, 168–170
persistence, 171–174
coping skills, 141–154
age and experience, 127, 154
cognitive skills, 149–153
hope, 144–149
judgment, 144
perception, 141–144
  see also coping
counseling programs, 239–245,
  250–255
  see also self-esteem construct
creative process, artistic vs
  scientific, 28
in problem solving, 170
as productive functioning, 7–8
  see also ordering ability

creativity, in children, 30
early studies, 3–4
and independence, 155–158
and intelligence, 26–28, 218
measures of, 27–28
and self-esteem, 31–33
creative person, characteristics of,
  25–33
personality types, 28–30
  see also productive personality
creative thinking   see creative
  process; divergent thinking;
  ordering ability
curiosity, and achievement
  motivation, 212
and perception, 142–143
decision making, and impulsivity,
  162–164, 176
as mastery, 174–176
defense mechanisms, 110–111
in dependent persons, 113,
  160–161
as early coping devices, 59,
  136–138
  see also independence; memory
delay   see impulse control
dependency, and affiliation, 94,
  158–159
and low self-esteem, 159–160
punishment of, 86, 204
and shame, 113
divergent thinking, 25–26, 31
  see also ordering ability
divorce, of parents, 194–195
  see also father absence
divorce rate   see sex identity
effectance, 6
ego control   see impulse control
ego identity   see identity
ego strength . see self-esteem
emotional security, fostering
  conditions, 190–193
empathy, as affective interaction,
  60–61

as basis of identification, 62
as basis of social responsibility,
  88–89, 101–102, 104–106,
  133–134
establishment of, 59–63, 243–244
as factor in leadership, 33–34
as *Gemeinschaftsgefühl,* 46, 134
and parental discipline, 118–123
  see also identification; social
  responsibility; socialization
ethics   see values
ethnic factors   see family
  environment
facial expression   see identification
family background, academic
  achiever, 200–214, 223, 233
creative person, 31–32, 214–219,
  223, 233
leader, 219–234
family environment, 188–199
child-rearing attitudes and practices, 107, 119, 183, 195, 197,
  201–203
family authority patterns, 128–131,
  178–179, 183, 192–193, 204–205,
  210–211, 218–220
parental discipline, 119–123, 219
self-esteem of parents, 119–120,
  128–129, 183, 185–186, 196–197
parental values, 178, 180, 182,
  202–203, 207–208, 213, 215,
  221–224, 233–234, 254
stability of home, 191, 193–194,
  200
warmth of family relationships,
  86–87, 128–129, 132, 191–195,
  201, 220, 222, 224
family size, 178–180
authority and discipline patterns,
  178–179
parent-child interaction, 180
  see also birth order; socioeconomic level

father, competence of, 87, 186,
    191, 194, 196–197, 206–207,
    215, 221
  influence on cognitive skills,
    82–83, 210–211
  and moral development, 79, 85
  and sex identity in daughters,
    83, 85
  and sex identity in sons, 77, 86
  role in family structure, 67–68, 78,
    181, 182
father absence, effect on
    cognitive development, 82–83,
    205–206
  heterosexual adjustment in
    daughter, 84
  impulsivity in son, 81, 167
  masculinity in son, 80–81
feminity   see sex identity
field dependence   see depen-
    dency
first-born child   see birth order
flexibility   see cognitive patterns
gender identity   see sex identity
generative empathy, 60–61
    see also identification
genius, 2, 6
    see also intelligence
group interaction   see leadership
guilt, 108–112
  and altruism, 102, 105, 108, 110
  defense mechanisms, 110
  and empathy, 108, 111
  as internalized behavioral
    control, 100, 111, 133–134
  moral judgment, 109, 112
  and self-esteem, 16, 50, 110
  and shame, 112–113
health, 234–235
    see also mental health; psycho-
    somatic disorders
heredity, 1–2, 18
homosexuality   see sex
    identification

hope, 144–149
  as affective response, 146–147
  and aspiration level, 144–145, 149
  as assumption of effectiveness,
    141, 145
  and expectation, 145–146
  and persistence, 174
  as self-fulfilling prophecy,
    147–148
    see also coping
identification, 51–57
  as basis of identity, 45–46, 51,
    54–55, 61
  as basis of socialization, 54,
    99–100, 114–116
  coping skills, 65–66
  dynamics of, 53–57
  early forms, 57–64
  generative empathy, 60–62
  infant feeding experiences, 54–55,
    57–58
  and introjection, 59–60
  and modeling (imitation), 51–53
  as response to expressive cues,
    62–64
  selection of identifications, 54–57
  and self-esteem, 49–51, 66
  superego identification, 56, 66
    see also sex identification;
    socialization
identity, 43–45
  age of formation, 45, 48
  effect of guilt, 50
  and identification process, 51,
    53–55
  integration, 45
  and perception of self, 47–48
  in productive persons, 11–12, 28,
    43, 88
    see also sex identity; social
    responsibility
  and self-esteem, 49–51
  and social responsibility, 45–46,
    99

imitation see identification
impulse control (ego control),
  161–167
and academic achievement,
  165–167
capacity for postponement, 65–66,
  77–78, 162, 164, 167
and cognitive skills, 164, 166
as control over outcome, 161,
  165–166
and creativity, 166–167
development of, 65–66, 77–78
and learning, 165
and self-esteem, 162–164
and social responsibility, 161–162
  see also persistence
impulsivity, and alienation, 162
cognitive approach, 164
and decision-making ability, 163,
  176
distractibility, 162, 165
effect on academic performance,
  163, 165, 166
effect in girls, 166
in father-absent boys, 167
and frustration tolerance, 164–165,
  167
hyperactivity, 162, 164, 167
and intelligence, 18
and judgment, 161, 162–163, 167
need for closure, 152–153,
  162–164, 176
as predictor of underschievement,
  166
and sex identity, 165
and socialization, 126, 167
and spontaneity, 163
  see also sex identification
independence, 155–161
in academic achiever, 157–158
in creative person, 25–26, 29,
  156–157, 219
and identity, 43
independence training, 204

and intelligence, 158
and judgment, 156, 161
in leader, 35, 39–40, 158, 175
mother-child relationship,
  59–61, 191–192, 193
and perception, 160–161
pseudo-independence, 156
and self-esteem, 33, 159–160
sex difference in, 113, 132
and social responsibility, 90, 155,
  159
  see also dependency; family
  socialization practices
intelligence (IQ score), and
  academic achievement, 17–18
and creativity, 26–28
changes in, 94, 151, 212
and family size, 180–181
and coping characteristics, 22, 94,
  151, 158
parent-child relationship,
  210–212
and productive functioning, 11
and self-esteem, 22, 151
and socioeconomic level, 209–211
  see also cognitive skills
internalization of values, 90
age of, 131–132
as goal of socialization, 90,
  113–114
and inductive discipline, 123
and introjection, 59–60
and social responsibility, 92–93,
  132–134
  see also socialization; values
interpersonal competence (social
  competence), 89, 91–92
in academic achiever, 19, 93–95
in creative person, 30–33, 95–97
in leader, 34–39, 97–98
marital stability, 70, 72–73, 75
  see also social responsibility
introjection, 59–60, 113
  see also independence

judgment, and cognitive development, 65–66
moral judgment, 109–110
as leadership characteristic, 34
in problem solving, 144
value judgment, 91–92, 132
  see also coping skills; in dependence; value system
language   see verbal skills
leader, characteristics of, 33–41
  see also productive personality
leadership, and academic achievement, 4–5, 35–36, 37
in children, 2, 35, 36
and competence, 4, 34
and empathy, 34–36
as function of group interaction, 33–35
and interpersonal competence, 34–36, 38–39, 40
and self-esteem, 36–41
sex differences in, 222–223
masculinity   see sex identity
mastery   see coping
maternal employment   see mother
mathematical skills, and coping ability, 149–151
as masculine characteristic, 82–83
  see also cognitive skills
maturity, 6
  see also internalization of values
memory, 150–153
and academic achievement, 18, 150–151
and associative thinking, 153, 170–171
and attention, 29, 153
defensive forgetting, 152
and impulsivity, 152, 153
and language, 118
interference with, 152
  see also cognitive skills; perception

mental ability   see intelligence
mental health, 2, 6
and family environment, 191–193
and self-esteem, 24–25
and social responsibility, 92
  see also personal soundness
merging, 58
model, basis of selection, 55–56
influence of, 55–56
influencing characteristics, 66, 126–128
  see also identification; socialization
moral development   see sex identification; socialization
moral values, 91–92, 109, 116–117
cultural basis, 100, 114
  see also family environment; values
mother, early identification processes, 54–64, 137–138
empathy of, 59–62, 86, 183, 191–193, 198
maternal control, 87, 191–192, 202, 204–205
maternal employment, 184–186
role in family structure, 68, 183, 196, 218–221, 231
self-esteem of, 62, 196–197, 201,
  see also parent
motivation, 20–21, 40–41
  see also family environment; ordering ability
oedipal period   see sex identification
ordinal position   see birth order
ordering ability, 168–171
association of ideas, 153, 170–171
flexibility, 169, 172
integration of nonconscious material, 170–171
intellectual ordering, 29, 168
pleasure in manipulating ideas, 29, 168–169

preference for complexity, 29, 168
tolerance of ambiguity, 168–169,
171
   see also judgment; memory;
   perception
productive personality, 4–5,
11–12, 17–41, 225–229
coping characteristics, 155–175
family background, 200–224
development of, 188–199,
230–235
identity, 11–12, 71–75, 88
self-esteem, 13–14, 21–25, 32–33,
36–42
social characteristics, 31–35,
93–99
value system, 89–93, 98–99,
133–134
   see also self-esteem construct
productivity, 6–8
and creativity, 7–8
criterion of, 8–9
enhancement of, 243–245,
250–255
and intelligence, 11
levels of, 9–10
measures of, 10–11
and self-actualization, 7
   see also academic achievement;
   creativity; leadership
psychosomatic disorders,
234–235, 250
psychotherapy, cognitive
requirements, 239
current approaches, 237–239
results of, 238–239
   see also behavior modification;
   self-esteem construct
self, 47–49
and identity, 48, 49
and perceptual process, 48
self-actualization, 7, 15, 46
self-actualizing person,
   see leader

self-esteem (self-concept,
   self-confidence, self-image),
   14–16
and aspiration level, 38–42
ego strength, 14–15
as basis of internal value system,
91
and family background, 194–199
and identity, 49–51
and identification process,
55, 58
influence of report card, 252
and mental health, 23–24, 37
as perceived evaluation of others,
17
as predictor of academic
performance, 21–23
self-actualization, 14, 20, 22
stability of, 16–17
   see also academic achievement;
   creativity; leadership
self-esteem construct, in
   behavior-modification
   programs, 242–243
in parent-child counseling,
243–245, 251–255
as personality theory, 235–237,
245–250
psychosomatic disorders, 234–235,
250
   see also psychotherapy
sex identification, 75–85
age of onset, 75–76
in boys, 77, 79–80
effects of father absence, 80–83, 84,
167
in girls, 83–85
and moral development, 77–78,
79
oedipal conflict, 76–77, 85
role of father, 78–85
role of mother, 84
   see also identification;
   socialization

sex identity (sex-role identity), 67–88
anxiety over, 70
as aspect of personal identity, 67, 71, 88
confused sex identity, 86–87
in creative artist, 218
in creative scientist, 72, 73–74
as diagnostic label, 44, 67
femininity and education, 74–75
masculine-feminine role perceptions, 67–71, 76–77, 78, 83–84
heterosexual adjustment, 72–75
homosexuality, 87
as personality description, 70–71
see also sex-identification
shame, 112–113
and dependency, 113
and guilt, 112–113
sex differences in, 113
social competence, *see* interpersonal competence
social responsibility, 89–93
and altruism, 89–90, 92–93
and conscience, 90, 131
as *Gemeinschaftsgefuhl*, 98, 134
and internalization of values, 89–90, 131–132
in productive persons, 89–90, 93–99, 134
see also altruism; empathy; interpersonal competence; sympathy
socialization, 113–115
cognitive development, 117–118, 132, 134
conditions for, 123–126
dynamics of, 116–123
effectiveness of models, 126–128
and empathy, 114–115
family unit as basis of, and identification, 99, 114
impediments to, 125–126, 232

internalization as goal, 90, 132
observational learning, 117–118
parental discipline methods, 119–125
reward and punishment, 115–116, 118–119
see also family socialization practices; identification; parental values
socializing agents, 100
see also model; parent
socioeconomic level, 178, 181–186
and academic achievement, 178, 209–211, 253–255
authority and discipline patterns, 181, 183
competence of father, 181–182, 186
educational level of parents, 182, 183
see also family environment; family size
spontaneity *see* interpersonal competence
superego *see* conscience; identification
superego identification, 66
see also conscience; identification
sympathy, 105–107
acquisition of, 106–107
and altruism, 105–106
and competence, 106–107
and empathy, 106
selective expression of, 107
sex differences in, 107
see also social responsibility; values
teacher *see* socializing agents
time perspective *see* judgment
trust, and hope, 145
and impulsivity, 162
infant-mother identification, 57
and self-esteem, 199

290

values, 91–92, 116–117
acquisition of, 55–56, 66, 77–78
of academic achievers, 93, 95, 248
basis of selection, 90–92, 116, 132
of creative persons, 95–97
internalization of, 90, 131–133
of leaders, 98–99
parental, 133, 215
   see also altruism; conscience;
   guilt; sympathy

verbal communication, as
   empathic response, 64, 128, 242
in socialization, 119–120
sex of child, 64
socioeconomic differences, 64, 254
   see also identification;
verbal skills, and creativity, 28
and effective coping, 149–150
sex differences in, 64, 82, 203–204
   see also cognitive skills